"Accessing information and inspiration from our deeper levels of consciousness not only can improve our organization's outcomes, but can catalyze new approaches, products, and services that serve the greater good—leading to a triple win for the organization, its stakeholders, and society as a whole. The time is now for this important work by Tsao and Laszlo!"

—Claire Lachance, CEO, Institute of Noetic Sciences (IONS)

"Tsao and Laszlo's *Quantum Leadership* offers us a powerful vehicle for seeing and acting on the possibilities for our transformation as spiritual beings—becoming leaders at all levels of our lives and in our organizations and societies."

—Jim Stoner, Chairholder: James A. F. Stoner Chair for Global
Sustainability, Fordham University

"As an individual and in our human groups, when we are in sync we function at our peak in innovation, creativity, and compassion, and expand our possibilities. At a moment of awakening, we rediscover a universal truth. It gives us a deep sense of purpose and a grounding in reality. Tsao and Laszlo have created one of these moments for you."

—Richard Boyatzis, Distinguished University Professor, Case Western
Reserve University, and coauthor of *Primal Leadership:
Unleashing the Power of Emotional Intelligence*

"Business leaders who harness the science of connectedness presented in this book will be poised to function at a higher level of creativity, productivity, and profitability while transforming the world around them in a way that typical corporate social responsibility initiatives cannot mimic. Kudos to the authors for presenting a complete how-to framework for business that places the heart of transformation right where it should be: within you."

—Dr. Anoop Kumar, MD, author of *Michelangelo's Medicine: How
Redefining the Human Body Will Transform Health and Healthcare*

QUANTUM LEADERSHIP

QUANTUM LEADERSHIP

New Consciousness in Business

FREDERICK CHAVALIT TSAO
AND CHRIS LASZLO

STANFORD BUSINESS BOOKS

An Imprint of Stanford University Press • Stanford, California

Stanford University Press
Stanford, California

Special discounts for bulk quantities of Stanford Business Books are available to corporations, professional associations, and other organizations. For details and discount information, contact the special sales department of Stanford University Press. Tel: (650) 725-0820, Fax: (650) 725-3457

Printed in the United States of America on acid-free, archival-quality paper

Library of Congress Cataloging-in-Publication Data

Names: Tsao, Frederick Chavalit, author. | Laszlo, Chris, author.
Title: Quantum leadership : new consciousness in business /
    Frederick Chavalit Tsao and Chris Laszlo.
Description: Stanford, California : Stanford Business Books, an imprint of Stanford
    University Press, 2019. | Includes bibliographical references and index.
Identifiers: LCCN 2019009008 (print) | LCCN 2019009650 (ebook) |
    ISBN 9781503609167 (e-book) | ISBN 9781503600331 (cloth; alk. paper)
Subjects: LCSH: Leadership. | Industrial management. | Consciousness. |
    Social responsibility of business.
Classification: LCC HD57.7 (ebook) | LCC HD57.7 .T86 2019 (print) |
    DDC 658.4/092—dc23
LC record available at https://lccn.loc.gov/2019009008

Cover design: Cadence Design | Preston Thomas

Text design: Kevin Barrett Kane

Typeset by Newgen in 11/15 Minion

CONTENTS

PREFACE

The world is facing many challenges—sustainability, globalization, and myriad technological developments that will change everything. Challenges in fact define the direction in which we evolve. Business has a key role to play in overcoming these challenges, and to succeed, business leaders must evolve a new consciousness, one that is collaborative, that better balances "I" and "We."

Business has become the most powerful institution of the era and with that comes a new role in society aimed at solving the problems facing humankind. Furthermore, as Albert Einstein is believed to have said, "The problems that exist in the world today cannot be solved by the level of thinking that created them."[1] We can and must evolve in the direction of our perceived challenges.

Consciousness is the mother of all capital, the source of all wealth, and mindfulness is the tool that provides access to it. With mindfulness practices comes an expansion of consciousness that in turn changes our worldview, providing us with a fresh perspective on the challenges we face and granting us the gift of intuition and the intelligence to generate creativity. Creativity in business is the entrepreneur's true mission, one that is the source of all new capital. We all have the potential for infinite creativity—which in the final analysis is love. "Quantum leadership" is about cultivating consciousness to celebrate the creation of life, and business creativity—entrepreneurial activity—expands the scope of possibilities for humanity.

My quest for new consciousness in business has been ongoing for a quarter of a century. In 1995, I took over as executive owner of IMC Pan Asia Alliance Group (IMC) and was fortunate to be able to grow it during a period when the Asian shipping and real estate markets, although exceptionally turbulent, were brimming with opportunity. Over this period, IMC grew multiple times in size and value. It has been a journey without a final destination but also one that has produced extraordinary rewards of personal struggle and growth along the way.

My primary goal as founder and currently chairman of Family Business Network Asia (FBN Asia) and the FBN Foundation is to help shape the next generation of business practices. I want to promote a new leadership model that offers those working in for-profit enterprises a powerful guide to a more holistic, life-centered way of being.

What we call quantum leadership is the product of elements that are often seen as disparate: family and business, wealth and well-being, scholarship and practice, and Western science and Eastern philosophy. Quantum leaders are stewards who create prosperity rather than only short-term profit. They produce holistic well-being rather than meet only material needs. They contribute to a regenerative natural environment instead of only doing less harm.

There are many stories of business leaders who succeeded in creating their own path with great personal cost and episodic failure, but I believe that the lessons from my own journey have a value during a time when existing corporate practices are failing to produce the desired results either for business or for society. Businesses should be more than places to earn a living. They are a platform to pursue self-actualization, both individually and as a community. When you do it right, embracing the challenges of leadership becomes the best opportunity to evolve your consciousness, and raising your consciousness provides the highest leverage point for meeting today's business challenges. In other words, business becomes a place where leaders produce economic outcomes that cultivate well-being and promote a culture of stewardship for others and for future generations.

At IMC, we tried many Western leadership theories and their gurus, but none of them took hold. International consultancies were brought in, but ultimately all proved unable to gain the kind of traction I was searching for. I wanted business to contribute to economic prosperity in a world in which both people and nature flourish. I wanted an alternative to traditional management theories that serve short-term profit without attention to pressing human and environmental predicaments.

Social entrepreneurialism, "conscious capitalism," and similar ideas are steps in the right direction. They embody business as a force for good. They reflect the *outer* transformation of markets, with business required to meet rigorous standards of social and environmental performance, accountability, and transparency. Quantum leaders do all that, but they also go much further—they embrace the *inner* transformation of business leaders: the global mind shift, the consciousness that we are deeply connected to others and to nature. Such inner transformation brings out from an authentic place our natural tendency toward creating prosperity and flourishing. Business in such a situation becomes a positive institution with leaders who are not choosing to be in service of others as much as they are manifesting a new way of being.

As integrators of wealth and well-being, quantum leaders bring together seemingly disparate roles to harness the collective energy of the organization in service of society. Such integration can come only from a transformation in consciousness—the awareness by the mind of itself and the world—which in turn has the potential to lead to a genuinely new way of being. This way of being is also thousands of years old, based on oneness and wholeness, but it must be continuously reimagined for today's context. Transforming our consciousness to one of wholeness erases the distinction between the person or organization doing good and the person or community who is the recipient of the good. It lessens the tendency to nationalism and tribalism. It helps us avoid the more extreme "us-versus-them" cleavages along political, ethnic, cultural, and national lines that mar human affairs. It enlivens a much earlier mindset in which our ancestors saw themselves, intrinsically and indivisibly, as part of nature.

For some in my management team, this emphasis on transforming consciousness was initially difficult to accept. At best, it seemed to them to be a distraction from pragmatic business realities and, at worst, a waste of time. But eventually it had a profound impact on their lives. Managers who were initially resistant but stayed with it ended up making a huge difference to the success of the business. What surprised me most was to hear how many came back over the years to tell me what a pivotal influence it had on their personal lives.

The Quantum Leadership Model is now drawing adherents around the world. At a recent FBN summit, which I hosted at my company's Sangha Retreat on Yangcheng Lake in Suzhou, new consciousness in business permeated the summit conversations with nearly six hundred multigenerational business leaders from forty-four countries. There was a major focus on POLARIS, a movement within FBN to foster transformation of family business as a force for global good.

In 2014, as I was contemplating how best to share with others what I was learning about business leadership, I came across the philosophical treatises of Ervin Laszlo, who put me in touch with his son, Chris Laszlo, a noted business academic and author. Although Chris grew up nearly six thousand miles away from me, in Switzerland, it became quickly apparent that we had similar perspectives on business and synchronistic life experiences. While I was searching for how to communicate the new consciousness leadership paradigm, he was seeking a business leader who practiced it. We began weekly conversations over Skype and eventually began traveling between Cleveland, Ohio, and Shanghai, China, to collaborate.

Chris had started his career in merchant banking on Wall Street, then went back to school to pursue a doctorate in economics before moving on to management consulting. He spent five years at Deloitte, followed by nearly a decade in the multinational construction materials company Lafarge, S.A., and then returned to management consultancy. Through it all, he found himself increasingly dwelling on how best to weave social responsibility into corporate life. Social and environmental performance, he believed, was something that would increasingly have to be recognized as core to the strategy of any flourishing business.

Throughout that period, bridges were being built between business and society in ways that paralleled my own evolution in thinking. Chris realized that this was a time to bring together the main two facets of his career: social responsibility and corporate performance. In 2002, he cofounded Sustainable Value Partners, LLC, a management consulting firm helping clients including Bayer, Cisco, Lafarge, L'Oréal, UBS Bank, and Walmart to create competitive advantage by embedding sustainability into their core businesses. He wrote about sustainability for business advantage, first in *The Sustainable Company* (2003) and then *Sustainable Value* (2008). But after publishing his third book, *Embedded Sustainability* (2011), he began to have doubts about the prevailing reliance on a business-case approach to sustainability. It became increasingly clear to him that business could no longer be said to be serving society well, in spite of self-congratulatory reports about corporate social responsibility (CSR). In an interview published by the Rocky Mountain Institute in 2013 and later reprinted in *GreenBiz*, Chris said,

> I have spent the last twelve years developing the business case for sustainability from a strategy, finance, organizational and operations perspective. Having spent all that effort over those years, it really struck me a few years ago that something was missing: Most importantly, the way sustainability is typically addressed in most companies is not producing the kind of results either business or society is expecting. . . . What I'm talking about is [the need for] a completely disruptive approach. . . . The next wave in sustainability will have to do more to raise the bar from mere survival to economic and environmental prosperity; it will also have to pay more attention to individual well-being. We cannot expect to have a thriving business in a flourishing world without individuals who are also able to experience a greater sense of well-being and connectedness to their self, to others and to the world around them.[2]

I realized then that Chris had a vision of business in society that was closely aligned with my own. A few years later he was given an endowed professorship at Case Western Reserve University and appointed to lead the Fowler Center for Business as an Agent of World Benefit. I accepted an invitation to join the Fowler Center's advisory board and later established the AITIA Quantum Leadership Initiative with help from Chris to advance the scholarship and practice of quantum leadership. Our collaboration brought together a business leader seeking to articulate his vision and a management scholar seeking to demonstrate a new and emerging paradigm of business. This book is the product of that multi-year collaboration.

In the pages ahead you learn that the greatest point of leverage for a new leadership orientation is a transformation in *consciousness*. This may seem surprising to people who are committed to having a positive social impact and want practical advice on how to do it. Of course, the business case for environmental and social performance remains essential for taking action. Using financial metrics, any business leader can now show that, through the process of innovation, there is no *necessary* trade-off between economic and social or environmental benefits.[3] But in addition to changing what leaders are *doing*, we need to change who they are *being*. That is where a shift in consciousness comes in. Evidence from current trends suggests that without such deep-rooted change, businesses are condemned to continue today's strategies that, at best, reduce social harm or ecological footprints and, at worst, contribute to growing social crises and environmental disaster.

Having a consciousness of connectedness changes how we think and act. We become more empathetic and compassionate. When we see ourselves as an integral part of the natural world rather than separate from it, we become more attuned to how our actions affect not only people but all life on earth. Mindfulness practices—in this book recast as "practices of connectedness" to encompass both Eastern and Western forms—quiet the mind and expand our consciousness so that we are more aware of the truth about our experiences. Through such practices, we connect to the origin of consciousness itself, slowly awakening to holism. From that "We" space, we grow in personal power, we clean up our traumas and trapped emotions from the past, and we discover our gifts and purpose in life.

The *inner* transformation of business leaders toward wholeness and connectedness and the *outer* transformation of business toward sustainable value are both needed for a business-led future of global prosperity and flourishing.

The time is now for a new role of business. Quantum leadership has the potential to become widespread. Its tremendous appeal comes from a business leader being able to create economic value consistent with

greater purpose and personal well-being. It offers businesspeople everywhere a pathway to a world in which businesses prosper, people flourish, and nature thrives.

Frederick Chavalit Tsao

January 12, 2019

ACKNOWLEDGMENTS

The authors are indebted to the following individuals for contributions to the book's research and project management.

Sook Yee Tai, overall project head and executive director of the AITIA Institute

Joseph Leah, project head West and colead researcher

Maria Muñoz-Grandes, colead researcher

Rosseana Wong, project member and head of Chairman's Office IMC Pan Asia Alliance Group

Lingkang Gong, researcher

QUANTUM LEADERSHIP

PART I TRANSFORMATION TO QUANTUM LEADERSHIP

1   A NEW CONSCIOUSNESS IN BUSINESS

WHAT IS IT that drives people to care for the well-being of others? What motivates them to invest in their communities and to be good stewards for future generations? How do we get more of this kind of leadership in for-profit enterprises?

We are often asked these questions at a time when business is increasingly expected to solve all kinds of social and global problems. Fifty years ago a Nobel Prize–winning economist wrote that the only social responsibility of business was to make a profit, and, it was assumed, from profits would flow jobs and consumer satisfaction.[1] Back then, the public looked mainly to government and nonprofit organizations for social welfare and national security. Legislation was only beginning to protect citizens from the smokestacks that spewed airborne chemicals and from the industrial effluents that blackened rivers and lakes.[2]

Now business is expected to play a much bigger role. "Legitimacy [of business] has fallen in tandem with rising expectations," say leading management scholars Thomas Donaldson and James Walsh. "Society expects more from business these days than simply creating wealth. . . . Entirely new legal entities have recently emerged to serve this kind of ambition. The low-profit limited liability corporation and the benefit corporation, for example, are innovative attempts to create companies that pursue profit and social good simultaneously. . . . Change is in the air."[3]

Today business is on the hook for everything from climate change and income equality to education and personal well-being. These are just a few of the startling UN Global Goals for 2030 engaging the business community.[4] Rising demands from consumers, employees, and investors are forcing chief executives into unknown territory. Corporate social responsibility (CSR) was once focused on doing less harm (a.k.a. footprint reduction). A company was free to pursue profit as long as it obeyed the laws and, where possible, minimized environmental damage and social injustice.

Leading companies are increasingly expected to provide *solutions* of public interest (a.k.a. a positive handprint) by creating disruptive innovations that not only are profitable but also benefit society and the environment: for example, Patagonia's business strategy to give back to nature more than it takes, Unilever's Sustainable Living Plan, IKEA's People and Planet Positive strategy, Greyston's Open Hiring employment practices, Warby Parker's Buy a Pair, Give a Pair program, and Natura's "Well Being and Being Well."

But is it realistic to expect business to be a force for good? Other than a few specialty companies, can for-profit enterprise ever really become an agent of world benefit? Some may believe that business, as an institution, can never act as a responsible custodian for future generations, given its single-minded pursuit of financial gain.

Business leaders have gradually warmed to the idea that they are tasked with greater social responsibility. However, their efforts have almost always been framed in terms of financial calculation. What is the return on investment of converting to renewable energy? How can investing in the local community enhance a company's reputation? Will sustainable packaging increase a retailer's shelf-space utilization? No matter how noble and inspired the CEO or founder's vision, the central operating question eventually devolved to whether such efforts increased the bottom line.[5]

Periodic surveys of business, starting in 2010,[6] showed a steady increase in the percentage of CEOs who said that environmental and social sustainability is critical to competitive advantage, rising to an astonishing 80 percent a few years later.[7] The same surveys showed that as soon as the business case for sustainability proved difficult to make, interest began to wane among business executives.[8] By 2018, survey reports were documenting a decline in the number of companies engaging employees in sustainability strategies.[9]

Perhaps more troubling, when you look at the sum total of economic activity across all business sectors, you see that corporate sustainability efforts are only *decelerating* the growth of many social and global problems.[10] Stress and disengagement at work,[11] income inequality, chronic hunger, climate change, and biodiversity loss (species extinction) are getting worse, not better.[12] CSR and corporate sustainability are at best mitigating these trends but not reversing their direction.

The conclusion of any objective observer has to be that the business-case approach to sustainability is not enough—and never will be enough as it is currently practiced—to create prosperity and flourishing. Nor is it sufficient to teach people ethical behavior or to disseminate moral injunctions against irresponsible conduct,[13] even when using sophisticated corporate training programs employing shared vision and values processes.[14] Even the best-intentioned leaders are struggling to engage their organizations in making consistently positive impacts that materially contribute to stakeholder well-being.

A Fresh Approach to Flourishing Enterprise

Our contention is that we need to change leaders at their most fundamental level of being—at the level of their consciousness. *Transforming consciousness changes us at the deepest level of our self-identity.* It must always be built on a foundation of principled leadership accompanied by a credible and compelling business case for social responsibility. When business leaders have strong guiding values and are able to articulate a persuasive business case for social responsibility, they have the groundwork for a new awareness of how their actions affect others and future generations.

So What Is Consciousness Anyway?

Consciousness is the awareness by the mind of itself and the world. This awareness is not only of the Cartesian "I think, therefore I am" variety. It also includes subjective experience, the raw feelings and emotions immediately present when we taste chocolate, smell coffee, or feel love for someone. Beyond this simple definition, a debate currently rages about the very nature of such awareness. We explore this in greater depth later in the book, but, put simply, one camp sees consciousness as the product of the brain and explains selfhood in purely physical terms; the opposing camp argues that consciousness is not reducible to physical phenomena: no reductive physical explanation can ever account for the *feelings* that accompany sensory experience.

In Chapter 6, we provide growing evidence for the idea that consciousness might in fact exist *outside* the brain rather than be generated *by* it. While still hotly debated, this paradigm-shifting view is based on recent developments in quantum physics and consciousness research that suggest that quantum-level vibrational fields lie behind (and are the source of) all reality as we know it.

Also in Chapter 6 we suggest that such findings have huge implications for leadership practices. Spending more time in silent retreat, practicing mindfulness meditation, or immersing oneself in nature can lead to an experience of wholeness and of greater oneness with the world. Such practices may allow us to process information at the quantum level,[15] information that is normally inaccessible when we engage the brain's neocortex in the dominantly analytic-cognitive mode of the workplace. In other words, we feel more centered after moments of silence, or more upbeat after spending time in nature, because we are tapping into a source of evolutionary coherence and interconnectedness (what quantum physicists call "entanglement"), not only in a metaphoric or conceptual sense but also in terms of actual energy and information flows at the quantum level.[16] The title of this book reflects this interconnected quantum reality and the benefits of the practices that tap into it.

To accept that the fundamental nature of reality is other than we have been led to believe is potentially destabilizing. It also presents an unprecedented opportunity. The consciousness of the Western mind that has served us so well in business since the beginning of the

Industrial Revolution is no longer serving us in the twenty-first century. To progress as a species and to be a force for positive change, we have a choice before us of whether to embark on a path of transforming the way we see the world around us, informed and supported by new empirical insights into the nature of reality. The proposed path of transformation has the potential to bring out intrinsic care and compassion and inspire us to do good because that is who we are. The good that we do will come from a more authentic place and is not just the by-product of a financial calculation.

Such a transformation toward care and compassion is often presented in spiritual terms as a journey toward awakening or enlightenment, a human development dynamic that science is now affirming.[17] The lower stages are centered on the ego and are the sources of our human suffering. As we evolve, we move through an awareness of the self as not absolute reality. We experience life as something more than our self. We have an increased experience of nonattachment, which leads to less suffering and greater freedom and peace. Ultimately, we move toward the experience of oneness, where we are able to be "fully awake," a state that encompasses empathy and caring of others. While many people have an intuitive understanding of this spiritual journey, what is exciting now is that science is converging on and validating perennial insights into our ability to experience it.

In our journey toward awakening, we each have a story about what it means to be human and the nature of reality. We might see ourselves as spiritless biophysical entities, existentially alone, selfish and competitive, born into a cold mechanical universe composed of clumps of matter subject to forces immutably driving us toward meaningless extinction. Or we might see ourselves as spirit-infused beings living in a world that is alive with meaning, demonstrably interconnected through energy and information flows, with human natures that are essentially compassionate and longing for mutualism and cooperation. These alternative stories of what it means to be human are no longer only a matter of belief; as we show in later chapters, they reflect competing paradigms in the natural and social sciences.

The Role of Transforming Consciousness

To understand the power of transforming consciousness, we turn to systems scientist Donella Meadows. Sustainability pioneer Ray Anderson, the founder and former chairman of Interface Inc., often said that her article "Places to Intervene in a System," written in 1997,[18] was the most insightful treatise ever written on business transformation.[19] In it, Meadows observes that the highest leverage point at which to intervene in a system is in "the mindset or paradigm out of which the system arises":

> The shared idea in the minds of society, the great big unstated assumptions—unstated because unnecessary to state; everyone already knows them—constitute that society's paradigm, or deepest set of beliefs about how the world works. . . . Growth is good. Nature is a stock of resources to be converted to human purposes. Evolution stopped with the emergence of *Homo sapiens*. One can "own" land. Those are just a few of the paradigmatic assumptions of our current culture, all of which have utterly dumfounded other cultures, who thought them not the least bit obvious.[20]

In reflecting on how to change mind-sets or paradigms, she points to Thomas Kuhn's seminal work *The Structure of Scientific Revolutions*,[21] saying that "you keep pointing at the anomalies and failures in the old paradigm . . . [and] you insert people with the new paradigm in places of public visibility and power. You don't waste time with reactionaries; rather you work with active change agents and with the vast middle ground of people who are open-minded."[22] That is what we are doing: pointing to failures of an old paradigm based on separateness and selfishness while proposing a new paradigm of connectedness and wholeness. Living the new paradigm requires a *transformation in the consciousness* of who we are and the nature of the world we live in. It invites what Peter Senge and others have referred to as systems leadership aimed at flourishing for all.

> Though they differ widely in personality and style, genuine system leaders have a remarkably similar impact. Over time, their profound commitment to the health of the whole radiates to nurture similar commitment in others. Their ability to see reality through the eyes of people very different from themselves

encourages others to be more open as well. They build relationships based on deep listening, and networks of trust and collaboration start to flourish.[23]

Consciousness and Purpose in Business

Quantum leadership is a learning journey to elevate a person's consciousness as the most powerful lever for unlocking his or her leadership potential to drive creativity and innovation. It changes people at a deep intuitive level, combining embodied experience with analytic-cognitive skill development. The culmination is *flourishing enterprise* with significant business benefits to any organization. These benefits include greater authenticity and collaboration along with an increased capability to inspire people and produce lasting change in turbulent environments. Along this journey people learn how to authentically cultivate personal well-being and a deep connection to others for shared prosperity and genuine flourishing. Figure 1.1 shows the Quantum Leadership Model (QLM). (The underlying research conducted between 2015 and 2018 is described in more detail in Chapter 5.)

To read the QLM, begin at the far right of Figure 1.1. The goal of quantum leadership is to generate positive economic outcomes, defined as above-industry-average profits along with prosperity in the communities in which the business operates. The goal is also simultaneously, and without trade-offs,[24] to generate positive social and environmental outcomes, by which we mean contributing to a healthy natural environment and improving human well-being. The leadership to pursue these outcomes requires not only technical skills but also emotional and social ones, exemplified by shared vision, compassion, and relational energy.[25] Such leadership generates intrinsically greater insight and creativity.

So far so good. But what are the antecedents to such leadership? Based on our research, they are mindfulness-type practices—defined broadly as "practices of connectedness" that encompass both Eastern and Western forms—which elevate our consciousness of connectedness and increase our sense of purpose. Such practices are the independent variables on the far left of Figure 1.1. They are the drivers of the adaptive and direct-intuitive skills needed to succeed in today's turbulent market environments and are essential to entrepreneurial creativity.[26]

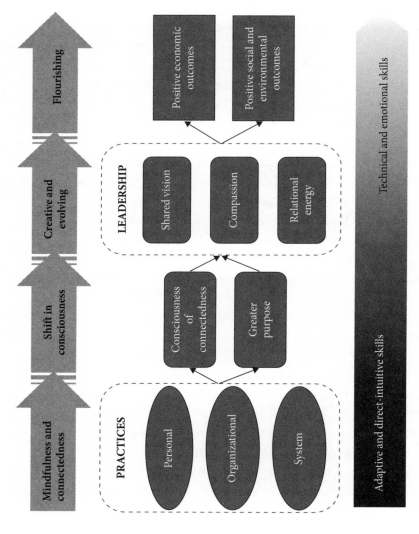

Figure 1.1. The Quantum Leadership Model (QLM)

Practices of Connectedness

Our business experience and multiyear research into leadership as a force for good led us to explore the primary value of practices that elevate our consciousness of connectedness and increase our sense of purpose. The gateway to these practices is mindfulness, but our contention is that they are not limited to popular techniques such as meditation, yoga, and other contemplative schools of practice that most people think about when they hear the word "mindfulness." Changing who we are can start with any of thousands of possible practices that can reconnect us to what is important and make us whole again. They range from music, gardening, and physical exercise to Hakomi therapy and appreciative inquiry, along with a host of other activities that help quiet our five senses and slow the analytic cognition of the brain. Jeremy Hunter, an expert on mindfulness in business, notes that such practices can include everyday activities from mindful eating to how we sit or walk.[27]

Such practices have three characteristics in common.[28] First, they are part of a well-documented upward spiral in positive emotions that increase our sense of well-being and build consequential resources to handle life's challenges. Second, they expand our awareness of being one with the world, helping us get in a state of "flow" where creativity and productivity emerge effortlessly. Third, they engage the whole person rather than only the analytic rational self.

The practices are a healing antidote to today's fragmented multitasking behaviors in which we self-interrupt our attention every few seconds, often as a result of jumping from one phone screen to another electronic device, in urban environments largely devoid of nature. The practices help cultivate broader perception and greater awareness of our life purpose in relation to our community and the natural environment. They offer an experiential path—not one of words or concepts—that leads us to a more meaningful life in which we pursue legacies of lasting positive impact.

The Role of Practices of Connectedness for Business Leaders

Why are such practices vital to the development of business leaders capable of exhibiting relational intelligence and creativity in the pursuit of flourishing enterprise? Because they are an action-oriented pathway to changing the mind-set or paradigm out of which we fashion the world. In reviewing Daniel Wahl's book *Designing Regenerative Cultures*, Jonathan Porritt writes that "no serious attempt is made to explain how this demonstrably preferable worldview [of caring for life as a whole] is ever going to gain traction in the world as it is today."[29] According to Porritt, calls for a new narrative are frustratingly lacking in a theory of change. This criticism is often leveled at individuals and organizations trying to change the world for the better: they are better at diagnosing problems than offering solutions and more effective at describing the desired future of flourishing than proposing meaningful pathways to achieve it. *We believe that it is time to change the narrative about change itself by turning to embodied practice rather than only analytic-cognitive approaches to learning.*

There is a growing body of clinical neurophysiological evidence that demonstrates the power of practices of connectedness for business leaders.[30] The evidence suggests that such practices strengthen a leader's ability to deal with situational complexity and increase empathy and a sense of human connectedness.[31]

Practices of connectedness help leaders develop critical skills: to be present and aware of themselves and the world around them, allowing them to recognize in real time their own perceptions and feelings so that they can take immediate action to address complex realities more effectively.[32]

While transforming business can be facilitated by tinkering with government subsidies and taxes, revising corporate incentives, or overhauling strategic objectives, *it is the power of the practices of connectedness to change our consciousness that is likely to have the greatest and most enduring impact on business leadership.* The literature on leadership tends to emphasize emotional, technical, and cognitive skills.[33] Quantum leadership focuses on adaptive skills that change who the leader is *being* rather than only what the leader is *doing*. The practices change who we are at a deep intuitive level, combining technical skill development with an embodied learning of what it means to be deeply connected to others and future generations.

A final introductory observation: When we say that consciousness is the ultimate form of business capital, we mean it in the Donella Meadows sense of the highest point of leverage. Although rarely considered in this context, consciousness is a unique resource for business leaders. Individuals and organizations that master the shift in consciousness are accessing a difficult-to-imitate form of business advantage. It also requires "right motive." A person cannot manipulate his or her consciousness or that of others for instrumental reasons alone, such as for power or money. It must be done for its own sake, as an end in itself.

To illustrate the different types of consciousness existing in the business world today, we now present two stories, featuring lead characters based on composites of actual people we have worked with. We feel certain that readers will recognize in these characters someone that they have known or experienced at work. As you read these two profiles, ask yourself what aspects of them ring true for you, as well as for the colleagues you work with.

Dieter's Story

Dieter woke early, roused by the buzz of his alarm clock. He felt a familiar and sickening pain behind his eyes. He had been out late again with clients. It had been well past midnight, and he had had one too many vodka gimlets. He was surprised to notice Anne-Marie lying next to him, her arm resting lightly across his midriff. He sat up heavily, shook his head twice, and lumbered into his home office. He turned both computers on at the same time, closing his eyes until the night's e-mails had downloaded. He checked the markets in Asia before looking at anything else. Despite thirst and a headache, he spent an hour in front of the two screens: when a file took too long to download, he scanned the CNN headlines; when his financial spreadsheets failed to tell him what he wanted to know, he browsed YouTube videos of fine art auctions. He finally stumbled half-awake into the kitchen. A quick scrabble around in the fridge, a fumble at the espresso machine, and he was back in his office again, chasing down leftover sausage and potato spätzli with two cups of bitter coffee, his eyes never leaving the screens.

By 6:30, he was showered and shaved. He picked his way down the stairs to avoid waking Anne-Marie; he had no desire to talk to her right now. Outside, he paused, took a deep breath of the cold Düsseldorf air of late October to ready himself for the day, and allowed himself a satisfied backward glance at his glass-fronted townhouse. Across elegant and exclusive Königstrasse was an equally elegant and exclusive red Italian sports car. Nestling into its firm leather seat, he felt his headache beginning to dissipate. It was a thirty-minute drive to his office in Ratingen, an industrial zone on the outskirts of the city, and while driving, he checked his voice mail and put through several energetic calls to his company's Warsaw and Belgrade offices.

As the elevator doors swished behind him, he cast his eyes over his already industrious staff. "Where's the final agenda for tomorrow's *Vorstand*?" was his cold greeting to Marcus, a research assistant who was helping him prepare for the upcoming management board meeting. He ran down his list of appointments for the morning, issuing clipped instructions to his secretary, Jana, then called down the hallway: "Why are our inventory numbers up again this week?" It was loud enough to make the whole office pause and look at him. Dieter had a habit of pulling at his left eyebrow when he was about to blow up at a subordinate, a cue for trepidation for those in his sights. It was Frank's turn today, and it landed especially badly: Frank had put in a lot of overtime to move the company's flagship product, in spite of having recently lost his father. He had said nothing about it to his boss.

Lunch for Dieter consisted of a club sandwich and a cold Weiss beer—and the relaxation of scouring websites for bespoke shoes. Could he find time to fly to Milan next weekend to get measured up at that amazing boutique store on Via Montenapoleone? He already had a dozen pairs of fine leather shoes in his wardrobe, but buying them gave him a real buzz. A daydream about tasseled loafers in crocodile leather was jolted by a knock on his office door. "Our bank auditors are expected next Wednesday at five," said the assured face leaning in at the door. Heidi was head of treasury and in line for divisional president. That job was rightfully his. To make matters worse, her smile always infuriated him. "Have we resolved the debt restructuring with our Brazilian suppliers?" he shot back icily, aiming to throw her off balance. "Yes," she replied coolly, "as a matter of fact, I sealed it last night. The Brazilians signed off on it." Dieter nodded, trying not to look disappointed.

At 2:00 that afternoon, he was in planning mode. The next quarter needed a sense of crisis in the company that he would artificially create by hiring a management consulting firm to justify firing the bottom-performing 10 percent of employees. That would immediately lower costs and boost productivity, burnishing his reputation as a hard-driving manager who got results fast.

He grabbed his antacid tablets from the desk drawer. With a little push from the markets, his stock options would rise another tenth of a percent, and then, time to say hello to that solid-gold Rolex he had his eye on. Some obstacles remained. Not least the hippie activists. To get the Naturschutzbund off his back, he would have to find unbudgeted funds to hire an aggressive Zürich PR firm he had used previously on the case. The furniture division had been doing well but only with the help of cheap lumber, some of which came from old-growth forests in Indonesia. Now several nongovernmental organizations had gotten wind of it. A serious massaging of the company's public image would be required.

On his way home Dieter lit a last cigarette, then threw the carton out his car window. For him it was a small act of rebellion, though he always looked around anxiously before doing so: he didn't want to get fined. He'd never been moved by nature; he actually got a sense of satisfaction seeing green spaces making way for industrial development. He had no time for parks and trees. He was a busy and successful man: the steady march of economic progress was what made him tick.

He pulled into his personal parking space, looking forward to another evening of business entertainment—another postdinner meeting with clients at a posh downtown bar. First, he would need to get the argument with Anne-Marie over with. But instead of Anne-Marie, he found a note, written in black lipstick and propped up on a chair against the inner door of his townhouse: "We are over." Dieter sighed. She had always been unreasonable. He carefully moved the chair back to its proper place. It didn't matter. He would succeed no matter what,

through determination and hard work. And he could do without anyone standing in his way.

. . .

Dieter's life is accessible to only a small percentage of people—perhaps
less than one in a hundred worldwide—yet it remains an aspiration for
many. Parents of pre-school-age children are already pushing them to
excel so that they can be fast-tracked to top universities with a chance
of securing Dieter's kind of job. High school graduates dream about
Dieter's salary and what it could bring. MBAs imagine themselves in his
executive office, directing others and influencing markets around the
world.

Dieter's kind of hard-driving, manipulative, and materially excessive lifestyle was celebrated in *The Wolf of Wall Street*, starring Leonardo
DiCaprio. The movie became a cult favorite among young professionals, earning more than US$392 million worldwide and having the du-
bious honor of being the most illegally downloaded film of the year,
shared more than thirty million times[34]—one indicator of its appeal to
the tech-savvy younger generation. In the real world, we are engrossed
by the rise of a figure like Donald Trump with its story of manipulative power and glitzy excess. While such wealth chronicles may fasci-
nate us, they rarely lead to more than a transitory feeling of reward. A
growing number of aspiring businesspeople know this to be intuitively
true. They are searching for greater meaning at work, in purpose-driven
careers that offer the potential for enduring happiness and well-being,
without compromising their professional success.

Lihua's Story

As Dieter was throwing back his third vodka gimlet of the evening,
halfway across the world Lihua opened her eyes. She was the first of
her household to awake. Rising from her simple mat of reeds covered
with worn cotton swathing, she went straight to the garden and picked
her way carefully through meticulously tended flower beds. Among
the plum blossoms, a red hibiscus—the "rose of China"—was getting
ready to bloom, bloodshot petals unfurling in the receding darkness. A

smile lit her face. A new day was beginning. Lihua gratefully breathed in the smell of the sparse, dusty plot of land. In the faint morning light she pulled some weeds, inspected her pale green shoots, and readjusted their slim bamboo stakes.

She stretched and straightened her back, working out the kinks from her long hours of sleep. As she methodically swept the footpath that led outward to the main road, the back-and-forth undulations, coaxing the broom along the pebbly trail in first one hand and then the other, helped her see the day's circumstances more clearly, without scrutiny or anxiety. As she swept, she observed each pebble, each root and fallen twig, letting the visual frames wash over her and slowly enrich her sense of being. The edges of the path became suddenly more visible, the chirping of rose finches more acute, the scent of plant decay sharper. She paused only to give thanks for all that was good. She walked back to her thatched roof dwelling to wash her face and make her first cup of tea.

Her three sisters were still asleep. Chun Jiao, her oldest niece, had managed to push a back door open, as independent, curious two-year-olds will do, and was navigating the eight wooden steps to the garden, sliding backward on her stomach from one slat to the next. "Good morning, Chun Jiao," Lihua said, greeting her usually chipper morning helper, before noticing the dirty cloth diaper hanging perilously on chubby infant legs. At the sound of Lihua's voice the child turned and fell the rest of the way down, screaming and tearing her diaper on the lowest step. Lihua scooped her up and carefully dislodged the soiled cloth, all the while whispering reassuring words that soon turned wracking sobs into noiseless whimpers. The soft black curls tickled Lihua's face and made her giggle. Soon they were both in fits of laughter. They headed to the garden spigot to wash up. Feeling playful in the cool spray, they turned their cleanup chore into a few moments of noisy delight.

Yu-Ren, Lihua's middle sister, appeared in her crimped cotton shift and slammed the screen door. She was angry about being woken up. "Why do you always do this to me?" she yelled, storming off. Lihua dried Chun Jiao and took her by the hand. Making a pot of tea was a ritual they liked to share: Lihua poured the boiled water into delicate teacups layered thinly with green leaves carefully chosen by Chun Jiao's little hands.

"Here's your tea," smiled Lihua at Yu-Ren. "Please forgive me for not being quieter." Lihua ambled off to find fresh clothes for the two-year-old, leaving Yu-Ren to sigh as she gratefully drank the steaming cup and wondered how Lihua always seemed so unruffled. She was different from the others: calm, steady, impervious to unkindness or defeat, and always ready to smile at friend or stranger.

Lihua worked eight kilometers away in Suzhou. One hundred kilometers west of Shanghai, this burgeoning industrial city stretches from the lower Yangtze River to Lake Taihu. Visitors might come to look at its historic Song-dynasty gardens and eat the squirrel-shaped Mandarin fish called *song shu gui yu*, but today's reality was one of huge steel structures, expressways, traffic, and overcrowding, with industrial parks springing up like weeds. On winter weekdays, commuters wore face masks to escape the foul air: armies of surgeons prepped to operate beneath the sulfur and nitrogen oxide blankets hanging thick with industrial soot. But economic development meant jobs—lots of them. And Lihua and her siblings were thankful. Their parents had scraped by on farming rice and vegetables on a meager half hectare. That would not be their destiny.

New manufacturing and construction companies offered jobs that paid cash at the end of the week. The work was hard and repetitive, quickly tiring body and spirit. Lihua's first year at a local electronics supply company had consisted of tedious ten-hour shifts soldering connectors onto miniature circuit boards. Somehow she found a way to stay engaged, making the most of her short breaks, stretching her limbs and clearing her mind, encouraging others—and always meeting her daily quotas in a game of speed and accuracy. Her employers soon noticed. They saw her attentiveness and positive energy as a source of organizational resilience, as she spurred those around her to do better.

Lihua was promoted to team leader. And she hadn't served quite three years at the company before she was hired away by a Singaporean family-owned business that had recently branched into China. This was a new world. There were flexible working hours. There were mandatory fifteen-minute Tai-Chi sessions every day at 10:00 a.m., signaled by the boom of traditional bronze gongs. She was given technical training in precision machining and, after a nine-month apprenticeship, given responsibility for a giant lathe and metal stamping tool that produced car parts destined for export. Her precision work and productivity were exemplary, as they always had been, and acknowledged throughout the company. Being humble, she was quite often embarrassed about it.

Her reputation wasn't earned just because of her meticulous attention to quality and quota fulfillment: She was also judged to be a model team leader, always seeking to help others and bringing a sense of personal care to each personal interaction, whether with the latrine cleaner or the CEO. Before long, her bosses were fighting over who could have her on their team. Lihua was promoted to machine shop production supervisor and, eighteen months later, to chief manufacturing executive. She was now part of the senior leadership team: a C-suite executive and officer of the company. She was dumbfounded. How had this happened so quickly?

Lihua received special recognition for an after-hours project in which she worked with an engineering team to redesign an injection-molding machine capable of using fully compostable bioplastics—modified starch formulations—instead of oil-based polymers. Her team's efforts led to new business contracts in the highly competitive, but increasingly environmentally conscious, automobile parts industry. She enjoyed the recognition, but she got more satisfaction knowing that she was contributing, in some small way, to reducing the drifting piles of plastic garbage she saw every day on her way to work.

Lihua felt an innate inclination to protect and restore the natural environment. She had become entranced by the beautiful forests that lay outside the industrial city. As she walked by her favorite pear blossoms and sakura trees, she felt as if she were soaking up their ancient energy. Sometimes she would turn her hands outward, palms facing the trees, imagining an unseen force connecting them to her, giving her renewed strength to face the challenges of each day. Such regular connections with nature inspired her to seek out opportunities at work to care for the environment, but, more than that, they helped her maintain her sense of well-being. They made her feel more comfortable in her own skin.

She ate simply and mindfully, rejecting processed meats in favor of mostly vegetarian fare. She rarely spent more money than she needed for her daily existence. When buying durable products, she sought ones made of steel, bamboo, or other natural materials, avoiding plastics made from synthetic oil-based polymers. On Sundays, she would meet with a group of neighborhood volunteers who picked up trash and trimmed the trees and bushes along the local roads.

At work, Lihua served on a human resources team to offer employee perks such as English lessons, table tennis, and yoga classes. She was terrible at table tennis but went to all the tournaments anyway to cheer on her coworkers as if each game were an Olympics final. In team meetings and on the factory floor, she motivated and encouraged her coworkers, always with her trademark bright smile.

Lihua's behavior was not a lifestyle choice; she was not interested in being seen as "green" or socially responsible. She was guided instinctively by a desire for wholeness. Those choices of simplicity and social awareness increased her sense of well-being—in a private and personal way. In practicing acts of kindness and care for others and the natural environment, she grew more fulfilled and at peace with herself. What others thought of her became less and less important as time went on.

A year later Lihua found her life partner, Zhi Ming. He was outgoing and hardworking and had recently been hired at an engineering company across town. Zhi Ming came from a poor farming family in the inner part of the country. Through sheer grit and determination he had excelled at school in a village where education was not encouraged. Soon after earning his technical degree, he got a highly coveted job at a software company in Zhangjiang Hi-Tech Park, the so-called Silicon Valley of China, before transferring to Suzhou. Lihua and he met through mutual friends at a favorite karaoke bar where they both let loose after work. His party piece was Joe Cocker's version of "The Letter," which he sang in perfect English. She put her heart and soul into "New Endless Love" (新不了情). When Zhi Ming sang Jay Chou's "Cute Girl" and Richie Ren's "Hey Girl Look Over Here" (對面的女孩看過來)

without once taking his eyes off her, they both knew they had fallen in love.

After two years of seeing each other, mostly on weekends, they became engaged. They saved what they could, planning to marry as soon as they could afford an apartment with a terraced garden inside the city walls. Like the new generation of upwardly mobile professionals of which they were a part, they would manage to balance work and personal life while earning enough to live well. Although their combined income was relatively high among young people, if they ever wanted to move to Shanghai, it would look like chickenfeed against the inflated city prices. But they refused to yield to the real estate panic that was overwhelming many of their friends.

Lihua remained untouched by much of the fast-paced life of urban China. She cycled the hour-long trek to and from work. She smiled at strangers and spoke to them only when she had something kind to say. She was compassionate to herself and to others, following a way of life exemplified by her Tao and Confucian ancestors. She practiced the ever-popular Hatha yoga at home and on weekends, using its breathing exercises throughout the day to reduce the inevitable pressures. Colleagues followed her example and took up yoga not only for the physical exercise but for what they saw as a source of social harmony and moral rightness.

. . .

Lihua's story, unlike Dieter's, is one that a majority of the world's population could pursue. If every person in the world were to emulate Lihua, we would have a lifestyle for humanity that would be sustainable for generations. Yet many cannot aspire to lead even such a simple life. A billion people—more than one in seven alive today—have a daily struggle for their most basic human needs.[35] They face chronic hunger, lack of access to clean water and sanitation, and threats to their physical security. To expect them to attend to inner fulfillment is perhaps unrealistic. Or is it?

No matter what our circumstances, we are mostly free to choose the rituals of daily existence that create order in our lives, to engage in the moments of silence when we feel deeply connected to something greater than ourselves, to be compassionate to others, to perform unsolicited acts of kindness, and to care for our little corner of nature. There is little personal cost in making these choices, and the benefits to our happiness and well-being are enormous. Such benefits are being increasingly well documented by psychologists and neurophysiologists,[36] though generally they remain little known in the business world.

The stories of Dieter and Lihua are, of course, more than a little exaggerated. A happy existence and sustainable lifestyle are not necessarily dependent on saintly behavior or a materially deprived life, just as professional success is not automatically an indicator of unkindness to others, excessive material consumption, or antipathy to environmental causes. But the two opposing ways of being do present an interesting paradox: Dieter is materially more successful, and his life appears more desirable by the monetized standards of many people the world over; yet Lihua is the happier person and lives more sustainably. Does one have to choose between Lihua's way of being and Dieter's? Can one be hard driving and focused on wealth creating while tending to one's health and others' well-being?

In the next chapter you learn of a "third way of being" told in the first-person voice of Fred Tsao. His life story offers insight into a way of life and enduring set of practices that are a powerful guide to flourishing enterprise,[37] no matter where you live or work. As money manager Joseph H. Bragdon concludes in his study of companies that mimic life, "When people work with their hearts as well as their minds, they engage the powerful heart–brain neurology that is the source of their highest (spiritual) intelligence. . . . [Those] that use it effectively achieve higher returns on equity in spite of using less mechanistic debt leverage than their industry peers."[38] It is, in brief, about doing well by doing good.

A PERSONAL EXPERIENCE: THE FREDERICK CHAVALIT TSAO STORY

IN THIS AND THE NEXT CHAPTER, we hand over sole authorship to Frederick Chavalit Tsao, whose story is of central importance to our discussion of quantum leadership. Fred Tsao was born in 1957 into a well-known family: his father is the respected shipping legend Frank Tsao, the tycoon who led the high-profile Hong Kong consortium that built Suntec City in Singapore. Fred joined the family business in 1977, taking over in 1995 at the age of only thirty-seven to become the fourth generation at the helm. Under his stewardship, it has expanded from a traditional shipping company to one focused on integrated industrial supply chains; it has diversified from maritime interests to encompass lifestyle/real estate, investments, community development, and leader health and well-being.

In this chapter we hear Fred's story in his own words. Important for us here are not the accounts of business adventures and successes, formidable though they are, but Fred's personal journey, which has been one of transformation, inspired by Eastern philosophy and Western science. We learn how it underpins his approach to business and leadership. We present this as a first-person narrative and, in so doing, allow the reader to appreciate that the aspects of leadership that define Fred as a quantum leader do not derive from management literature or training courses but rather from a fundamental and original exploration of what it means to be a business leader today.

. . .

As a young man in my twenties, born into a wealthy and successful family, I found career success early on. Borrowing money from my father, I made investments in the family business and watched them grow. Maybe I had a knack for it, or maybe conditions simply worked in my favor, but my early efforts soon yielded big dividends. I got used to getting exceptional results—in one instance watching US$8 million balloon to more than US$200 million in a relatively short period. In the years that followed, as a full-time member of the family business, my role expanded: I helped reorganize our shipping operations and developed profitable new businesses in Thailand and Hong Kong. I felt like I was conquering the world and could live forever. Now, at the age of sixty-two, with experience and hindsight, I can see that much of this was a form of ego gratification.

Today, my preoccupations are very different. As I describe in the following pages, my life has taken me on a journey not only through a sometimes cutthroat world of big business but also on a personal transformative path. It is this transformation in being that I wish to convey here, specifically with regard to how it affects my current approach to business leadership.

I believe I am well placed to offer my story as an example to other business leaders, because it is based on a fusion of Eastern and Western ideas grounded in experience. Neither an American nor a Chinese approach has thus far offered a clear-cut path to global prosperity: we must bridge these two worlds and integrate elements of both to truly succeed.

Now is the time for such a transformation across the world. There is a growing momentum in search of fundamental change, driven by China's leadership in the world as much as by the United States and Europe. It has become clear to me and colleagues across my business and industry networks that many people are seeing the need for a new consciousness in business. I am witnessing a growing desire to cultivate the self to experience the essential oneness of life in a way that spans respect for one's ancestors and care for future generations. I see this process of awakening in others, and I am experiencing it myself. Those of us on this path should investigate it together and share our experiences to facilitate the growth of a community so that others may benefit.

We are on the threshold of imminent global change—which will be either for the better or for the worse depending on the path we choose. I believe we can cocreate a tipping point in business, one that leads to a path of greater self-awareness and to a heightened perception of how our attitudes and actions in business can affect others, indeed all life on earth, and future generations. Many are rising to meet this challenge—if you are reading these words, you are likely among them. This book itself is an exploration of what it will take for each of us to contribute to an emerging reality of global prosperity and flourishing—an invitation to engage in dialogue and to take action.

To help you understand my approach to business leadership, I describe the events and experiences that shaped who I am. In the following pages you learn something of my background and the challenges I faced in an often turbulent economic and business environment. But my central message concerns a more inward journey, an awakening of my consciousness, and how that informed all aspects of my leadership and decision making.

My Early Years

There have been many apparent contradictions in my life. I grew up in Hong Kong, the fourth generation in a family business whose cultural roots are in China. I am Chinese but feel at home in many countries. I am as comfortable in Tokyo or Bangkok as I am in London or Los Angeles.

As a small child, I was influenced by both Chinese and Western cultures: Hong Kong was then a British colony. My ancestors came from Shanghai, which, since the Treaties of Nanking and Whampoa in the 1840s,[1] has been China's international city. My grandfather attended an English middle school there, and my father graduated from St. John's University, an American-style institution. So among Chinese families mine was more Westernized than most. My family's aspirations—especially those of my grandfather—found expression in the opportunities of the free market. This was a turbulent time in China: many Chinese people were rejecting their traditional culture yet desperately conflicted about doing so.

I went to university at the age of sixteen and graduated from the University of Michigan with a bachelor's degree in naval architecture and a master's degree in industrial engineering. My interest in Chinese culture was revived in the mid-1990s when I began to investigate what might be called cultural sustainability. As a family, we often felt culturally displaced: we didn't live in China, and we had to assimilate into local cultures wherever we went. It became clear to me, especially after attending school in Canada and the United States, that I was different. I was Chinese, but the question "What does it mean to be Chinese?" took on a new importance for me around that time.

I returned to Asia when I was twenty to work for the family business, starting off in engineering and in the maintenance section of the shipping business, then the dominant portion of our family's holdings. I questioned everything, too often committing the Socratic mistake of asking "Why?" and "Why not?," which was unsettling for my coworkers, especially as I had already been identified as the successor to the family business. I was passed through various departments and eventually assigned to manage two small cargo ships and a somewhat larger twenty-two-thousand-ton vessel. The attitude was, "Let's give the boss's son something to occupy him so he will stop meddling in our work." But, as it turned out, my bosses were agreeably surprised by the unexpectedly high economic returns I managed from those first ships.

A couple of years later, I was in Thailand attending to the discharge of cargo from our vessels docked in Bangkok when I met one of our agents who handled the palm oil distribution for our Malaysian refinery. This agent introduced me to a palm oil plantation in southern Thailand that was looking for capital. It was far from obvious how this plantation would integrate with our refinery, but I showed an interest, probably being mostly enthused by the idea of having an adventure in a remote jungle where my father could not find me. I borrowed US$3 million and became a partner in the newly formed Thai company and eventually its CEO, even though many people had warned me that southern Thailand was a dangerous place to do business.

There was little law and order, and, at times, it felt like Hollywood's version of the Wild West. The challenges were many, a few of them even life threatening, but to build the business, I had to overcome them. One of our villages was raided by bandits. I had to deal with communist revolutionaries in the mountains. And in the worst incident of all, our plantation manager was shot and killed by five hired gunmen on our own housing estate. His death had a profound effect on me. I was only twenty-six, and the murder was a personal warning to scare me away from the business. I did what I could to care for his family in the years that followed, but the incident was emotionally distressing and left me with many questions about the nature of business and the value it placed on human life.

A few years later, the plantation company was listed on the Bangkok stock exchange. I sold my controlling stake in it to a British concern looking to do a backdoor listing by injecting its local assets into the company. We got a good price, and for sentimental reasons I kept a 1 percent share. It still yields good dividends.

In the mid-1980s, a number of national shipping lines around the world collapsed, and my family's company, at the time called International Maritime Carriers (IMC), was asked by the Thai government to step in to help rescue its national shipping line. I was in Thailand at the time working on the palm oil plantation, so I was the obvious candidate for the role. That was when I first experienced what it's like to be a wounded animal preyed on from all directions. It was not pretty. I witnessed it again in 1997 when the Asian financial crisis hit, and the value of the Thai baht plummeted. Our company in Bangkok was in good shape, but because of the currency devaluation its financial books were not. We were borrowing in US dollars, and almost overnight the value of the dollar went from 25 to 72 baht, so our loan was no longer serviceable from our operating cash flow. I decided to wind up the loan, which we had been using to build our Bangkok container terminal. That experience introduced me to the shadow side of bankers, of whom it is rightly said that "they give you an umbrella when you don't need it and take it away when you do."

With the intention of repaying the loan in full, I paid a visit to the lending bank in Bangkok. I was met at the door by enraged bank officers behaving like mad dogs. Welcome to the enforcement team: intimidation was the name of their game. I was being given a hard time under the assumption that I couldn't pay and had come to renegotiate. I could have diffused the situation instantly, but I chose to hold out to see how far they would go. When I had had enough of this "entertainment," I said, "I've come to pay back the loan in full." In an instant, their fury melted into obsequiousness. The enforcers withdrew to be replaced by a different team, who eventually accompanied me back to my car, continually thanking me, smiling and bowing all the way. It taught me a lot. A good hardworking businessman on the wrong side of a devaluation will go to a lending bank on his knees and get roughed up. That's the game. What I learned was that if you are down on your luck, they will send in the dogs. That's not a position you ever want to find yourself in (unless, of course, your debt is so large that your default could threaten the bank's very survival).

There were many other such stories: setting up a shipyard in a community where violence was routine; dealing with the Thai mafia; working out how to catch thieves in the warehouses; witnessing gun battles in the shipyard. We left some of the machine-gun bullet holes on the dock as a reminder. These early experiences played out against a background of incredible growth, which peaked in the 1990s and made for a business environment that I can describe only as the Wild East.

I saw the rise and the fall of the Asian economic miracle, which first emerged during my Thailand period in 1988. And I saw the damage that irresponsible economic growth was inflicting on society. People were going crazy with their financial deals and stock market speculation. They were ignoring their day jobs. Employee turnover was high because nobody wanted to do an honest day's work: everybody was going to make a fortune playing the market instead. Many young people abandoned the fields in a rush to cities, only to find themselves in dire straits, and this led to the unraveling of the rural communities' social fabric. In

1997, I watched it all fall apart again: the big-money guys pulled the plug on the market and left everyone else high and dry, which led to more confrontations with bankers.

All this provided much food for thought about the role and purpose of business and the way in which it was conducted. How far will people go to clinch a deal? How far will *I* go to create value for my family business in such an environment? It then became clear to me: *The fundamental purpose of economic activity has to be to serve human well-being.* Business is a human construct; it is worthwhile only if it is run for the benefit of people as a whole—it must work to maintain relevance in pursuit of social goals. In 2018, as we completed this book, the conclusion may seem obvious, but at that time and for much of my career in business, the behavior I was seeing in the marketplace was the polar opposite of this.

Succession

In the early 1990s, I was spending increasing amounts of time in Hong Kong helping my father restructure the family's core shipping business, looking at how to achieve economies of scale by pooling assets with other people's ships and improving logistical supply-chain operations. I was made managing director, a sort of co-CEO role in which I shared responsibilities with my father. My job was to reorganize and transform our operations in line with Asia's boom and to build IMC into a differentiated shipping enterprise. We added more specialized vessels, including self-discharging ships and chemical tankers. This transformation of a traditional family business to a more professionally managed organization allowed us to expand when Asia started to really take off a few years later.

Sharing leadership responsibilities with one's father is often a challenge, and so it proved to be. I remember having dinner with him to talk about how difficult it was to manage as co-CEOs. "Two pairs of chopsticks in the same bowl of rice is a problem," I said. "And, on top of that, you want me to eat with my left hand, even though I am right-handed." The conversation continued for years with no clear resolution. During that time our company headquarters relocated to Singapore while we continued to reorganize shipping operations and expand our fleet. At one point I said to him, "This really isn't working too well." Neither my elder brother, who had become a renowned architect, nor my sister had any appetite to manage the family business. So I made a suggestion to my father: Since it was undesirable to divide up a family business between siblings when some are not involved in its management, it would be better if he gave me whatever he intended to give me as his legacy, and then I could finance a buyout of the rest of the business using the capital I had built up, along with any financial leverage I might need. We finally reached agreement in late 1994, and, as of January 1, 1995, I became the fourth generation to head the family business.

There was a lot of talk at the time about the opening up of the Asian markets and the emergence of China as a global economic power. With family and colleagues, I looked at the implications of evolving IMC into a global business. We began by looking at the very meaning of such an undertaking and how to make use of the wisdom and resources of both East and West in search of our own identity and sustainability. That led to the establishment in 1995 of the East West Cultural Development Centre, which we describe in the next chapter.

IMC's Origins

To fully understand my ideas of business sustainability and its stewardship of society, you have to look at the legacy I inherited. Each generation of my family evolved the business and shaped it to thrive in the particular era in which it found itself. But consistently applied across every era have been the three values of our founder, my great-grandfather: integrity, hard work, and prudence.

My great-grandfather Tsao Wa Chang was a sampan boatman in Shanghai at the turn of the twentieth century. One day, a drunken captain left a bag full of cash and documents in his boat. My great-grandfather could have kept it; it would have represented a fortune for such a poor boatman. Instead, he chose to seek out the captain, but his ship had already sailed. Months later, when the ship returned, my great-grandfather was waiting for the captain with the bag and its contents intact. It turned out that many of the documents were bills of lading and titles for cargo in a warehouse. The captain, a Westerner, was impressed with my great-grandfather's integrity and gave him a large reward—a sum of money that would allow him to establish his own waterfront transport business. And so our family business was born.

With each succeeding generation, the business grew exponentially and often against all odds. Under my grandfather, Tsao Ying Yung, and my father, Frank W. K. Tsao, it expanded in shipping and real estate, through two world wars, and against the backdrop of China's transition from empire to republic and thence to today's more market-based socialist regime. As the Tsao family grew, members migrated from China across the globe—my grandfather died as a citizen of Brazil. By the time I was born, our business headquarters had moved from Shanghai to Hong Kong.

The story of the Tsao family business is one of rising to the challenges of the world around it, adapting to the changing needs of society while observing consistency in its three main corporate values. Among them, prudence has been key. It has prevented the family from becoming too embroiled in the past century's turbulent events, and it continues to guide us now. Rather than fail during the third generation's tenure, as family businesses are statistically prone to do, we have flourished. IMC was listed on the Hong Kong and Singapore stock exchanges, but in 2002 I made the decision to take that public part of the company private to give the family enterprise more freedom to evolve with creativity and imagination, answering to no one other than ourselves.

My Years as Head of the Company

In the years since I took over the business, it has gone from being a regional shipping company to an integrated multinational service-based solutions provider—a complex multi-billion-dollar business operating across many geographic markets. In the mid-1990s, China's industrial development meant an increased demand for raw materials, and there was a tremendous shortage of cargo capacity to ship these raw materials into China. But markets are inherently cyclical, and at the height of the boom in 2005–2007, when the value of all ships was hugely inflated, I urged my managers to sell a few of our vessels. This was met with formidable resistance: "Why sell when the market is so strong?" While it is hard to anticipate a downturn when the market is hot, selling ships during peak times is what made it possible for us to expand once the market had cooled.

Over the past couple of decades, we continued to diversify our portfolio and add new ventures, from equipment and ports to marine offshore engineering services. We transformed our business model from ship owner to solutions provider through multiple industry supply chains. At the heart of it was the emergence of China as a trading powerhouse and the growing requirements of its booming market of more than a billion people. The China miracle forced changes to the shipping industry in ways never seen before.[2]

I shied away from speculative windfall deals, instead concentrating on the business's long-term sustainability. Although some advised against it, in recent years I broadened the business beyond our core industrial and real estate activities by creating Octave, a division encompassing businesses that promote health and well-being in line with quantum leadership.

Today the IMC business is about evolution and creativity, which is a reflection of my own personal journey. IMC continues to practice an inclusive business philosophy of creating value for all stakeholders in what is still very much a dog-eat-dog world. I believe that this philosophy is what allows IMC to outperform companies who pursue short-term profit whatever the cost to society and the environment. The focus for us is on *sustainability as flourishing*.

What Is a Business For?

As my own journey progressed, I began to see more clearly that the role of a business leader is to serve human well-being while also creating wealth. And wealth in this case does not only mean profit for the owner but also prosperity for all. A resource without a social purpose is not wealth. Businesses have to add wider social value as they create enterprise value, through which they contribute to serving the needs of society. This is the essence of Adam Smith's phrase "the interests of the producer ought to be attended to only so far as it may be necessary for promoting that of the consumer."[3] And in today's world the continued evolution of business requires greater value integration and support from all stakeholders.

To understand business, one has to start with its purpose. Business is an integral part of society in which markets—at least in today's capitalistic system—play a major role in meeting people's needs and wants. It is the willingness of people to pay for goods and services that converts economic resources into wealth. Economics should be understood, fundamentally, as activities that satisfy human desires. But in the age of unbounded consumerism and materialism, human desires do not necessarily align with well-being.

Business is thus far the most efficient mechanism humans have devised for deploying resources to create value. It is a conjunction of people and institutions with two primary roles: to serve humankind and to generate wealth. A business that is well aligned is more than just a place to earn a living; it is also a platform for leaders, managers, and employees to pursue development, creativity, and self-actualization, individually and collectively as a community.

Insights from Those Years

As it grew, IMC's businesses ranged from agriculture to investment management and spanned trading, construction, manufacturing, logistics, and mining, among other activities. This range, plus our geographic diversification, exposed me to the full spectrum of human behavior. Ultimately, it allowed me to see the bigger picture of social and economic change in our times and offered me the experience of and sensitivity toward a wide range of cultural perspectives. It taught me that globalization and global integration have brought great material benefits but at the same time contributed to the weakening of human relationships. While the world is getting smaller, people are drifting apart. An overly developed notion of selfhood and materialism has emerged that has contributed to a narrowing of the global business mind-set.

At every step, we looked at IMC's economics to make sure we were adding value for our customers while ensuring capital was used efficiently. A creative approach to the challenges to the company's bottom line helped us overcome an inevitable institutional resistance to new ideas. That resistance often meant slow execution and timing missteps and realizing our mistakes only in retrospect.

Why do we resist change until it's too late? Because of a lack of contextual awareness of the times and of the broader market environment. Constant "terrain analysis" is required, and in today's era of swift change and market turbulence, a higher level of awareness is more important than ever before. Leaders and management teams need to be vigilant and on a continuous quest to understand the complex economic, political, and social systems in which they participate to achieve safe transit into the future, even if it means putting ourselves in vulnerable situations. If we are reacting only to the here and now, it will be too late for proactive decisions, and opportunities to flourish will pass us by.

My early life experiences raised questions about purpose, and when I took the helm in 1995, I was already asking myself questions about the deeper meaning of leadership—questions such as "Where am I leading the business?" and "What does sustainability really mean?" Existential concerns about the social role of business preoccupied me. And that is how my quest began: how to sustain a business that works not only *in* society but also *for* society.

I began by studying Western leadership practices and management theory. I spent the early years of my career reading and questioning in this area but ultimately found the dominant approaches neither holistic nor particularly effective. Many pieces are missing; and even those approaches taught in leading business schools and practiced by the highest-performing companies are still fraught with negative implications for society and the environment. The managerial mind-set has to evolve to be ever-more sophisticated in its ability to produce flourishing enterprise. Business as an institution now has a direction provided by the United Nations' seventeen Sustainable Development Goals (SDGs), signed by 193 nations, which is an excellent opportunity to speed up its own evolution to meet the challenges facing humankind.[4] It is an opportunity for business to increase its already positive impact in alleviating poverty, developing wealth, and raising standards of living. As this new awareness becomes prevalent in society, business should also work to achieve a higher level of consciousness to create the businesses necessary to take on this challenge. Meanwhile, business life cycles are getting shorter, the nature of competition is increasingly disruptive, and ecological and social issues intensify. Industry leaders are finding it difficult to weather the perfect storms they are facing with increased frequency, unable to meet the needs of either their shareholders or stakeholders.

How could I lead my business through such times in ways that contribute to well-being, prosperity, and flourishing?

Learning from Traditional Eastern Cultures

Having explored quite deeply the Western leadership models without finding satisfactory answers and solutions for my endeavours, I turned to the teachings of Eastern sages whose wisdom has stood the test of time, measured not in decades or centuries but in millennia. I began by seeking an understanding of the Eastern thought systems of Lao Tzu, Confucius, and Buddha. This led me to realize that in every system, whether business, marriage, or any other relational arrangement, each participant must have a specific role. Without defined roles, the players in a system have no relevance and the system itself ceases to have value. When a system has no value, it declines and eventually ceases to exist: not only will it fail to flourish; eventually it will be unable to sustain itself.

I found myself on an exciting journey of discovery. I was seeking the key to whole-person well-being, looking for a way to flourish in both life and business. *You cannot lead a flourishing organization unless you learn to flourish as a person.*

Ch'i (the Life Force)

In 1992, I began exploring mindfulness, first in terms of the Chinese concept of Ch'i or Qi (pronounced "chee"). This lies at the heart of ancient Chinese philosophy. What drew me to Ch'i was the realization that I could experience it physically. Ch'i literally means "breath" or "air," and figuratively it stands for the life force, the energy flows that circulate in every living system. As my Ch'i practice began, I could feel it moving in my body. I began to comprehend that this energy is a hidden treasure to be used in daily life. Ch'i is the essence of life and also something that can be cultivated, a force to be used in pursuit of our health and well-being. Most of all, it is a creative power inside us.

My active exploration of Ch'i energy goes back to 1993 when I met a Chinese doctor trained in traditional Chinese medicine as well as Taoist traditions. This doctor had come highly recommended by a family member. He was a master of Qigong, an ancient Chinese health-care system that integrates breathing techniques and focus. On the day of my first appointment, I found a long line of people waiting at his office. When my turn finally came, he examined me and gave me a prescription for a potion of traditional Chinese medicine (TCM). "You're going to lose your voice, and then you're going to have terrible headaches and probably feel awful for some time," he said. "But don't worry: then you're going to get better." On the way out, I went to pay, but his assistant said, "Oh, you don't have to pay him anything. It's up to you. There's a little red box by the door. Just pay whatever you think it's worth."

I was highly skeptical about the potion's medicinal properties, so when I got home, I faxed the prescription to my Beijing office to have its formulation analyzed. It turned out to be mostly seaweed and other plant-based ingredients. I decided that it should be relatively safe and tried it for a few days, even though it smelled awful and tasted worse. The first day, I lost my voice singing karaoke, right in the middle of a song. I flew to Thailand soon after and developed a splitting headache. I persisted with the prescribed doses even though it got so bad that I couldn't get out of bed for three days. But then, on the third day, it started to clear up, and by the fourth day I was feeling great. I lost ten pounds and was sleeping better than I ever had. My mind was clear, and my emotions were more in check. This doctor had really got something.

"You were right: I feel great!" I said to him on my return visit. "How can I progress further?"

"Go and practice Qigong," he replied.

Qigong (life-energy cultivation) is a system of body posture and movement, breathing, and meditation—a practice to cultivate and balance the Ch'i. As soon as I began, all the energy in my body started moving. I could feel it acutely—where it started, where it stopped. I was intrigued. This experience with the Taoist doctor had put me on a path to meditation, and I could feel the energy flow just by opening the palm of my hand.

From those first steps, I began doing meditation for longer and longer periods. One afternoon, I went to visit my sister's home. She and her family were out, so I let myself in to wait for them and started meditating. Evening came and still I was alone. I felt hungry, but I continued to meditate until 3:00 a.m., sitting there the whole time and feeling the energy flow through me.

I enrolled in the doctor's Qigong classes and paid the fees for many years, but I was able to attend only a few classes because of my crazy business schedule. One day I invited him to lunch, expecting an interesting conversation, but he would not talk about any of his theories or concepts. Every time I asked him anything remotely philosophical, he would interrupt me. "Stop talking and start doing," he would say. He taught me the importance of practices and knowledge through experience rather than through words and abstractions.

Exploring Spirituality and Philosophy

There was little obvious Taoist influence in my childhood. I went to Christian schools, and my mother was a fervent Buddhist. I spent years exploring Buddhism and the practices of many other religions and spiritual traditions. I understood that all the world's major religions share a common spiritual essence aimed at peace and harmony. My purpose here is not to compare them or to persuade you that one is better than another.

Spiritual traditions and their practices, however, are a different issue. I find Taoism and its practices to be appreciably relevant to today's world because Taoism focuses on dealing with the truth about materialism, and through materialism, an understanding of spirituality and its origin, what the Chinese call the Tao. A lot of what is written in the Taoist canon, the *Daodejing*,[5] is about management and leadership. Taoists focus on understanding the nature of reality, especially the material world, and on living in a way that is in harmony with nature. Some of its foundational notions include *Wu wei* (action through inaction), *Ziran* (naturalness), and the ineffable, mysterious *Tao* (the Way) itself. The *Daodejing* declares that, if you lose the Tao, you can at least have virtue. If you lose virtue, you can still be benevolent. If you lose benevolence, you can have ethics. And if you lose ethics, you are left with protocol. After that, you are left with nothing but the messiness of life.

Taoist philosophy as it relates to leadership is often surprising and counterintuitive. For example, the weak but pliable sapling is acknowledged as being more able to weather major storms than is the rigid oak tree. "Weakness overcomes strength; softness overcomes hardness" is a key tenet of the *Daodejing*. Taoists value the power of apparent weakness: rather than the more primitive concept of power deriving from strength, we may understand through the Tao that true power comes from an understanding of the connections between disparate things, situations, and people. But a sapling, in the end, sways with the wind and is destined to grow into a tree. Human beings can do far more. We are capable not just of understanding connections but also of making new ones to generate entirely new realities and new worlds. Here, I find inspiration from the Buddhist *Fahua jing* (Lotus Sutra), which assures us that Nirvana is attainable in our own material world.

In the West, we seek truths in the external world: we tend to look outward. Chinese traditional culture tells us that self-cultivation involves looking inward by means of mindfulness and energy practice. According to the ancient Chinese worldview, our eyes are closed, looking inward and evolving from that space. If we look inward deeply enough, we might find that everything we want in life is already encoded within us. Having experienced the holistic nature of reality, by means of continuous self-cultivation, one comprehends that impermanence and suffering are fundamental properties of reality. Having become aware of this, the way one thinks begins to change. This approach, constantly looking inward, investigating reality through meditation and related practices, is a path to understanding oneness.

I now pause for the benefit of those for whom such practices and insights are unfamiliar, who may be puzzled about their relevance to business leadership. My attempt is to make clear that only by means of a transformation in consciousness can we aspire to lead businesses fit for the challenges of the twenty-first century—businesses that serve the interests of humanity as a whole. It is this consciousness, this alignment with our inner purpose, that allows passion and love to be expressed and creativity to match the transformation that is going on, available for humankind's evolution. All reality happens in our inner world, and our perception of the outer world also happens in our inner world, so the practice is both what is happening as we deal with the movement of information in and out, of awareness and consciousness, and our response to it. The significant implication of quantum science is a change of direction from one that is in separation and becoming more divisive into one that is more integrative, holistic, and systemic. It is holistic in its formless energy, and it is systemic in its material expression. In other words, at a quantum level, it is holistic; but at a material level, it is systemic.

My own personal journey, and one that I can recommend to others no matter where they live and work, has centered on traditional Chinese culture, which emphasizes the importance of harmonious transition, of taking the middle way by centering one's actions on the right principles, the right practices, and the right behaviors. It does not require sophisticated learning. While studying philosophical texts is helpful, without practice one can never fully grasp the right way of living. In Chinese, the word "life" (人生) also means discovering what it means to be human, understanding the mind-body-spirit connection and that the past, present, and future all exist simultaneously. How might we live if we gave ourselves the freedom to see the past and the future as resources for the present?

Anyone can easily begin a journey based on mindfulness-type practices. It simply requires you to know yourself in the moment, to have awareness of your own self, which is constantly changing as you interact with the world. We can access the outer world through our inner world. There is a direct two-way communication between our inner and outer worlds. By cultivating our inner world, we tune in to the fundamental nature of the outer world. *With success in the inner world, we can become outwardly influential and impactful.* That is how we become one with the Tao. It just requires practice, practice, practice.

Over many years I learned about emerging Western scientific discoveries, especially with regard to quantum physics,[6] quantum biology,[7] neuroscience, and consciousness research.[8] Quantum science tells us that the fundamental building blocks of nature are not particles but energy fields: matter, including our own bodies, is held together, and interacts, using energy. Every particle in the universe is in fact a ripple of the underlying field of energy, molded into a particle by the machinery of quantum mechanics. Some interpretations of quantum theory assert that there exists a universal quantum energy field.[9] This has a strong correlation with the Eastern notion of the Tao—that the coherence and vitality of life comes from an ineffable connection to a deeper nonmaterial reality. It is my view that modern science's universal energy field and the god of many of the world's religions converge into a single description of the true nature of reality. As we show in Chapter 6, science is now providing evidence of the interconnectedness and essential oneness of the world, validating the traditional Chinese worldview in which mind and matter are seen as unitary.

There is only one consciousness. This view is expressed in ancient texts such as the *I Ching* (also known as the *Book of Changes*), the *Daodejing*, the Buddhist Sutras, the Hindu Vedas, and the oral traditions and later written scrolls of Jewish mysticism known as the Kabbalah. The *I Ching* anticipated Western scientific theories of an interconnected reality by more than 2,500 years, and it is not the oldest of the texts by any means. Its teaching are about the alignment of our inner and outer worlds to create a unified reality in which individuals and groups are interconnected and made whole. *This* is the universal principle we need to use to elevate human behavior—and business leadership—in the twenty-first century: a path made manifest by both ancient wisdom and the implications of emerging science.

For decades now, I have been experimenting with practices to evolve my consciousness, and what I have found can be summarized in these four words: "oneness," "wholeness," "discovery," and "evolution." All the great sages from Jesus to Buddha to Lao Tzu have expressed the same essential truths.

I have logged more than a thousand hours of healing practices, in retreats and with accompanying discussion. It has helped me identify and release trapped emotions in attachment and traumas, and in the process I have discovered that sadness is inexorably at the core of my being. It is a sadness of personal loss in experiencing the shift from the "I" to the "We" space, a sadness for humanity (the "All of Us" space) and its continuing crises of existence. Unlike anger and fear, sadness was an emotion that for many years I could not work through. Then, one day I realized that sadness was the starting point of all my other emotions and that I can transmute its falling energy into rising energy through which comes the motivation to act with compassion. From that came the sudden realization that the transmutation of negative energy to positive emotions and the cycle of development and love are expressed through our own self-compassion turning into compassion for the world. This energy is also the energy of creation from which the world can evolve into a more flourishing place for all life and future generations.

At that point, I realized that I now had an answer for those who asked me why I do what I do, why I work so hard to develop new businesses aimed at well-being and being well. I had previously offered a variety of responses, but now I knew what was really driving me. I was dealing with sadness in my life, and the only way for me to work through it was by taking actions that benefited the world. We are all in the same place; we all have the same issues; we all want to be well and to experience well-being.

Unlike many older Chinese people today, who were profoundly influenced by the Cultural Revolution of the 1960s–1970s, I turned my gaze to earlier times in Chinese civilization. I find that the teachings of Confucius strongly influence my outlook. From Buddhist teachings, I have incorporated elements of the "eightfold path," which encompasses the right view, the right intentions, the right speech, the right action, the right livelihood, the right effort, the right mindfulness, and the right concentration. From Zen, I have learned mindfulness through concentration meditation, where you train the mind to observe what arises in your consciousness, to concentrate without distraction, and to go where you want your consciousness to go. Insight meditation is a nonattached examination and exploration of our own experience and conceptualizations.

In traditional Chinese culture, the purpose of life is to elevate one's consciousness. The aspiration is, over the course of your life, to reach oneness with the Tao. Buddhist teachings establish the philosophical framework, Confucian teachings act as a kind of standard operating procedure, while Taoism provides the "policy menu." Policy menus are not heavy on theory; they are not prescriptive. Thus, Taoism can be thought of as a powerful, if somewhat oblique, guide to living life the right way. I should add that I learned much from Christianity and its practices of surrendering to God. And among its many virtues, the chants of the Islamic tradition touched my soul profoundly.

There are misconceptions about Chinese traditional culture. While we might seem submissive to notions of a collective, we see our care for this collective not only as a condition for holistic health but also as a good evolutionary practice to refrain from overattachment to individual desires. Refraining from pleasures for certain periods helps us understand the Tao and illuminates our attachments. But it is also true that in Eastern wisdom there is no Protestant- or Islamic-like injunction that we must live without sin as the price of entry into heaven. Instead of denying our human urges and avoiding the messiness of life, the Eastern approach encourages us to embrace them. Worldly desires are not only accepted; they are considered necessary, because without them there is no movement toward emotional and spiritual growth. There is no motivation without desire.

Cultivating the self changes what we desire. For example, if you have been meditating long enough, you will realize that there is no need for stimulants to achieve a sense of bliss. You may think you want many material things to satisfy your worldly desires. But when you cultivate your desires through inner mindfulness, you realize you don't need so many material possessions to feel satisfied. When you can go anywhere through inner reflection, why watch a Hollywood movie? Instead, you can *be* the movie.

What I Learned for Business

A central view in traditional Chinese thought is that everything is relational and that reality is holistic. Historically, over much of the last 2,500 years, we Chinese have lived our lives in conscious awareness of our relationship to the heavens, to nature, to other people, to family, and to our inner self. Seeing the world in that way—in relational terms—is itself transformative. When you live your life in a healthy relationship with others and with the world around you, you have a greater likelihood of achieving harmony.

As a businessman in the twenty-first century, I interpret harmony as a dynamic state that enables authentic collaboration. Once you achieve harmony, you are better able to collaborate with others, and *authentic collaboration* is one of the keys to meeting the challenge of business as an agent for social change.

The key influences in my life have not been businesspeople. My mentors include Lao Tzu, Jesus, Confucius, Buddha, Krishna, and other great sages. These are my role models. They still exert an incredibly strong influence thousands of years after their deaths. But the intersection of Western science and traditional Chinese philosophy remains a source of inspiration for me. As discussed earlier, emerging fields of research offer evidence of the essential oneness of the universe, mirroring the ancient Chinese view. This is the reason I have sponsored research and conferences worldwide on these new sciences and invited world-class researchers from both East and West to explain their findings to a broader business audience.

Worldviews are important. A worldview is an assumption about reality. We need a right worldview for us to flourish in the era in which we find ourselves. A worldview creates a language and a structure in which to express our ideas, understand the world, think, act, and communicate. We all have a worldview, consciously or not, but often it is incomplete, incongruent, or obsolete, which leads to inner conflict. When the many cognitions we hold about the world and ourselves clash, a state of tension results, known as cognitive dissonance. Our urge to maintain cognitive consistency can lead to irrational and sometimes dysfunctional behavior. Harmonizing our conflicted beliefs, developing a worldview characterized by oneness and connectedness, and exploring its details are essential in achieving congruency in the way we engage in relationships and the attitudes we adopt in responding to the world. It is how we cocreate a flourishing world.

I see a need for business to upgrade learning for management. But business also needs to address human development more holistically. We need to promote a new work lifestyle to support emotional and spiritual growth as part of business. This will eventually result in more authentic collaboration and creativity, and thus—as I have experienced and as we aim to demonstrate here—in business sustainability. My leadership approach over the years has led to periods of confusion for those around me; yet my guiding star has always remained constant: my belief that *business leadership is not about maximizing shareholder returns or transactional success but about stewardship and creating value for society over a sustained period of time.*

I describe myself as a pragmatic person, and I aim to be quick to take action when business opportunities or risks arise. Nonetheless, at times, some may find my approach mystifying. Looking at the hidden elements below the surface in a managerial situation, I may offer direction along these lines: "Gradually develop your skills and relationships, and your awareness of the changes you need to make. It is all linked in body, mind, and spirit. Evolution, or the freedom to create, doesn't come suddenly; it is a gradual process. Clean up your trapped emotions, your mind-set, and your prejudices. Continually rewire your neuroconnectors." Not everyone is able or ready to accept such guidance in a management review.

What I find important today is not *vision* especially—vision is a recurring theme in Western management approaches—but rather directionality and evolution. The "how to do it" that I promote involves meeting our daily challenges through a *continual process* of reenvisioning the future. It is important to avoid fixed projections of the future. I am wary of definitive answers to complex problems. I am more likely to address such problems obliquely with reference to scientific principles, perennial spiritual insights, and social trends that suggest the direction in which solutions might be found.

Living and Working Toward Well-Being

I am convinced of the relevance of traditional Chinese wisdom to the here and now, even though Chinese people themselves have tended to reject it over the past century. Reinterpreted for the twenty-first century, traditional Chinese thought offers us a path to experience higher forms of consciousness. The first form of consciousness is simply to be centered. This centeredness derives from the state of equilibrium and harmony that comes when we are integrated within our self and in our relationships to society and nature. When there is clarity and everything is aligned, all things can grow and flourish. Consciousness in its most holistic and natural state expresses love, enabling us to realize our fullest potential: freedom, joy, and peace. With a rise in consciousness, we all have the potential to gain the wisdom and courage to shift our business in a more meaningful direction toward prosperity and flourishing.

Thoughts on Personal Growth

We all continue to grow and develop throughout our lives. In 2013, I had another epiphany: a sudden realization that there is no shame, no guilt, not even fairness or forgiveness at a deeper existential level. None of these feeling are real, so we are called on simply to let them go. They are emotions we experience when we are being conditioned by others. At that point, I felt I was more able to accept life for what it is rather than for what others want it to be for me. Ego is the negative projection of our social needs: It functions in a continuous state of fear rather than love. The nature of ego is always seeking validation, building loops of repetitive conditioned programming in our minds based on our upbringing and on our dogmatic beliefs. Instead, we should learn to accept ourselves without judgment and to have compassion both for ourselves and for others. Only then can we develop the engagement, connectivity, generosity, and kindness that we need to function effectively. I have learned to accept that whatever happens is what it is. Every challenge is a gift for personal growth. Resistance takes on a different nature when I embrace it. Everything then seems to flow better.

Actually, before acceptance there is courage. I have learned through meditation practice that courage is a matter of becoming comfortable with uncomfortable feelings. Mindfulness is the process that will lead you to it. With courage comes the realization that emotions are provoked as a response to feelings of vulnerability. The ability to deal with vulnerability comes from seeing a given situation with yourself in it. Rational analysis and vigilant study of the terrain are required. Over the years, I worked on my emotional and spiritual growth, but I didn't listen to or learn to love my body as much as I should. Perhaps I am blessed with a strong constitution. But nowadays I am connecting with and listening to my body much more.

In putting what I have learned into practice, I am not constantly thinking about how I should be doing things that are compassionate or caring; I am not thinking about the Tao every time I make a management decision. As I venture into my exploration of life, first comes courage, then acceptance, and then a realization that love is resonance and that, if you work on your connectivity, love will be present. Starting from a place of loving ourselves as part of acceptance allows us all better connectivity. At the age of sixty-two, like many others, I have finally comprehended the meaning of the phrase "all you need is love."

3 AN ORGANIZATION'S JOURNEY: THE IMC STORY

IN THIS CHAPTER Frederick Chavalit Tsao explores his evolutionary journey in more detail and its relevance for a new kind of leadership. He enlarges on his views about the transformation in consciousness required by managers to be guided by a congruent worldview while being able to embrace change and continuously evolve. This is the essence of the quantum leader. IMC has undergone continuous evolution under his leadership and developed a core philosophy based on traditional Chinese wisdom. Fred argues that quantum leadership is the only response to managing in an era of exponential and bewildering change. We learn how AITIA, an institute to support the evolution of consciousness in the context of business and to develop quantum leadership through mindful awareness and connectivity, was established to promote flourishing. The culmination of the IMC journey so far is the creation of Octave, a transformational business model based on the promotion of a consciousness of oneness in a twenty-first-century global context. Octave is a for-profit business comprising three main parts—AITIA; Octave Living, focused on wellness and the journey of life; and Octave Space, for a community seeking a lifestyle of shifting consciousness.

·   ·   ·

Our modern management theories reinforce a fairly standardized set of corporate behaviors. These behaviors are predicated on an economic system that dictates the way management is measured and rewarded. We live in an era of leaders focused on creating short-term financial value and siloed organizations driven by narrowly defined key performance indicators (KPIs). In many cases, those with a financial interest in the business, the shareholders, are represented through financial institutions that have little concern for the business other than the maximization of short-term economic returns. Executives' incentives are not aligned with the long-term interests of society. Visioning and collaboration—processes that are crucial in making the business a cohesive whole that functions for society—are often absent or ineffective. As leaders of teams and organizations, we are failing to draw on our creative energies.

Business leadership is more than a science or even an art: rather, it is an evolutionary way of being. It is the effective deployment of knowledge and experience to achieve congruent goals (short and long term) that give managers their role and thus their relevance. The key task of leadership is to organize and deploy people and resources to respond to change. Management must embrace entrepreneurship and innovation. Failure to innovate is the most important reason for the decline of an organization; and failure to manage effectively is the key reason for the failure of new ventures.

A manager is primarily an integrator, the aim being to align, deploy, and operationalize seemingly disparate elements and to harness the collective energies of the organization. Managers throughout society—in government, businesses, or NGOs—too often operate in silos. But now, more than ever, collaboration is needed to harness the holistic energy of entire business ecologies. Leaders must understand the big picture and exercise creativity to fulfill the purpose of business as an institution that serves people's well-being. The fullest expression of management as an integrator is to be an entrepreneur with the competence to evolve and integrate business models relevant to the needs of society embedded in nature.

Leaders and managers, therefore, must develop the competence to recognize and respond to the dynamics of change. They must have heightened awareness, of both the inner spirit world and the outer material and social worlds, through which they can manage the dynamics of the evolutionary process. They must be guided by a congruent worldview, a worldview capable of perceiving and expressing oneness and wholeness in the business context. They must be able to continuously evolve in a constantly changing environment. To guide their thinking and action requires a transformation in consciousness, to see the world from a holistic, dynamic, evolutionary perspective. An increase in awareness through practices of connectedness is an ongoing commitment and investment that fulfills its own potential—evolution and creativity—through *consciousness, the mother of all capital.*

It is ironic that human beings create societies and systems that enslave and oppress them. But the very challenge that these systems present becomes the opportunity for their personal evolution toward flourishing. As leaders evolve their selves, they contribute to a transformation in the collective consciousness, which again changes the system. Then the new version of the system will enslave them once again and thereby stimulate them to develop a further transformation in consciousness. An understanding of this dynamic changes the way we look at problems, because problems are the basis on which we evolve toward flourishing. We elevate our consciousness to solve the problems we are faced with at a given point in time; then a new set of challenges arises, requiring a further shift in consciousness. So we know where we are evolving toward: the next challenge. It is a yin-yang dynamic of challenge and evolution spiraling up toward oneness. It is like swimming: it is through the resistance of the water that we learn to swim. If you can swim, you can progress; but if you can't, you sink. So it is the resistance that propels us forward.

What leads and guides us is ultimately at the spirit level: the connection to the deepest source of being, the force of creation—whatever you wish to call it.

If I had to pick one fundamental characteristic for leadership, I would say it is humility. With humility, you are more willing to change yourself, to learn, and to see the environment in a mindful manner. This is the basis of the self-cultivation at the heart of the evolutionary journey.

We are constrained by human constructs and beliefs that arise from our ego. We are conditioned by them, and we function according to the preferences and judgments that derive from them. These constructs and beliefs are barriers that prevent leaders and managers from expanding their realities. They limit our ability to engage with authenticity, creativity, and meaningful relationships. We see things as *we* are and not as *they* really are. When you are deeply connected to yourself and the world around you, you are able to embrace both your light side and your shadow side, by which I mean the parts of yourself you do not normally accept in your everyday life. Such unaccepted aspects of oneself will usually trigger defense mechanisms, such as justifications, falsehoods, the construction of alternative narratives, or simply shutting down. Quantum leaders, however, connect to the life energies within them and transmute that energy into positive action.

Loving yourself is important. This is an oft-cited truth. True love means accepting yourself as you are. Mindfulness helps us become aware of and understand our beliefs and assumptions, our preferences, fears, and desires. Sustained change can be realized only if we are able to rewire our behaviors so that we evolve in a manner sometimes referred to as "being in flow," which is what is meant in traditional Chinese culture by following the Tao.

It is clear to me that organizations can flourish only when their leadership evolves in such a way and managers create this kind of culture. It all begins with self-cultivation: the development of a mind-set that is truly open to change. Elevating our consciousness means being able to see clearly and to distinguish between what is in our wider interests in the context of organization and community and what is in fact only our distorted self-interest. This is fundamental to our ability to lead and manage sustainable change. An evolved self can perceive the distinction between objective reality and our own perceptions of self-interest. *Even a small team of mindful managers can create a workplace and organization capable of extraordinary achievements.*

But leaders are consistently challenged by systemic drag, because existing organizational structures and processes act as unintentional barriers to evolution. So how can business be organized to encourage new mind-sets and deal with the rapid changes in social and economic structures throughout the world? What will convince businesses to address the needs of—indeed, to serve—society? Identification of such needs is not the issue: we need look no further than the seventeen SDGs that define our aspirations for the world in the year 2030.[1]

Organizations' behavior and culture are driven by how people are organized and rewarded, which is an expression of our collective consciousness of who we are. So the structures, policies, and processes must change to allow sustainable evolution and enable innovation, while still maintaining the integrity and effectiveness of the larger business system. An organization with a culture founded on mindfulness and a consciousness of connectedness will be a collaborative and authentic workplace, one that promotes systemic innovation and has congruence of values, mission, and pathways. And an evolving organization continues to raise the consciousness of its members in response to the contemporary challenges it addresses. In this way it creates what I have already described as the mother of all capital—consciousness. Over half a century ago, Peter Drucker described the shift from manual workers to knowledge workers.[2] Today's opportunity is one of a further evolution—to "wisdom workers." We all have access to the knowledge required to prosper and flourish. What is needed is the wisdom to use that knowledge effectively.

IMC's Evolutionary Journey

I now offer some insights into how positive organizational change was brought about at IMC. As long ago as the early 1990s it was clear that, looking at IMC's structures and procedures, the management team needed to embrace some major changes: in its very mind-set and how we were organized, how decisions were made, and how actions were taken. In 1993, our top management team began a series of learning journeys to different countries as part of an endeavor to reenvision the very future of our organization. The idea was to expand their horizons of thinking while discussing the vision of our future organization. Vietnam at that time was just beginning the process of opening up. We went to see some state enterprises, met government officials, and talked about

Vietnam's situation and prospects just at that moment of opening when its potential was greatest. Then we went to Australia to see an entirely different situation, one that was already well developed. It allowed us to discuss the CEO guidelines in different environments. We were absorbing many factors related to a changing business environment and how we needed to address it. Recently my CFO pulled out the guidelines we put together at the time, which I still use regularly, and said: "Wow, we basically had it already twenty-five years ago." The guidelines forecast pretty accurately how the world would develop in terms of foreign exchange, stock markets, valuations, and the like. In those guidelines, we basically described the environment we now live in.

But it wasn't until after many years that we finalized the guidelines. In 2004, we resumed the exercise and took our fifty top managers on a five-day retreat to explore life, work, and community. This undertaking was then cascaded down the IMC organization. The final day of the exercise, March 9, is commemorated as our day of rebirth; every year since then we have made it a day of reflection throughout the company. In 2016, we established a further retreat program, with a similar cascading process across the organization. *For any business to flourish, ongoing evolutionary journeys of the self, team, and organization as a part of larger social and ecological systems are necessary.* The goal of such journeys is to develop the capacity for transformation at multiple levels.

Gatherings of managers can be—and should be—the catalyst for people to start evolving in their own direction. Many of them don't like it when they are there, but there is always a potential for positive impact. There was a manager who didn't work out, and she left us, but a year later she still hadn't found a job that she wanted. She had been affected by the experience of working with us. Our evolutionary learning journeys leave many people in the position of feeling they have to rethink their lives before they jump back into the race. Another manager commented that it was only after she left and went to work for another company that she understood the "chaotic" situation at Octave. Because it is not boring with us, it is challenging. Our working environment "disturbs" or "disrupts" people in a certain way, which can lead to self-discovery. So-called chaos is necessary in the process of change. Many people who leave us have a love-hate relationship with the company. We see conversations on social media from people who left us years ago. They can't stop talking about the experience, positively or negatively, which reflects the impact it had on their lives. In the end, it is a positive sign with regard to what we are trying to achieve, which is constant personal and institutional evolution. When they were at IMC, they may have resisted the approach, but when they returned to the outside world, they found they were no longer the same person.

The worldview we promote at Octave has, at its core, oneness and evolution. Recognizing it is first and foremost a business, we are continuously and unremittingly aware that it exists in a global context, designed to address social and global challenges. Business has an important role to play in how humankind deals with these challenges, and Octave offers a model we believe needs to be rolled out all over the world. Not of course in terms of its specific business activities or corporate structures but in terms of the basic philosophies that underpin everything we do.

At IMC we developed a core philosophy expressed in seven phrases, consisting of four words each in Chinese, and based on traditional Chinese wisdom. Together they make up the evolutionary model needed to transform our business. They are a guide to leadership and a source of wisdom for evolution of both self and system. The seven phrases have become progressively integrated into our leaders' lives and into the processes and structures of IMC's businesses, allowing them to flourish in unison:

- Investigating to understand our true nature (格物致知)
- Achieving integrity (至诚为本)
- Holistic interconnectivity (整体依存)
- Proactive adjustment (主动调整)
- Dynamic and complementary balance (相辅相成)
- Creation toward harmony (和谐创造)
- Liberation from ego (解脱自我)

The phrases were chosen to guide evolution at every level: from the self to increasingly complex teams, business units, divisions, the IMC group, and the larger communities in which it operates. Growth starts from within, and I want all members of the management team to join me on an individual and collective journey, as members of a business community. It is above all an opportunity for self-development. When one feels well inside, one can govern oneself, lead teams of coworkers, nurture a sense of community, manage an organization, and build a harmonious society (修身齊家治國平天下). Such was the teaching of Eastern wisdom in the university (大学), which guided the learning for adults of China for thousands of years.

The seven phrases have prevailed through the years and continue to play a foundational role in IMC's relational practices and core values. They are at the center of the company's culture and the processes that guide leadership and management: they direct us to be mindful in every moment, to be aware of how each of their actions affects and is connected to the broader community and business system, and to avoid being blinded by our individual realities while being open to new possibilities.

I believe that business sustainability cannot be achieved without leadership proactively embarking on a journey of evolving consciousness and leadership change. As part of my endeavor to transform the leadership mind-set, in the early 1990s I developed the IMC Sustainability Model. This model enables the organization and its members (collectively and individually) to collaborate and evolve to achieve their full potential. The essence of managing for long-term sustainability is to continually drive alignment of the organization (its people, structures, and processes) with the environment. An effective and flourishing organization is always evolving and adapting. Collective and individual potential need to dance together, and clarity of roles and purpose becomes critical.

The IMC Sustainability Model helps align an evolving leadership with flexible organizations and adaptive action, allowing the whole to shift holistically in response to the constancy of change. This can be experienced only as a transformation in consciousness to one of wholeness and connectedness, enabling creativity to emerge as a unique strength.

The IMC Sustainability Model remains an abstraction until it is enlivened by a set of management practices that enable it to exist and evolve as a living system. Eastern philosophies can help guide this evolution; mindfulness-type practices make it real for people—and from a combination of these two come congruent worldviews, values, and culture. Such congruency is critical in guiding decisions and actions that are in alignment with an organization's mission, especially in turbulent market environments: they drive organizational identity and community. In a constantly changing environment, the philosophical underpinnings of leadership combined with mindfulness practices ensure organizational alignment and cohesion. This is absolutely key for leaders who wish to lead a flourishing organization in service of a flourishing world. In the words of the Tao, when everything is aligned, there can be harmony. Isn't harmony what we are all seeking?

Between 1995 and the mid-2000s, the model went from conceptual to operational, and we now have over a decade's experience of integrating these philosophies and practices into every aspect of our strategy, structure, people, and process. But we were confronted with many challenges along the way. Soon after we began, there was an extraordinary and unprecedented boom in the shipping industry. Earnings and profitability soared, and it became hard to distinguish financial performance resulting from our Sustainability Model from what was simply a consequence of favorable market conditions. During this period, IMC experienced such a rapid expansion that, in 2005, I felt compelled to hire a team of managers to take over the operations of IMC's Industrial Group. These were world-class people with extensive and proven track records, many of them graduates from elite business schools. I empowered them and gave them a clear mandate to lead the Industrial Group to a flourishing future.

The experiment proved to be a failure. I felt like I had invited friends into my home and left the premises, only to find, on my return, the house totally remodeled—with the underlying presumption being that I could accept the new situation or leave. I chose instead to ask my new friends to go, leaving me with the task of remaking the house into a place I could call home.

But I was not discouraged. On the contrary, it made me more committed than ever to push forward with my goal of transforming consciousness at IMC. I no longer sought to rely on a change of leadership at the top or on superficial management frameworks and tools, because I had now experienced firsthand the misalignment that can result between leadership and prevailing market needs.

These days I actively engage with all of my managers and encourage them to embrace mindfulness and the goal of evolving, of striving to see past the constraints of human constructs to explore new possibilities, to engage in effecting external change from a place of inner transformation. To become a leader with humility and to possess a willingness to evolve the self are not attributes that happen overnight.

As a result of our ongoing efforts, we have a few core designs, including the three levels of leadership, which we call the "accordion" structure. It is an organizational design to buffer the impact of external rapid change with the inner stability of system and process. The goal is to create a layer of flexible leaders that is agile enough to absorb the external volatility and capable enough to lead a relatively more stable internal system. At a working level, standardization drives efficiency, but at the strategic level, change needs to be addressed on a continual basis.

Traditionally, businesses have been organized as hierarchies and as matrix organizations, but both of these approaches, in our view, fail to address the challenge of alignment. Hierarchical organizations tend to be rather rigid because of the increased standardization needed to drive stability and efficiency. Yet businesses need to be constantly changing to adapt to the shifting external environment. To overcome this weakness of hierarchical systems, we created the matrix organizational structure to better deal with change. But in practice, the matrix structure has also failed in many instances. General Motors was a pioneer in matrix organization and also demonstrated that it is not the answer. What is the flaw? Just because a structure allows the possibility of flexibility does not mean the organization will actually leverage flexibility to solve problems. Specifically, structural flexibility is like a tool, and there must be a will to use it. The organization has to be aligned to be aware, willing and able to change to make use of the organizational flexibility to change.

Structural flexibility is of no use if the organization cannot reach internal consensus and alignment to change.

The result is IMC's Triple Organization structure, which adds a third approach to the mix, a community organization, the Work Community, which operates in tandem with and is embedded in the hierarchical and matrix structures. It is specifically designed to address the alignment challenge. Values and culture are driven through this community organizational design, in which communication and dialogue permeate the hierarchy and silos to create an IMC culture that is inclusive and collaborative in support of the company's goals. The three elements—hierarchy, matrix, and community—come together and help attain both the internal stability needed for operational effectiveness and the flexibility needed to adapt to the changing external environment. The Triple Organization adds a network and community base of organizational structures to the hierarchy structure. In the hierarchy, the matrix is a normal structure, and the network base is a design to deal with developmental resource deployment, executing different pieces of the strategy. The accordion within the various organizations deals with strategy formulation and execution that puts a layer of flexibility into the process so it can be more dynamic, more able to handle complex challenges.

Direct linkage between the internal and the external needs causes stress that can result in cracks in the internal system. Internal operations cannot handle constant external volatilities without compromising efficiency. IMC's Triple Organization is designed with an absorber system to interface between the slow-to-change internal environment and the rapidly changing external environment. The team-based network organization formed by the IMC senior leadership and management team acts as a flexible interface layer to absorb the external disruption from the changing external environment and to keep IMC strategically aligned with external realities while interfacing with internal operations. The hierarchy team is technically grounded and thus able to translate the strategic responses into practical operations adjustments that minimize disruption; the network team is able to integrate and lead resources across different parts of IMC to implement complex strategies; and the community base is a hub for the work teams to align within the organization as it adapts to change. This arrangement achieves both learning agility and operational efficiency for the overall system.

I often explain the accordion as being like a ship next to a dock. The dock is fixed, and the ship parked beside it is moving. How do you match the two? You have a flexible pipe linking the fixed pipes on the dock and the ship, and the flexible pipe takes the shock from any movement and compensates. That is the accordion, the way we handle the interface between internal and external change. This is a level of leadership that needs to have a collaborative mind-set and be able to interchange roles constantly. Getting that accordion working is an ongoing process, and today there is still room for improvement. But the idea is to insulate the dynamic-change element from the accordion portion of the leadership. There can be a lot of emotion and even turmoil in that sphere, but it is still business as usual for most staff. The business and cash flow are not affected by the volatility because of the buffer in the accordion. Experimentation occurs at the accordion level and is not rolled out to the rest of the organization until there is a consensus on the success of an approach. For example, we may want to make management changes to bring the business closer to the market. That needs to be done in a way that doesn't negatively affect daily production. A buffer ensures that changes decided on are implemented smoothly throughout the organization. If the senior manager raises the implications of all sorts of strategic changes taking place in the market with the manager in charge of daily operations, that could be disruptive. Managers at the senior levels need to experiment and see how change can be gradually implemented throughout the operating units.

The Tsao Family Legacy Charter

While the IMC Sustainability Model was being developed, I was working on a succession structure for both the business and family. Similar to a business mandate, we needed a family charter around which we could build a consensus with regard to the company's direction and culture. It would need to define the governance process for the family's aspirations and for the use of the resources built up over many generations. My family and I—my father, mother, siblings, and other core family members—conversed over many years, exploring the greater purpose of our business, and in 2012 finalized the Tsao Family Legacy Charter, in which the family declared that they wished to be an evolving unit, a community of related people supporting each other on a journey, sharing a similar worldview on the path to greater awareness and wisdom.

The family legacy is not just wealth but responsibility as a guardian of the family's aspirations and the intangible resources of the generations that preceded. It is about how we relate to wealth. I view myself as a steward of wealth, seeing it not as an entitlement but as both a responsibility and an opportunity. When wealth is taken as an entitlement, it becomes a burden; but when wealth is taken as a responsibility, it becomes purposeful.

The norm in family businesses is a three-circle relationship, with the interests of "family," "ownership," and "business" overlapping. I have removed "ownership" and left it with just two circles, "family" and "business," because our motivation is connectivity of relationships and evolution of the business rather than financial interest (see Figure 3.1). It is not an easy model to implement, as it needs the proper alignment of all family members. The business is in a separate trust that has its own purpose. It becomes an opportunity for family members to express themselves rather than to claim their rights to the business as an entitlement. They are encouraged to participate and to contribute by being

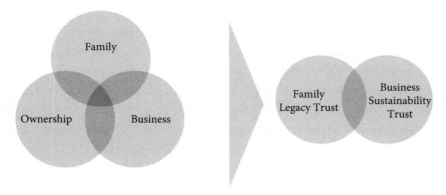

Figure 3.1. The Tsao family governance model. Used with permission from IMC.

good stewards of the business on behalf of society. The responsibility that I took on when I became head of the family business was one of stewarding its continuous evolution in the context of the world we live in. That purpose is one that I hope the following generations will adopt: continuing in the role of steward of the business as custodians for their children's and grandchildren's generations.

The resources of a family business are for the use of family members for their own growth as well as for the growth of humanity. We came with nothing and we leave with nothing. We have each one of us just a lifetime to experience and evolve to serve others from a place of wholeness and connectedness.[3] By taking out the ownership element, these two resources are very clearly separated for the evolution of the family and of the business. While these two elements are separate, there is a relationship between them, to support each other on this journey of evolution.

The charter is administered by a family council with various committees, including those concerned with learning, social needs, investment, and philanthropy. There are funds allocated to support entrepreneurship and to support family members who need assistance. Freed from the distraction of ownership issues, family members can concentrate on resources: how they should be deployed and their governance. The approach is enshrined in the Business Sustainability Mandate as well as the Tsao Legacy Charter, and each is held by a trust.

This is not only a matter of leaving a personal legacy but a recognition of a journey that extends back to my great-grandfather and his start-up waterfront business in China. Those humble beginnings have afforded me a unique opportunity to be both a practical and a philosophical businessman. More important, my aim is for future generations of my family to continue this quest, to see that the journey of evolution toward oneness and wholeness continues through the business.

In 2008, I was appointed president of the Family Business Network Asia (FBN Asia), which included family-based companies from ten countries. We conducted extensive research to better understand the growing needs of this sector and its potential to influence social change.

The Business Sustainability Mandate

IMC's Business Sustainability Mandate states, "This is not a static world, nor one that is stable and fixed. Change in each era, for each generation, will present challenges. These challenges are welcomed because they clarify our personal role and purpose, and present an opportunity to evolve." I came to realize that I am not passing on a business but developing the role, purpose, and culture of an evolving enterprise—one that exists to serve others, and in turn to serve ourselves.

In the IMC Sustainability Mandate, business is described as an institution that is currently misaligned with the long-term interests of humankind. We are facing challenges and stresses (individually and socially) that are unprecedented in human history. Our mandate is a call for all of us to engage and fully participate in a different future, powered by a shift in consciousness toward wholeness and connectedness.

Communities as social networks are required for us to prosper, and those communities need a common culture to facilitate communication and common purpose. The pillars of the culture we have developed in IMC are built from aspects of traditional Chinese culture and address the foundations of building a learning and evolving institution.

I have developed cultural pillars that embed guiding principles distilled from Chinese wisdom to help us raise our consciousness and develop a worldview of oneness and harmony, a desire for personal responsibilities and for freedom. There are many dimensions to my worldview, which can be summarized by this Buddhist saying:

> We are what we think.
> All that we are arises from our thoughts.
> With our thoughts, we make the world.
> We do not see the things as they are, we see them as we are.
> Our eyes form the world and the world forms our eyes.

·   ·   ·

The Sustainability Model translates into a general management model. There is a cultural side to it and a process side, and then there is the spirit wisdom embedded in it. Ultimately, effective management development is about the self-cultivation of leadership qualities in an organization that is a living system with a continuously evolving culture.

Unlike public companies, family enterprises have the unique ability to change their constitution and articles according to the changing needs of the times. Furthermore, multigenerational family enterprises need to not be fixated on delivering short-term results, which in public companies are often achieved at the expense of long-term sustainability. Family enterprises therefore have the potential to be a very important agent of change in the years ahead. They have more freedom to evolve to become enterprises that truly serve societal needs.

Our business will continue to be successful as long as we follow the path of transforming consciousness, as long as our collective leadership has the wisdom to evolve and adapt with creativity and innovation, making sure that our business models stay relevant to societal needs and are not confined to profit targets or burdened by history but instead evolve as a living system toward oneness and in balance with the whole.

Dealing with Continuous Change

Social and global change is inevitable, and there is a clear need to embrace it at the most fundamental level of our being. If we don't, we're in trouble. The list of problems is long, and today most people are aware of the predicaments we face—from climate change to social injustice—but the speed of change is such that existential challenges are now emerging simultaneously in the spheres of politics, economics, the environment, technology, and personal health and well-being. No one is shielded from these challenges that affect the rich as well as the poor. But there is also the opportunity for this to be the most creative era in the history of humankind.

Industrialization has been one of the top drivers of social change and has led to higher standards of living, eradication of diseases, and a doubling in human longevity, among many other benefits. Postindustrialization can continue the trend toward prosperity and flourishing. What might the new economy look like? Let me paint some scenarios for you.

We are facing a future in which fossil fuels will be gone. Solar, wind, and geothermal energy, and perhaps even nuclear fusion, will provide all the energy we need. Energy will become more localized and may even be free. What impact will this have on industrialization? We will also be able to create more intelligent materials: for example, organic constituents embedded with biocircuits as 3D printing continues to become ever more sophisticated. These materials may completely replace existing ones that depend on raw materials extraction, meaning that there would no longer be a need for the petrochemical industrial complex that is still such an important part of today's economic system.

The world is moving toward a web of urban nodes and metropolises linked by high-speed trains—and perhaps soon the Hyperloops imagined by entrepreneur Elon Musk[4]—separated by nature spaces for recreation and farming. It is already happening fast in China, and it is a mode of living that can be more rewarding for us and strengthen our relationship with nature in increasingly urban environments.

In such a future, we have the potential to wake up to the fact that material consumerism does us little good, either mentally or physically, and it is not helping the world with its endless landfills and garbage-strewn oceans, which, according to some projections, will contain more plastic than fish by 2050.[5] Fortunately, younger generations appear to be less interested in buying stuff and are more interested in experiences through the sharing economy.[6] What if, worldwide, people began to say, "I don't want to be sold things on the basis of vanity or conceit"? What would happen to luxury and branded goods?

A move to healthier and less materially encumbered lifestyles would mean that we might all live longer. Cancer would no longer be such a terminal threat thanks to scientific advances and a decline in harmful environmental factors. Huge progress has been made in the application of naturopathy and self-healing medicines. Life extension, life enhancement, and life quality are all improving. The trend in terms of the entire life science area is toward treating the whole person energetically with less reliance on allopathic treatments.

There is a trend toward shorter working days. Technology, especially artificial intelligence, will assist us with many routine tasks. There is also the issue of equitable distribution—of income, of education, and of health and well-being. Big changes are afoot in this area too. Barriers are falling as access to education becomes easier. New learning platforms such as massive open online courses (MOOCs) are enrolling millions of students who could not otherwise afford access to top-flight education. Location is no longer a critical determinant. You don't need traditional bricks-and-mortar schools in a networked and connected world, only a supplementary offline learning infrastructure. Six billion people are rising to join the 1.5 billion who are globally privileged. Facilitated by this emerging reality, by this paradigm shift to flourishing, such change can only accelerate.

As intelligent technology reduces the amount of time we spend in the production and consumption of *things*, our life goals will change. It will mean more interpersonal and communal activity. Just as in the twentieth century, economic activities were designed primarily to meet our individual material desires, in the new paradigm, once a person's basic Maslovian needs for food, shelter, and security are met, the focus will shift to meeting intangible desires: human relationships; a sense of community; connection to nature; and our emotional, social, and spiritual well-being. Children will learn from an early age how to collaborate, and parents will become more aware of and play a different role in the education and learning process as facilitators of whole-person learning and experience. Mindful parenting, as we become more conscious of connectedness and the importance of holistic well-being, will be very different from parenting as we see it now. All this, and much more, will transform economic activity in the years ahead, and business must be able to transform along with it.

The leading edge of technology today is affecting the world through developments in domains such as artificial intelligence, robotics, genomics, and nanotechnology. In the end, machines may replace most of what we call work. It is already having a huge impact in areas that relate to parts of our own family business, specifically logistics. And the trend now is into the logistics of decision making, information triage, and the use of big data.

All these changes have the potential to be positive for society as a whole. We cannot be sure about the pace of change, but it will probably be faster than most of us expect. The process of development was previously linear and localized; now it is complex, networked, and universal. So many disruptive innovations and seismic developments are happening simultaneously. IBM's Watson supercomputer is revolution-izing medical diagnostics. Self-driving cars are in the offing and will drastically reduce traffic fatalities, and floating farms are being devel-oped to meet the needs of coastal megalopolises.

Everyone and everything are talking and networking; the level of connectivity is astounding. Innovation no longer means someone toil-ing alone in a garage, inventing a product, and then taking it to market. Innovation results almost instantaneously from collaboration between entrepreneurs, investors, customers, science and technology, and global markets. It can occur much faster, more unpredictably, and ahead of expectations than has historically been the case. The whole develop-ment process is more interconnected and integrated in circular supply chains and, therefore, much faster—and a lot more creative in terms of the configuration and customization options for commercialization.

Exciting as these developments are in technological innovation and economic activity, their ultimate benefit to us and to future generations will depend on the capacity of our consciousness to keep pace with the rate of change. We must evolve a consciousness of connectedness to prosper and flourish in a world of economic, political, and technologi-cal interconnectedness.

I am not predicting that all these things will happen, but I believe that many are likely to happen. And they will have a huge impact on how the whole world operates, both locally in the communities in which we live and globally in the social, political, economic, and natural systems of which we are a part, whether we want it or not. It is plain to see how global reality is integrating and interconnecting, and we need to have a common worldview based on oneness and not separation, a common value system, a common language in which to collaborate for a future of flourishing. The fact is that much of the world is already af-fluent, and therefore humankind is faced with a new challenge to our creativity, triggering or demanding evolution.

Quantum Leaders Rising to Meet Tomorrow's Challenges
The quantum leadership approach is about evolving leadership from the inside out. It is about aligning motivation with creative energy, the

energy of love. Most of us would acknowledge that you cannot create enduringly positive benefits out of fear. And many people already accept the idea that great creations come from a place of love. If you align your energy as a leader, then you have the creative power to change the world for the better. And we need leaders who can evolve the world in this direction. In fact, *if we do not change the world, then the world will change us—most likely in a direction we do not want.* That is an important message for businesspeople.

Quantum leadership will continue to emerge because of a collective desire to bring about positive social benefits from new innovation, new technology, and new challenges. Our role is to facilitate awareness of its emergence. It is a new way of being, a response to change through elevating our consciousness. Those who share this idea are beginning to see the world differently. To paraphrase Marcel Proust, the real voyage of discovery consists not in seeking new landscapes but in having new eyes.[7] And as we share this journey of seeing with new eyes, our motivation grows with a process of mutual validation and support as we cocreate a future designed for the benefit of all people and all life on earth. In business, there are already many "conscious business" circles, and within such circles there is a clear process of awakening. There are "conscious*ness* business" circles as well. This is a rapidly morphing and growing area.

It is important always to emphasize that *the new consciousness makes good practical business sense.* A quantum leadership approach offers you a better chance of financial success because it improves your entrepreneurial skills. You become less restricted in your thinking. You can see better and more clearly, and you feel more courageous and adventurous. In short, it makes you a better entrepreneur or corporate leader. Conflicts between the short-term goal of keeping your company alive and financially healthy and the longer-term challenge of elevating consciousness and awareness are a matter of balance. You need to have both short- and long-term strategies in place. It is analogous to considering how much of your portfolio should go into venture capital risk—which is basically a matter of portfolio management.

I used to be pessimistic about the world's future prospects, but these days I feel very positive because I see the potential for all the necessary elements of flourishing to fall into place: the network support, the network development process, the way information will work in the future, education, the global sustainability mandate, and technology support. What I see now is a direction of evolution toward oneness that is truly global.

We all want to move toward greater collaboration, more meaningful relationships, and a more harmonized personal reality. Throughout human history, religion has been the route through which such personal development has been sought. But religions are limited to various extents by their belief systems. If you consider yourself spiritual but reject the sectarianism caused by a religion's intolerance of other faiths or of secular spiritual traditions, you are at liberty to avoid religion's packaging, labels, and restrictions. You don't have to become entwined in religious dogma, in its structure and identity. All religions in their different ways promote love and harmony and the idea of working together, but I think there is a growing desire, among those who seek spirituality without the constraints of organized religion,[8] for practices that speak to a universal sense of what it means to flourish as a human being on earth.

Relationships change when our paradigms about who we are change. To avoid the continued conflicts and degradation in human affairs, it is my belief that we will need to work toward a new spirituality based on the essential oneness of reality. Sages have a conception of reality that, at its essence, says that we can be deeply connected to our self, others, and the world only through love. Jesus, Buddha, Krishna, Muhammed, Lao Tzu—all these great figures, along with their spiritual traditions, have fundamentally the same message, which is the goal of oneness. They tell us of a reality with a spiritual dimension called god, or the Tao, or some equivalent and that, through various practices, we can be awakened so that we are gradually able to experience it. Such practices in one form or another—mind, body, and spirit—can be found in all religions. Every religion, for instance, addresses fasting and energy work, although under different names, and some equivalent of the Holy Spirit or Ch'i.

The East West Learning Centre and the AITIA Institute

In the early 1990s, when I was thinking about how I was going to steward my family business, I was concerned about developing and handing down a healthy, flourishing enterprise. Given the Chinese tradition of reverence for our forefathers and for future generations, I didn't want to be the one who screwed up. Where was I leading my employees, my customers, my family members? I realized that you cannot sustain yourself in an unsustainable world and that our sustainability as a family business was inseparable from the sustainability of the wider system of which we are a part. These considerations led me to found a small initiative based on the idea of combining the wisdom of East and West to address the challenge of flourishing. The East West Cultural Development Centre was set up as a nonprofit organization based in Singapore: a platform for individuals and public intellectuals to discuss topics such as collaboration, harmony, community, and the nature of leadership.

There is a pressing need for business to be seen as a community of people working with and for society rather than as an organization serving only its own ends. It was the East West's goal to promote this concept. If business development and investment strategy were the ostensible objectives of the IMC Group, the East West Cultural Development Centre became its spirit. If economics is the commercial activity to meet human desires, then social economics is about societal desires and needs, and that is the real essence of business purpose. In a flourishing enterprise, social economics are integrated into economics and form the fundamental reason for its existence.

The centerpiece of this initiative was the East West Learning Centre, which provided holistic learning for an inspired individual to work, live, learn, and play. It was founded in 2007 and promoted mindful learning for leaders as well as research and practices for organizational transformation. It proposed a journey of "Learning Life, Life Learning." If change is the only constant, then learning is the ultimate tool. The East West Learning Centre worked with professionals and corporations to consider notions of business sustainability and its impact on the global social economic system. It also promoted, designed, and delivered programs that focus on total wellness rooted in Eastern philosophies.

Concurrent with the IMC's organizational transformation in the mid-2000s was the implementation of a prototype township community development project. I discuss these in more detail in the section "Octave," but at its heart the aim was one of integrated living to build a harmonious society based on flourishing life, learning, and evolution. I selected the town of Dujiangyan, near the city of Chengdu, for this project in 2005. It is a beautiful location in a place famous for its ancient irrigation system, dating back more than two thousand years. It is quiet and pristine, a reasonable distance from Chengdu, and has a large forest reserve nearby. Added to these factors was support from the local government, making it an ideal location to showcase a new model of government and business collaboration. But nature had its own way of telling us that ideas, time, and place are not always in alignment. A major earthquake devastated the area in 2008 and caused substantial damage to the site.

I devoted a lot of time in the following years to finding alternative sites to build these harmonious communities. They were always placed under the East West Group, intentionally separating them from the operating businesses of IMC to allow the company to focus on its longer-term vision. My hope is for the East West mission eventually to be integrated into the business groups, but it first needs to be able to survive in the marketplace on its own transformational path.

The work of East West gave birth to the AITIA Institute in 2016, and the new organization superseded the old. The word "aitia" (αἰτία) was used by Aristotle in his philosophical writings to designate what we might translate as "cause" or "purpose." In 2018, AITIA was established as a nonprofit company based in Singapore, dedicated to the evolution of consciousness in the context of family businesses and quantum leadership development through mindful awareness and connectivity.

Sustainability, in the sense of prosperity and flourishing, is the main challenge for the twenty-first century, and meeting this challenge requires changing our nature to extend and improve our "being" rather than only our "doing." AITIA explores the gap between the business case for sustainability and the transformation in consciousness needed to effect lasting change. It integrates Eastern wisdom and Western scientific findings, using mindful practices through advocacy, research, prototyping, outreach, and training in the areas of stewardship, family business, leadership development, philanthropy, and sustainability. AITIA aims to direct humanity's evolution onto a more sustainable and more enriching path by emphasizing positive social impact as foundational to leadership and organizational evolution. It is an agent for individual and enterprise transformation. AITIA strives to be a leader in the practice of, training in, and research into relationships. It also participates in and partners with global initiatives on research and work on consciousness. It works under the principle that to live is to evolve and that evolution is the key to flourishing, whether for self, an organization, or society. Evolutionary leaders focus on connectivity and on building organizations that last. AITIA is a center for such research and learning—a place to transform. Only when one can see oneself clearly will one be able to resolve one's own conflicts and move toward harmony with others and the environment. With AITIA, we specifically address business leadership aimed at well-being and flourishing, although the concept is not limited to business. AITIA's mission is to be a platform for humanity to learn, grow, and evolve into quantum leaders. There are many areas of cultivation for quantum leaders. Fundamentally, they are all about relationships, with personal health and wellness, with family, with organizations, with community, with nature, and with the universe. AITIA training involves *rewiring* (helping us think in new ways), *reframing* (revisiting our database of experiences and revising our insights into what it means to be human), *reskilling* (working at collaboration so we can work better together), and *renewing* (working on a new way of relating to the world in service of flourishing).

Reality Is Relational

Relationship is all there is, and it is always cocreated. *Change yourself, and the world will change around you.* As the transformation efforts within IMC intensified during the early 2000s, I realized that the systemic drag within the organization was strong. After all, it was a family business, which inevitably tended to hold on to old patterns and habits. By 2009, I was facing another downturn in the business cycle. I then made the difficult decision to reorganize our industrial businesses, which created the opportunity to reignite the idea of building harmonious communities as one of IMC's central missions. People and organizations change when they are suffering, and without suffering the pressure to wake up and change is not strong. The opportunity to evolve lies amid the challenges we face.

When reality is relational, and our consciousness is what creates our reality, then what is most needed is work on relationships. Only when our relationships are positive and congruent can we be free from conflict. Reality is an expression of our connection to others and to the external environment. Over time, we have conditioned ourselves, thinking, feeling, and acting in iterative loops, such that we don't see the world *as it is*, but instead we see it *as we are*. If we are in a state of love, we express love; if we are in a state of anger, we express anger; if we are conflicted, we express conflict. We need to find congruency and harmony in our relationships with our self (internal) and with the people and world around us (external). This is not a new phenomenon. But resistance to change and the desire to live in our comfort zones are so strong that, even when the need for change is self-evident, people still find it hard to act.

Relationships need to start from the inner self and then move out into the external world. Sustainability is no longer only about our material existence: it is about shifting consciousness to meet life's challenges from a whole-person perspective. What we need are learning programs for leaders that help them see the essential oneness of being. These programs, which are already piloted at AITIA, will guide businesspeople to think and act from a place of wholeness rather than one of separateness.

Octave

Guided by the work I was doing to elevate my consciousness and to introduce practices of connectedness in the IMC organization, I felt that the time had come to create a business that would address the challenge of well-being and flourishing for others. I had transformed the model of our real estate business unit to focus on the concepts of mind-body-spirit and connectivity and had begun to scale up the building of harmonious communities into a functioning business. Real estate is like a bowl that is designed to hold soup: what we really want is the soup; and the hungrier we are, the more the design of the bowl becomes secondary. A subtle shift in business model requires a big shift in the mind-set of the leadership and organization. This is what led to Octave, which encompasses businesses aimed at both being profitable and helping build a harmonious society. It is a full-blown transformational business model, one that focuses on promoting a consciousness of oneness in a twenty-first-century global context. A quantum leader's journey is always anchored in an evolutionary consciousness-based way of life aimed at wellness for oneself and for others. We were developing a lifestyle business where the focus was on life and on styling the expression of the self, in distinction to other lifestyle businesses that focus on the consumption and possession of material things.

As part of my evolutionary journey, I began working on the development of a community to support the Shanghai region. Its main learning campus (or retreat), called Sangha, is in Suzhou, just an hour and a half from the center of Shanghai, near Yangcheng Lake, an integrated complex of wellness residences and learning facilities. It is intended to be the embodiment of a vision of how such a community might work and the distillation of decades of reflection—a consequence of my own evolution, if you like.

Octave as a business entity is an expression of a worldview where evolution is supported, where consciousness shifts to embrace wholeness and connectedness. With consciousness, we can lead with purpose and we are able to deploy all forms of capital responsibly, to embrace all as one and in an interconnected way.

We decided to build a prototype of an evolutionary worldview for the twenty-first century that supports freedom and creativity, and that is Octave. As we complete this book in 2019, there are three divisions—Octave Living, Octave Space, and AITIA—devoted to the business of transforming consciousness for well-being and flourishing. The Octave system supports a holistic life learning journey of cultivation that aligns the mind, body, and spirit of a whole person and community, where learning and evolution happen in the space that has been designed and crafted for this life journey. The structure of the IMC Group of entities is shown in Figure 3.2.

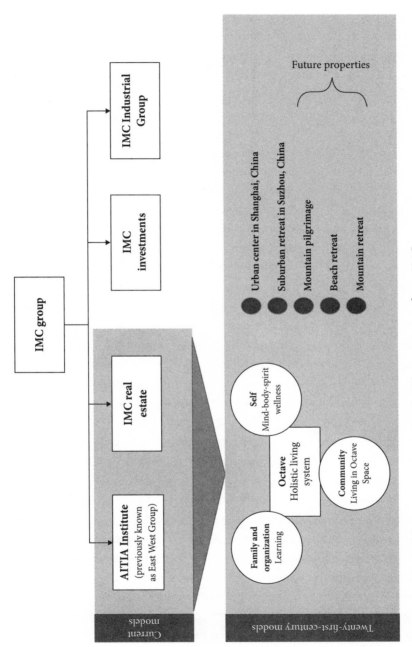

Figure 3.2. The IMC group structure. Used with permission from IMC.

Octave Living focuses on wellness and the journey of life. Wellness is not a single point; it is rather a direction, a continuous never-ending journey of evolution, based on the Taoist ideals of living according to what is called for in each moment and harmonizing the past, present, and future. The Taoist goal is to live a healthy and carefree life through to old age—to harmonize your relationship with heaven to achieve not extreme happiness so much as the absence of restrictions and fear. When you are able to go with the flow of life, you are free. If you swim against your desires, you will understand Tao—but only eventually.

Octave Living offers a whole support system to enable such a healthy lifestyle, including the infrastructure needed for a whole life journey with the goal of promoting basic ideas of consciousness, connectedness, evolution, and wellness. It is a lifestyle company offering a variety of mind-body-spirit programs and modalities. Eventually, it will consist of five centers with differing purposes, two of which we have built so far: one in Shanghai and the other in Suzhou. In Shanghai there is a day center supporting personal well-being practices, community activities, and continuous learning; the facility in Suzhou is residential and focused on deep learning and inner work. The third will be a pilgrimage location to visit for further self-development in deep nature immersion. The final two will be a mountain resort and a seaside resort: destination locations where you can take advantage of your leisure time to work on evolving your consciousness and wellness. The goal of Octave Living is very close to the catchphrase proposed by entrepreneur and thought leader Dustin DiPerna—wake up, grow up, clean up, show up.[9] By which, in brief, he means be aware, continuously evolve, be healthy, and be involved.

Octave Space is a property element in which I respond to the new challenges by changing the real estate business model to a lifestyle business model focusing on shifting consciousness. Sangha combines both Octave Living and Octave Space, allowing for residential, whole-person investigation, and deeper work, including medical procedures. It is a community for people who like to live this lifestyle, designed to enhance communality and built with natural materials. We rethought the whole idea of space utilization. In terms of the villa homes at Sangha, we emphasized the design of relational space, so that home is where relationships could be built and evolve. Most people go for taller houses, bigger gardens, and narrower streets, but we went with wider houses, smaller gardens, and wider streets, which means the common area is bigger. We wanted to create a greater sense of closeness, a relational and community-oriented space. The market wants a bigger garden, but what people really need is to have their kids playing together on a wider street. It is all about choices that connect. We could have chosen to make the hotel like most hotels, with rooms on both sides of a central corridor, but instead we designed it with the rooms on one side and nature on the other. As you go to and from the room, you walk along a corridor with windows, with light and nature beyond. The cost is, of course, different, but when you have nature, you have sunlight; it's a different feel when you walk into your room. And we make it up in other ways: no huge lobbies, a greater sense of communality and intimacy, and a heightened connection to nature.

Octave Living and Octave Space are both commercial ventures, based on the Quantum Leadership Model. All the Octave Living offerings—classes, therapy, education, yoga, practices of connectedness, the clinic—are fee based. The world is moving in this direction, and for-profit businesses have a new role to play in creating well-being and flourishing. Wellness is going to become increasingly important, and people will have more time to concentrate on it. I have taken a position on the future because by the time it arrives, it will be too late; and only those who are prepared will benefit.

So Octave is a worldview based on continual evolution, and therefore its expression is not fixed. It seeks an integration of quantum science and the Eastern esoteric tradition, the Chinese tradition in particular. Octave is a Chinese company, so it is natural that Chinese culture is featured prominently. Octave Living is the expression of how we live and where we define wellness as a life journey of learning and a way of living. The Chinese define wellness as understanding and illuminating Tao, because that is your spiritual expression and creation. Practicing energy and spirituality work and living according to your environment and your personal condition: that is the Chinese—in fact, Taoist—definition of wellness.

Octave has been created to provide support for and specific services to enable the journey of life, to change your lifestyle based on the Tao. The infrastructure has been designed to support the need for lifelong work on relationships both with our selves and with the external environment. We have designed urban, suburban, and nature retreat hubs to support the deepening of individual and group journeys. We basically have only one form of consciousness that is in a continuous dance with the touch points of our outer environment. Thus, Octave's software has an inner-self focus, which is the mind-body-spirit and its transformation and awakening to see the holistic and connected nature of all things. The keywords in the Octave community, our expression of creativity, are "mindfulness," "relationships," "connectedness," and "consciousness." The goal of Octave is to provide the knowledge, practices, and processes to stimulate learning to change our lives to express such oneness with the world. Octave's "Four Pillar" learning approach is rewire, reframe, reskill, and renew. We also have a mind-body-spirit wellness clinic to facilitate wholeness healing with integrated medicine. The goal is to know the Tao, the Way, through mindfulness. As Stephen Covey put it, "Between stimulus and response is our greatest power— the freedom to choose."[10]

In this community, discovering mindful self-love is often the start of the journey. We have designed the evolutionary journey to support the development of a process that will open the door to release the limitations and constraints we have on cultivating the self toward well-being and flourishing.

We define wellness as a system. As a lifestyle business, we are often challenged in ways that teach us more about how to style our life and our company, reminding us of the importance of discovering our gifts and our purpose in life and how we go out and create our life and the environment in which we live. With all the changes and development in the past century, we need a twenty-first-century global worldview that embraces the idea of moving toward holism and integration and collaboration. The twenty-first-century living model includes a design of wellness, for oneself, for the family, and also for business, all in the context of community and a community living lifestyle.

Octave Living is a system to support this evolutionary lifestyle, which is relational. Without stress and suffering, there is no evolution. But sometimes we run certain risks when stress and challenge are faced, and if we don't have enough time to evolve, we get eliminated. As leaders we have to create stress in the system and sense a perceived threat so that evolution can happen, even if we are not really that vulnerable. The process of creating stress in an organization to stimulate evolution is not an easy one. We have to have the proper skill sets of creating stress in the right way to help people evolve.

The Business of Helping Others on Their Evolutionary Journeys

These ventures are our response to current global pressures. Business models are called for that support individuals, families, business leadership and organization evolution, and practices that support mind-set change, which allow consciousness to shift and release creativity and innovation for the twenty-first century of quantum leaders.

Physical, emotional, and spiritual well-being—for myself and others—is more important to me now than material satisfaction. We are materially affluent, yet we are still not free and satisfied with what we have. We need to have a mind-set of abundance and a transformation toward emotional and spiritual freedom. I am interested in using my influence to transform the institution of business itself, starting with the stewardship of family-owned enterprises. Business as a whole has a huge responsibility in terms of the well-being of the world. Business leaders need to step up to their responsibility and unleash the creativity and power inherent in business to allow it to play its role in both serving human well-being and creating wealth. A business that prospers by continuing to evolve to meet the needs of society is a sustainable and flourishing business.

Of course, the implementation of these concepts in an organization can be painful. People are inherently uncomfortable with change. It is disruptive to wake up and reassess old habits. Shifting the system to a higher level of consciousness is not a sudden event. It is a continuous process involving the transformation of individuals in different ways at different times. It is dependent on the circumstances that make it possible for them to accept new ideas. But systemic drag can be overcome, and it is ultimately a positive and profitable shift both for the organization and its members. We have suffered the pain of being a pioneer, which meant less instinctive buy-in by staff, because our world does not yet automatically validate this approach. But our conclusion is that in the long term it is the only way forward for both wellness and flourishing.

What I Have Learned

The evolutionary process for humans is centered in our consciousness. That is the gift that we possess. Our genes encode only our potential, and we can now choose our own evolutionary speed and direction, because every thought affects who we are becoming. Our belief system is key to how we see things, how we think about things, and therefore how we act on them.

Among the most challenging touch points in our lives are our closest relationships, especially those with family members, with all the attachments and trauma, the experiences of love, rejection, and projection they involve. It affects our conditioning and our belief systems. Sentimentality, expectations, and other emotions can get mixed up with love, and sometimes our sentiments take over and are understood to be love. But love is more than a feeling. It is the essence of wholeness and connectedness.

I have learned the truth of the old saw that we are not really material beings having a spiritual experience but spiritual beings having a material experience. We are a mind-body-spirit being with a material existence we often confuse with life. Our past, present, and future exist simultaneously. There is a holistic internal-external flow of energy and information, where the internal reality is awareness of the flow of information back and forth with our external touch points. This is what drives the global mind change that futurist Willis Harman spoke about decades ago.[11] Our body will submit to the power of our mind (willpower), but the power of the spirit is so strong that both our mind and body will comply.

Connectedness is an energetic resonance, and it can be either positive or negative, coming from either our light or dark side. Many spiritual practices the world over are based on the same principles of oneness and love.

There are three contemporary worldviews rooted in science: the Newtonian physicalist view of atomistic particles and forces that act on those particles; the relativistic Einsteinian paradigm with time and space dilation and contraction; and the energetic worldview of quantum physics. The three worldviews range from a functional materialism to a more spiritlike reality where matter barely seems to exist, and certainly not in a form that we recognize. If you grasp quantum physics, you can understand Newtonian physics, but not vice versa. Similarly, if you have a spiritual worldview, you can truly understand the material worldview, but not the other way around. These three worldviews are now accessible to us all, and if we integrate and use all three effectively, then we have a better chance of living life from a place of wholeness.

Human beings, unlike other animals, are capable of conceptualizing our realities, like the Neolithic human who paints what she sees onto the wall and makes it into a story, making sense of her experience by contextualizing it and regulating her stress. That is the beginning of human creativity beyond the animal state, when we can conceptualize and create the world we desire.

Being willing to take responsibility is crucial, and I have learned that responsibility is fundamentally not something imposed on us by others. No matter what the circumstances, we accept the consequences of our actions. Blaming and complaining reduce us. This makes it harder for us to act proactively to correct situations and to take charge and make the choices for ourselves. In particular, in the name of love, we tend to project all our fears onto our children.

We live in systems: a company, a family, a community, an industry, a country, an ecology. Leveraging the system to shift the individual is very effective, but an individual shifting the system on his or her own is very challenging, so we need to work on our collective consciousness.

We have to change our worldview in a way that positively helps us evolve to a higher consciousness. This process parallels the way our gene expression and health depend on how we live and on what we put into our bodies and how we interact with the external world.

Talking of the knowledge and experience of sages and wise people from the past about the reality of oneness can help us frame an understanding that helps us make sense of our experiences as we go through the process of shifting consciousness. While reality is holistic, our thought processes are linear and fragmented. We need to translate them into an integrated frame and bring about consistency in that frame to allow us to think systemically, to allow us to think relationally. These are skills that we have to develop to help ourselves regulate our psyche more effectively and move to a new positive energy phase of evolution and consciousness.

Throughout history, people have appropriated worldviews from philosophers and sages and translated them into religious structures and practices that have gradually shaped our culture. If we retrace our steps, we can take pieces of our different cultures and remold them into a new culture more suitable for today's world—one that is global and not restricted to our own cultural or national contexts. This is the way to tackle the global challenges of prosperity and flourishing.

I see myself as being on an evolutionary journey, and I consciously work to break the numerous limitations of my own conditioning. I have taken pieces from the West and pieces from the East and whatever else I have come across in my sixty-two years of life, as I have traveled around the world so many times I cannot count. And ultimately, I have learned that it can be done.

PART II ATTRIBUTES OF QUANTUM LEADERSHIP

PART II TAKES a practitioner-scholar approach to quantum leadership by studying real-world examples of consciousness of connectedness and then building a theoretical model to illuminate the relationships between key variables. In Chapter 4 we profile some of the world's most forward-thinking and flourishing companies that are already exhibiting aspects of quantum leadership. In Chapter 5 we present what is the first published attempt to build a Quantum Leadership Model. It presents an evidence-based framework for the evolutionary progression that quantum leaders represent: an emerging fourth transition of business toward full-spectrum flourishing.

In Chapter 6 we look at the science underpinning the practices of connectedness and their benefits. Here we also seek to locate quantum leadership within the truly transformational epoch of scientific discovery in which find ourselves. We offer a multidisciplinary overview of the way new advances are changing our understanding of the everyday world and our place within it. Quantum leadership does not merely belong within this new outlook but is a necessary response to it.

4 SIXTEEN EXEMPLAR COMPANIES

IN THIS CHAPTER we seek to discover to what extent people and organizations are already embarking on the quantum leadership journey. Our aim was to find mainstream companies (by which we mean widely known or at least well established in their sector) within which a consciousness of connectedness was already in evidence: businesses and their executives for whom making a positive impact was intrinsically embedded in their purpose, strategy, and culture.

We studied hundreds of sustainable businesses and ended up selecting sixteen of them. We concentrated on for-profit companies with a particular set of attributes. We were looking for companies that had demonstrably *positive impacts* on a broad set of stakeholders and who *outperformed their peers in economic terms* but whose distinguishing features were leaders and corporate cultures that, in some observable fashion, *embodied a consciousness of wholeness and connectedness.*

The exemplars spanned fast-moving consumer goods (Unilever), banking and financial services (Westpac), food (Greyston Bakery), apparel (Eileen Fisher), athletic footwear and sports apparel (Nike), personal care (Natura), environmental services (Clarke), retail (IKEA and Woolworths South Africa), hi-tech (Schuberg Philis), industrial machinery (Tennant Company), heavy industry (Nucor), pharmaceuticals (Novo Nordisk), a diversified conglomerate (Tata Group), tea and coffee

(Starbucks), and transportation (Tesla). They were located in Africa, Australia, Asia, Europe, Latin America, and North America.

How Quantum Leaders Differ from Other Forms of Business as a Force for Good

Today there are many labels used to identify business as a force for good. Among them are B Corps, benefit corporations (which are different from B Corps),[1] and Conscious Capitalism, along with numerous forms of reformed capitalism (stakeholder capitalism, regenerative capitalism, natural capitalism, and humanistic capitalism, among others). So how are quantum leaders different?

Existing forms of business for good are all steps in the right direction. They reflect the *outer* transformation of markets that increasingly expect business to meet rigorous standards of sustainability performance, accountability, and transparency. They respond to the growing social and global challenges that are creating new market opportunities as well as threats.

For example, B Corps are defined as "for-profit companies certified by the nonprofit B Lab to meet rigorous standards of social and environmental performance, accountability, and transparency."[2] They are designed to address two critical problems: corporate law that makes it difficult for businesses to take stakeholders' interests into consideration when making decisions; and the lack of transparent standards in helping people tell the difference between a good company and just good marketing.[3] Benefit corporations are a type of for-profit corporate entity, authorized by thirty-three US states and the District of Columbia, which includes positive impact on society, workers, the community, and the environment in addition to profit as its legally defined goals.[4] Conscious Capitalism emphasizes a philosophy or ideology based on four tenets: greater purpose, stakeholder value, leadership, and culture. These tenets enable companies to be "the emotional common ground you need to level with consumers," according to John Mackey, the cofounder and CEO of Whole Foods and coauthor of the book *Conscious Capitalism.*[5] These four tenets bring Conscious Capitalism in alignment with quantum leadership, offering a valuable platform for us to build on.

But are such initiatives sufficient to create a tipping point of positive-impact companies capable of building a future of flourishing? MIT senior lecturer Otto Scharmer points out that "what's missing is a *systemic connection* between all these initiatives—an enabling mechanism that allows us to not only connect the dots, but also to *see ourselves*, and the significance of our work, *from the whole*."[6]

Quantum leaders, like other enlightened leaders, pursue outer transformation based on markets that increasingly require businesses to have a positive impact on society and the environment. But they go much further by embracing the inner transformation of people: the global mind shift, the consciousness that we are deeply connected to others and to nature. Such inner transformation brings out one's intrinsic care and compassion, inspiring us to do good from a more authentic place, not as a fortuitous by-product of a financially motivated decision. Quantum leaders build on the "business case" for positive social impact but are not limited by it. A holistic approach to the well-being of self, organization, stakeholders, community, and the environment is the only route to a full-spectrum flourishing that includes financial benefits. Otto Scharmer talks about the need to "build the capacity among leaders to co-sense and co-shape the future on the level of the whole system."[7] The inner transformation of business leaders toward wholeness and connectedness and the outer transformation of business toward sustainable value are both needed for a business-led future of global prosperity and flourishing. *This, and nothing less, is what is needed for business to transform into an agent of world benefit.*

The Sixteen Exemplars

Three main criteria were observed in finding exemplar companies: (1) the company is a sustainability leader that has a positive impact on society and the environment, rather than just "doing less harm"; (2) it is more successful, in economic terms, than its competitors; and, crucially, (3) there are signs of a consciousness of connectedness, evidenced by an enhanced awareness of the positive impact that the company has throughout its activities. The purpose of showcasing the exemplar companies is to shine a bright light on the characteristics of a new kind of emerging business that embodies a consciousness of wholeness and connectedness. In these companies, economic performance is a result rather than a purpose of their existence.

Among the exemplars, not all embody quantum leadership all of the time. This is one of the main findings of our field research: average companies can do extraordinary good, while leading ones can, on occasion and often unintentionally, engage in harmful activities in parts of their businesses. The Starbucks' 2018 incident of racial discrimination at one of its Philadelphia locations and accusations of improper conduct by senior managers at Nike that same year illustrate the difficulty of being a force for good on a consistent basis.

Every effort was made to weed out *greenwashing* impostors. We found many companies who claimed, on their websites and in their sustainability reports, to be exemplars of "doing good for society and the planet while doing well for their customers and shareholders." Such companies often put forth visions and missions supporting social good and exhibited aspects of quantum leadership, such as distributed decision making in networked operating units with high levels of employee empowerment. But on closer inspection, many of these companies proved to have a business purpose centered primarily on quarterly results or had sustainability efforts that were, for the most part, limited to doing less harm. To factor out such companies, we disregarded those whose sustainability initiatives were focused only on cutting carbon emissions, waste reduction, water recycling, employee safety, labor compliance, and other "hygiene" factors whose absence was a dissatisfier but whose presence was fast becoming standardized operating practice.

We made every effort to obtain sectoral and geographic diversity, and there were always more quantum leaders than we chose to profile. For example, in seeking African exemplars, we chose Woolworths South Africa, which operates in South Africa and eleven other sub-Saharan countries, because it met all the criteria we were looking for, but we could just as easily have chosen Tongaat Hullet, an agriculture leader in KwaZulu-Natal with a strong emphasis on the well-being of its employees and on restorative environmental practices such as improving soil health. We could have selected South African financial services provider

Nedbank with its business vision of "interdependence with people and planet."[8] Or Solms-Delta, a wine producer with a fifty-fifty partnership with the descendants of the slaves who helped build it.

We did not include Chinese exemplars for a variety of reasons, including the rapid transformation in the country's corporate employee policies, community responsibility practices, and environmental regulations. Nonetheless, several Chinese companies could have made our list. Good-Ark Electronics in Suzhou, founded in 1990 and now one of the largest diode manufacturers in the world, embeds a sense of cultural responsibility through its business practices aimed at creating both material and spiritual wealth. Employees are given paid time to learn traditional Chinese texts on self-cultivation and ways to live a meaningful life. The company invests millions of dollars annually in manufacturing processes that protect the environment along with boasting an organic farm and zero-waste kitchen. Another noteworthy Chinese company is the Haier Group with US$32 billion in annual sales and seventy thousand employees. On the cutting edge of robotics and connected home devices, the company's CEO, Zhang Ruimin, restructured the business into an entrepreneurial platform called *rendanheyi* in which every employee becomes his or her own CEO—creating value for clients and realizing self-achievement at the same time. Haier is profiled in Dana Zohar's *Quantum Leaders.*[9]

In summary, the sixteen exemplars are only the first buds of an impending corporate renaissance taking place across the world. Initiatives such as AIM2Flourish are beginning to uncover thousands of such stories of business as an agent of world benefit.[10] AIM2Flourish is the world's first higher-education story platform designed to recognize businesses that contribute to the seventeen SDGs,[11] using a process that gives students a transformational experience in how they see business as a force for good and their own potential to be agents of world benefit and thus helping develop a new generation. It is time for the world to become better acquainted with these businesses.

Unilever

One of the world's leading producers of fast-moving consumer goods (FMCGs), this company produces well-known brands such as Dove,

Axe, Knorr, Hellman's, Lipton, Vaseline, and Ben and Jerry's. It is regularly recognized as one of the world's most innovative and sustainable companies, with top ratings and awards each year in areas such as forestry, water, climate, nutritional health, transparency, and trust.[12]

Unilever's Sustainable Living Plan, launched in 2010,[13] was its blueprint for sustainable business. Its mission was to help one billion people improve their health and well-being by 2020. A big part of it was raising living standards and contributing to quality of life in the markets in which it sells its products and the countries in which it sources its raw materials. Dove has become well known for its Campaign for Real Beauty. According to Unilever, "The aim of the [Dove] campaign is to celebrate the natural physical variation embodied by all women and inspire them to have the confidence to be comfortable with themselves."[14] The men's-oriented brand Axe kicked off its campaign, "Is It OK for Guys . . . ,"[15] as part of the brand's new Find Your Magic positioning, launched in early 2016. The brand says it hopes to help "break the cycle of toxic masculinity by providing guys with resources to live more freely."[16] Another example is Vaseline, which is working with disaster-relief organizations to provide petroleum jelly to help treat wounds in war-torn areas.[17] At the corporate level, Unilever promotes initiatives such as Growing Roots, a program designed to improve access to fresh food and deliver education on how to cook in American cities' low-income neighborhoods.

Between 2000 and 2019, its stock price rose by 360 percent. By comparison, its closest competitor, Procter and Gamble, saw its stock price rise by 160 percent over the same period, while the Dow Jones Industrial Index rose by 200 percent.

To understand the company's leadership orientation to wholeness and to one of care for future generations, we need only turn to the company's former CEO, Paul Polman. When he took over in 2009, he did something rare for a chief executive. To the shock of many shareholders, he announced, on his first day on the job, that he was going to cease issuing earnings guidance and full quarterly reports. "The issues we are trying to attack with our business model and that need to be solved in the world today—food security, sanitation, employment, climate change—cannot be solved just by quarterly reporting. They require longer-term solutions and not 90-day pressures," he said.[18] Polman further stated,

> I don't think our fiduciary duty is to put shareholders first. . . . What we firmly believe is that if we focus our company on improving the lives of the world's citizens and come up with genuine sustainable solutions, we are more in synch with consumers and society and ultimately this will result in good shareholder returns.[19]

Elsewhere, he has said, "Above all, I think the main quality of a leader is to be a human being."[20] He has also been outspoken about the excess of CEO pay, telling the *Washington Post* that he is "ashamed about the amount of money I earn."[21]

The organizational structure of Unilever is set up to favor decentralized decision making and to empower frontline managers to create economic value in ways that are coherent with the life-affirming goals of its Sustainable Living Plan. The company is made up of two separate Dutch and British companies, Unilever NV (Holland) and Unilever Ltd (UK). Reporting to these two headquarters are hundreds of semi-autonomous companies operating in more than one hundred countries with a product reach into 190 countries.[22] With such a distributed, locally reliant structure, there is an organic self-organizing quality to how decisions are made. "The only way to engage the whole living system in which Unilever operated," writes money manager Joseph Bragdon, "was to engage the eyes, ears, and senses of the whole organization. That meant stepping away from traditional command-and-control policies and creating a radically decentralized network of self-organizing local cells, much like the organs of the human body."[23] Unilever is now integrating into its corporate strategy the seventeen SDGs, which it sees as a road map for achieving long-term growth and development, in a sustainable way, by 2030.[24]

IKEA

The world's largest furniture retailer is a Swedish multinational that designs and sells ready-to-assemble furniture, kitchen appliances, and home accessories. It has the ambitious goal of making a net positive impact on the environment. Not only does IKEA say its entire business will run on renewable energy by 2020, but it will produce more renewable energy than it consumes. It is investing heavily in its own solar and wind installations so that it can achieve such an energy goal.

IKEA's sustainability leadership is not limited to positive environmental impacts. In 2017, IKEA declared its objective to take two hundred thousand people out of poverty within a few years. An example was its efforts to employ a mixture of Syrian and Jordanian refugees at production centers in Jordan to supply woven products, including rugs, cushions, and bedspreads.[25]

IKEA's products aim for designs that are beyond green. The goal is *smarter* product designs, where sustainability drives innovation that its customers value. A typical example is the wedge dowel, a new type of universal snap-together joint that reduces the need for multiple product parts requiring lengthy self-assembly. This innovation reduces materials and waste while making it easier for DIY customers to assemble IKEA's products.

All these initiatives are part of the retail giant's group sustainability strategy for 2020, which it calls People and Planet Positive. Steve Howard, former chief sustainability officer, has stated repeatedly that "doing less harm" strategies are not very aspirational and leave everybody "completely confused."[26]

With worldwide revenues of US$44.6 billion in 2018, IKEA has grown rapidly and continuously since its 2001 sales of US$11.9 billion. Its net profits were US$2.4 billion, for the year ending August 31, 2018. In 2017, *Forbes* listed the company as one of the world's most valuable brands.[27] According to Millward Brown Optimor's BrandZ Top 100 Most Valuable Global Brands 2018 list, not only is IKEA the most valuable furniture retailer brand in the world, but it is also the seventh most valuable retailer in the world, valued at nearly US$18 billion.[28] The company exemplifies a set of corporate strategies aimed at creating prosperity and flourishing to drive business innovation and commercial success.

Woolworths South Africa (WSA)

This retail chain is headquartered in South Africa and operates in eleven sub-Saharan African countries. It is not to be confused with, and has no connection to, Woolworths in the United States, the now defunct five-and-dime chain store that went out of business in 1997.

WSA is part of Woolworths Holding Limited (WHL), which has three major divisions, two of which operate primarily in Australia and New Zealand. The southern African–based WSA is by far the largest of the three divisions with 55 percent of the WHL's revenues and 60.4 percent of its pretax profits. The financial performance of the WHL has been a steady upward march between 2000 and 2017. Over this seventeen-year period, revenues grew more than tenfold, and pretax profits grew more than twentyfold, from 6,693 million rands (Rm) and 290 Rm, respectively, to 74,273 Rm and 5,545 Rm.[29]

The company's mission is "to be the first choice for customers who care about value, innovation and sustainability in the southern hemisphere."[30] A consciousness of wholeness and connectedness permeates the organization and is enshrined in its Good Business Journey (GBJ). Launched in 2007, this initiative focuses on improving eight key areas of the business: energy, water, waste, sustainable farming, ethical sourcing, transformation, social development, and health and wellness. Specific goals include making positive impacts such as contributing to community well-being over the next five years, achieving 100 percent clean energy by 2030, driving responsible sourcing of all key commodities by 2020, and affirming that every private-label product it sells has at least one sustainability attribute by 2020.

The GBJ, combined with its values-based approach to employee development and supplier relationships, builds on a long history of openness, transparency, and positive social impact. "We have indeed been on this journey for over 50 years. We started in the 1960s by refusing to create separate amenities in our stores for people of different race. We pioneered black management development throughout the 1970s and 1980s—finding ways around the numerous draconian bits of apartheid legislation—to pursue our values and develop our people."[31] Throughout its sourcing and retailing operations, WSA continues to exemplify an integrated "do good, do well" approach to business success.[32]

Tesla

In a Bloomberg profile article, Elon Musk, the cofounder and CEO of Tesla, observed, "I came to the conclusion that we should aspire to increase the scope and scale of human consciousness in order to better understand what questions to ask. Really, the only thing that makes sense is to strive for greater collective enlightenment."[33] Between Tesla and Solar City, of which he is the chairman, he is doing exactly that. Even his skeptics might acknowledge that he is helping free us from our collective addiction to fossil fuels and carbon dependence.

In 2017, Tesla overtook General Motors and Ford in stock market value even though it was selling many fewer vehicles than the two established industry leaders. That year Tesla sold 103,000 cars, while General Motors sold ten million vehicles. In 2018, Tesla sold 245,000 vehicles, representing an extraordinary leap in unit sales. In 2019, despite widespread skepticism about the company's ability to meet production quotas, its stock price was still well ahead of that of both GM and Ford.

What made Tesla successful was not marketing a "green" product or fighting climate change as a core value. People buy a Tesla because it's a better car, and they invest in Tesla stock because it's a better financial bet. What is noteworthy is that sustainability performance—in this case, the potential to be a zero-emissions vehicle when charged from a clean energy source—is embedded in the company's founding vision. Elon Musk wrote Tesla's original 2003 mission statement: "to accelerate the world's transition to sustainable transport." In mid-2016, the company changed it: "to accelerate the world's transition to sustainable energy."[34]

Although he has a reputation for being difficult to work with, Musk is a hands-on leader who is willing to get down in the trenches. In an *Inc.* article titled "This Email from Elon Musk to Tesla Employees Is a Master Class in Emotional Intelligence," he emphasized the importance of employee safety and urged the organization to report every injury to him, without exception:

I'm meeting with the safety team every week and would like to meet every injured person as soon as they are well, so that I can understand from them exactly what we need to do to make it better. I will then go down to the production line and perform the same task that they perform. . . . At Tesla, we lead from the front line, not from some safe and comfortable ivory tower.[35]

Reputedly, Musk has a sleeping bag that he uses regularly in a conference room next to the production line.

For the most part, Musk is not vocal about his stated aspiration to elevate human consciousness. Nor is his business goal explicitly to do social good or to save the planet. Tesla's commercial success comes from having a smarter business model and better product designs. Social and environmental performance is simply seamlessly integrated throughout.

Eileen Fisher

The fashion company's mission is based on three pillars: "our clothing, mindful business practices, and support of every employee's purpose."[36] The three pillars speak to the founder's vision of purposeful engagement of all stakeholders in the production of its retail products by supporting women through social initiatives that address their well-being, practicing business responsibly with total regard for human well-being, and guiding its product and practice toward sustaining the environment.[37] In 2015, the company became a Certified B Corporation, formally committing to using business as a force for good. In 2017, it took an additional leap and became a New York State Benefit Corporation.[38]

In 2005, Fisher sold the company to her 875 employees through an employee stock ownership plan (ESOP). While it remains private and therefore does not publish its financial accounts, its growth has far outpaced the economy and its industry sector. Between 2002 and 2018, it more than tripled its revenues, from US$144 million to an estimated US$500 million,[39] and in a 2014 *Fast Company* interview, Eileen Fisher confirmed that her eponymously named company was financially profitable.[40] "We have a policy that we call 'good growth,'" added Fisher. "We don't want to grow if it's not sustainable, if what we're doing isn't good. We're proving there's a business case for this."[41]

As early as 1997, the Eileen Fisher Company had formally established an agenda focused on socially conscious business. Recognizing the need to invest in developing leadership across the company to support this endeavor, a department was formed that year and Amy Hall was appointed director of social consciousness. She was given the task of guiding the company's human rights work, supporting women and girls through strategic partnerships, and setting a vision and strategy for environmental sustainability in its production and manufacturing practices.[42] Eight years later the company established VISION2020, a bold plan detailing the steps it will take toward reaching a goal of 100 percent sustainability. The plan covers eight categories: materials, chemistry, water, carbon, conscious business practices, fair wages and benefits, worker voice, and worker and community happiness.[43] "VISION2020 is very much a work in progress,[44] and it will go beyond 2020, but the company's ideal destination remains the same—to be a truly sustainable business, *one that creates value while doing nothing to undermine the possibility that humans and other life will flourish on Earth forever.*"[45]

In all these ways, Eileen Fisher and her company exemplify a consciousness of wholeness and connectedness. She said recently, "I care more about the work itself, not just the product that we create but the whole of the work, from the way people work together, the way we treat each other, the way we try to create an environment where people can grow, and also the way we treat the workers and the way we care about the planet."[46] Financial success comes from the company's greater purpose of relational care, not from a single-minded focus on selling products or making a profit. "Repurposing [garments] can be made into a business that's profitable," Fisher said in 2018, adding, "We don't want sustainability to be our edge. We want it to be universal."[47]

The Tata Group

This Indian conglomerate, founded by Jamsetji Tata in 1868, puts making a positive contribution at the core of its reason for being. Its corporate purpose of "improving the quality of life of the communities we serve" and "ensuring that what comes from the people goes back to the people many times over" forms the basis of its business conduct.[48]

Karambir Singh Kang, an executive at Taj Hotels, a division of the Tata Group, says this about his company: "You will not find the names of our leaders among the names of the richest people in the world. We have no one on the *Forbes* list. Our leaders are not in it for themselves; they are in it for society, for the communities they serve."[49]

Like the other exemplar companies, the paradox of Tata's socially responsible way of doing business is the above-average economic performance that comes with it. Ratan Tata, the group's chairman between 1991 and 2012, and then again in 2016–2017, drew on the Tata family's 150-year tradition of social responsibility to transform the group into a highly profitable global powerhouse.[50] During his leadership tenure, he added US$100 million to the company's market value. In the most recent years for which figures are available, shares of the Tata Group companies have been among the star performers on the Indian stock market. The group's market capitalization grew from US$114.35 billion in 2014 to US$145.3 billion in 2018,[51] and by one account it is on a trajectory to reach US$350 billion by 2025,[52] which would make it one of the twenty-five most valuable companies in the world.

During the time that Ratan Tata stepped down between 2012 and 2016, the Indian powerhouse continued to invest heavily in its businesses and people. Cyrus Mistry, who took over the chairmanship during this interim period, exhorted the company's leadership to work with the Tata values of pioneering, integrity, excellence, unity, and responsibility for delivering sustainable and profitable growth. In 2016 Mistry announced a new leadership model, outlining a new framework focused on "happiness at work."[53] His successor, N. Chandrasekaran, former CEO of the very successful and profitable Tata Consulting Services (TCS), announced at his first town hall meeting his vision of a "digitally collaborative approach to build businesses that met the needs of the nation and community."[54] It was an aspiration that the company's founder would have recognized immediately.

Tata has a slew of products and services aimed specifically at low-income populations in rural India and other underserved markets around the world.[55] These include Tata BP Solar with low-cost solar home lighting systems, solar lanterns, solar cookers, and solar hot-water systems.

Considering only one of many such examples, Tata sells a twenty-two-dollar water purifier that works without electricity or the need for running water, designed to serve the nearly one billion people worldwide who lack access to clean water. As *Wired* magazine put it, with such products "Tata is saving lives and making a killing."[56]

Tennant Company

A Minneapolis-based producer of floor-cleaning equipment and related cleaning technologies, Tennant Company's mission is "Creating a Cleaner, Safer, Healthier World."[57] It sells to large commercial clients such as big-box retailers, shopping malls, and sports stadiums. In the year 2000, it found itself in an industry crowded with competitors all using a mature technology. At the time environmental efforts were directed at reducing the amount and toxicity of the cleaning chemicals used.

Then, in 2006, the company commercialized a revolutionary innovation that would almost overnight lead to a rapid growth in its stock price. Branded ec-H2O and tagged "chemical-free cleaning," this new floor-cleaning technology used regular tap water to clean as effectively as its competitors' chemical-based solutions. Through electrolysis, the tap water was oxygenated and ionized. The positively ionized water had acidic properties that helped kill bacteria, while the negatively ionized water had alkaline properties that cleaned floor surfaces.

The market reaction was instantaneous. Competitors decried Tennant's claims and publicly questioned whether a chemical-free cleaning solution was even possible. Commercial customers were cautious in adopting a solution that no longer required buying and storing cleaning chemicals or training employees in the use and disposal of the chemicals.[58]

Yet what proved decisive for commercial success were the many benefits ec-H2O offered its customers. It eliminated the amount of money customers spent on chemicals and training. Because water was the only input into ec-H2O, operators did not need to mix chemicals. The new process used water more efficiently, which meant the operator could fill up less often and clean faster. Ec-H2O did not leave any chemical residues on floors, which greatly reduced the potential risk of slip-and-fall accidents. Such incidents account for around 20 percent of insurance costs in retail environments, and their avoidance represented a significant cost savings to Tennant's clients.

Between 2000 and 2019, Tennant's market value grew by more than 300 percent, with much of the growth in value coming post-2006 when ec-H2O was launched commercially. During that same period, the Dow Jones Industrial Index rose 200 percent. Sales of the ec-H2O product line had skyrocketed, reaching US$130 million five years after its market launch.

In one of our interviews Tennant's CEO Chris Killingstad made it clear that becoming a green or socially responsible company was not his primary motivator for investing in ec-H2O and other chemical-free products. He simply believed that there had to be a better way to differentiate the company from its competitors and that sustainable cleaning technologies provided such a path forward. Doing good and doing well were integrated into a single value proposition.

Natura

This Brazilian natural cosmetics company features an innovative sales network of more than one million people, many of them poor residents of urban slums known as *favelas*. In 2018 it was ranked by Corporate Knights as the fourteenth most sustainable company in the world.[59]

Natura has always operated from a distinct and deeply felt sense of purpose. Its founder, Luiz Seabra, said, "At age 16, I was given this quote from Plotinus, a philosopher: 'The one is in the whole; the whole is in the one.' That was a revelation to me. This notion of being part of a whole has never left me."[60]

The company was started in a São Paulo garage in 1969 as a kind of personal protest against the chemical-intensive and elitist cosmetics industry of the day. Seabra wanted to "deliver cosmetics as a means for self-knowledge and promoter of well-being, powered by human relations as a way to express life."[61]

Natura's corporate purpose is concisely stated: "Well Being and Being Well" (*bem estar bem*). The company's goal is to cultivate healthy, transparent, positive relationships between the company and its stake-holders, among those stakeholders, and between them and the whole of which they are a part. *Bem estar bem* reflects Seabra's original vision, which "is infused throughout the culture and operations of the company today. . . . The eternal search for improvement is inherent to our existence. We believe that through the constant pursuit of innovation we will be promoting the development of individuals, our organization, and society as a whole. This approach to innovation is integral to our approach."[62] It's an approach that has worked remarkably well for the company. At one point it was chosen by *Forbes* as the eighth most innovative company in the world, just behind Apple, which ranked fifth, and Google, which ranked seventh.[63]

Although the firm is not widely known outside South America, it provides a formidable example of a company that does well by doing good. In 2017 it boasted a net profit of US\$203 million on annual sales of US\$3 billion. This profit level was up more than 100 percent from the previous year. The company had also been profitable for each of the prior five years.[64]

Schuberg Philis

This innovative Dutch information technology (IT) company focuses on mission-critical applications that its customers rely on to keep their operations running 24/7. It was the first IT supplier to win the European Good Practices Award, given for demonstrating that setting elevated performance standards alongside high levels of pressure at work does not necessarily have to result in work stress. Philip Dries, managing director and a company founder, explains:

> We consider it important that our colleagues make their own decisions—and also make their own promises to customers. As a consequence, colleagues here experience the freedom and autonomy that they get not as an added burden, but as putting them in control of their work. In our case, this leads to very high customer satisfaction and 100% availability for our IT systems. This sounds pretty obvious but usually, in the IT industry, it's the sales manager who makes the customer a promise and then passes the problem on to colleagues, who actually

have to solve it. People tend to get stressed by conflicts and frustration as well as by anger about unrealistic targets.[65]

The company's purpose-driven commitment to wholeness and caring is embodied in the twelve guiding principles on which the company was founded. One of these principles concerns love: "We have the desire for each person to flourish. We are all equal and unique. We see the whole human being—as a colleague, as a parent, and as a friend. When we connect at a deep level, wonderful things become possible."[66] In our author interviews with the company's founders, a consciousness of connectedness revealed itself in who they were as people, how they communicate, and what they do.

In 2017, Schuberg Philis's total operating revenues rose 18 percent from €50.3 million to €59.3 million, while net profits reached €3.2 million.[67] In one of our early in-person interviews, Gerwin Shuring, one of the company's cofounders, observed that profit margins for the business stood at that time (2014) at triple the European IT industry average.

Nucor

This leading steel producer is known for creating a highly profitable network of energy-efficient mini-mills feeding on recycled steel scrap. It represented a stark departure from established steel companies who historically invested in giant energy-intensive mills drawing on virgin iron extracted in often environmentally harmful ways. Yet this company has found its way into the sixteen exemplars not for its environment-friendly technology but for how it treats its people.

The company's egalitarian labor practices, its flat decentralized organizational structure, and its obvious care for the communities in which it operates help make it a quantum leader exemplar in what might be considered a sunset industry.

In 2017, Nucor was the largest steel company in the United States, ranked number 151 on the Fortune 500 list, with revenues of more than US$20 billion, up 25 percent from a year earlier. It reported consolidated net earnings of US$1.32 billion for fiscal year 2017, compared to US$796.3 million for fiscal year 2016. Between 2000 and 2019, Nucor's shares grew by nearly 400 percent, almost twice the Dow Jones Industrial Index over the same period. It survived and thrived during years in which dozens of American steel companies went bankrupt. It grew rapidly while the US steel industry declined from eleven thousand tons per month in the period 1967–1970 to under seven thousand tons per month in 2017.[68] By 2019, Nucor's market capitalization stood at US$17 billion, while global leader ArcelorMittal's capitalization was US$22 billion, even though ArcelorMittal's revenues were more than three and a half times higher than Nucor's in the prior year.

Ken Iverson, Nucor's CEO from 1965 (when it was still called Nuclear Corporation of America) to 1996, was the executive who made the company what it is today. His compass was the Golden Rule. "We believe in treating people the way you'd want to be treated. That's a fundamental building block of our company. It sounds simplistic, but it works."[69]

About his leadership philosophy, Iverson said, "Concede once and for all that employees, not managers, are the true engines of progress, and dedicate your management career to creating an environment in which employees can stretch for higher and higher levels of performance."[70] Under his guidance, Nucor transformed itself from an autocratic top-down organizational structure typical of the steel industry to a collaborative employee-centered networked organization in which local teams of employees were responsible for research and development, innovation, and operational performance.

Another distinguishing feature was the strategic choice to site its mills in small towns and rural areas where people cared for one another and their communities. Nucor's investments in these areas helped them support local businesses and municipalities, contributing to local schools, fire departments, disaster relief, and environmental projects with donations and employee volunteering. Such local investments were a source of pride to employees and helped Nucor maintain an exceptionally high employee retention rate. Like Unilever, its organizational structure was distributed and composed of semiautonomous operating units.

John Ferriola, CEO of Nucor since 2013, is continuing Iverson's legacy of emphasizing the importance of trusting, respecting, and empowering his teams across a distributed organizational structure.[71]

Novo Nordisk

A Danish-based global pharmaceutical company with a commercial presence in more than seventy countries, Novo Nordisk is a world leader in diabetes care, hemostatic management, growth hormone therapy, and hormone replacement therapy. It is also involved in researching and developing therapeutic treatments for autoimmune and chronic inflammatory diseases. According to Susanne Stormer, the company's chief sustainability officer,

> Novo Nordisk has a very clear social purpose, namely to help people with diabetes and other chronic conditions to live their life to the full. To do so, we provide them with medicines, but we know that it takes more than medicines and that is why we are engaged in driving change for the benefit of these people. This is why we are in business, and remains the focus for our business. Does that make us a social business? I would say yes. Some make a distinction that a social business is not supposed to operate with a profit. If a business doesn't earn a profit, then how is it supposed to be a sustainable business? We are a profit-generating business because we need the profit to generate more of what we do in pursuit of our social purpose.[72]

In January 2012, Novo Nordisk was ranked number one in the world by Corporate Knights in its annual list of the one hundred most sustainable companies. In 2018, *Forbes* ranked it the fifth most reputable company in the world.[73] The company's financial returns are among the highest in its industry. Between 2000 and 2019, its stock grew 1,721 percent, far surpassing that of competitors Amgen, at 325 percent, and Lilly, at 218 percent, over the same period. The shares of Merck and Pfizer, two other pharmaceutical competitors, showed little or no growth over this time.

Working in service of the social good and in harmony with nature is deeply embedded in the company's DNA. Its Blueprint for Change, a public-private partnership dedicated to reducing diabetes worldwide, is aimed at saving lives through early intervention. The company works with governments and health-care NGOs to reduce the diabetes epidemic and to provide access to basic health care as a universal human right.[74] It provides insulin to consumers in the world's poorest countries at 20 percent of the average price in the Western world. Through its

Blueprint for Change, it also trains doctors and caregivers in low-income countries where diabetes is often undetected at great human cost.

Along with pioneering the use of environmental profit and loss (EP&L) accounts, the company employs more than eighty bioethicists to address issues related to research involving people, animals, and, more broadly, ecological impacts of the company's operations. Employee engagement surveys show Novo Nordisk at 90 percent in 2017, well above the global average of 62 percent for large corporations in the Aon Hewitt surveys.[75]

Amid the rising concern of prescription drugs and the flagrant exploitation of price hikes by some pharma companies, Novo Nordisk former senior executive Jakob Riis promised not to raise the list price of any medicine by more than single-digit percentages annually.[76] This was only the latest evidence of a company that is, to a high degree, walking the talk of compassion and care.

Nike

In the 1990s this shoe and apparel giant faced enormous challenges in overcoming accusations of supply-chain sweatshops and human rights abuses.[77] It was blamed for violating minimum wage and overtime laws in Vietnam, ill treatment by supervisors, and the use of child labor in Cambodia and Pakistan. By 1998, Phil Knight, the company's legendary CEO, told the National Press Club that "the Nike product has become synonymous with slave wages, forced overtime and arbitrary abuse."[78] With much of Nike's sustainability efforts post-1990s aimed at labor compliance and reducing social harm, why include it among the exemplar group?

There are many reasons, almost all of them related to the changes Mark Parker made after he took over as CEO in 2006. He committed the company to a hockey-stick transformation toward positive impact. "[Sustainability] moved from being a risk and reputation function to being a business lever function to being an innovation function," said Hannah Jones, Nike's chief sustainability officer. While Nike's sustainability initiatives were launched as a response to scandals, they were now a tool for future-proofing the company.[79]

Nike has eleven maxims that drive its strategy, one of which is "Do the right thing."[80] The company's focus on building a positive impact for the community and environment is an example of this maxim in action. It has a range of business initiatives focused on increasing children's physical activity as part of promoting healthy and active communities. It is committed to greater inclusivity through which a healthy lifestyle is available to everyone.[81]

Collaboration with suppliers, customers, and even competitors is key to Nike's sustainability-driven innovation at the industry level. "Nike is a large company by most standards, but our ability to influence meaningful change at the systemic level has limitations," says Parker. "It is absolutely crucial that we work with other players to prompt real, sustainable system change. We embrace partnerships and open-source collaboration. We have proactively shared our sustainable design tools to help create an industry standard and continue to look for ways to scale innovations at Nike and across our industry."[82]

The company has teamed up with NASA, the US Agency for International Development, and the US Department of State, along with Nordic-region-based companies IKEA, Novozymes, Kvadrat, and Arla and a number of government institutions to announce LAUNCH Nordic, an incubator to engage local innovators and entrepreneurs in developing sustainable materials.[83] Nike is also a founding member of the Sustainable Apparel Coalition (SAC),[84] which launched the Higg Index to enable the industry to assess the sustainability of its products. The index covers three primary areas—brand, product, and facility—and is aimed at giving the apparel industry a way to assess the sustainability of any particular product throughout the supply chain.[85]

Through open-source collaborations, Nike has been able to articulate its strategic vision of a business capable of "meeting the challenges of a changing world—addressing climate change, preserving the earth's constrained resources, enhancing global economic opportunity—not by reducing growth but by redefining it."[86]

Nike has financially outperformed competitors and the stock market. Between 2000 and 2019, Nike's stock price rose 1,236 percent, while the price of Adidas's rose 685 percent over the same period. It should be noted that Adidas is also considered a sustainability leader who meets many of the quantum leadership criteria. Since 2007 *Fast Company* has ranked Nike six times among the world's top fifty most innovative companies. In 2019 Millward Brown ranked the company number eighteen on the list of the BrandZ Top 100 Most Valuable US Brands.[87]

Westpac Banking

This Australian bank was named the world's most sustainable company in 2014, beating well-known sustainability leaders such as Unilever and Novo Nordisk across all industry sectors.[88] An example of a positive-impact company, Westpac defines sustainability as "taking action to create long term value for the people who bank with us, work with us, invest in us or are part of our broader communities."[89]

Between 2000 and 2017, Westpac's shares rose by more than 255 percent, while its benchmark competitor JPMorgan Chase saw its stock rise 205 percent over the same period, and the Financial Select Sector Index (XLF) grew a mere 29 percent.

David Morgan became CEO of the bank in 1999. The following year he laid out his vision for a culture of service that would reenliven the bank's core-value proposition: "The future prospects for banks in Australia is not simply about how well we anticipate technological change, competition and globalization," he said. "[It is] increasingly more about how well we operate within the social and environmental constructs applying across our industry."[90] He argued for a "performance driven culture with strong vision and values" centered on employee empowerment. Morgan believed that "the staff are the bank . . . the ones, substantially, who rebuild the threads of common understanding and trust with the community."[91]

As author and money manager Joseph Bragdon observed, "By further inspiring employees with a vision of becoming more socially and environmentally responsive, [Morgan] created an organizational consciousness—and ability to see and sense the larger systems of which they and the bank are a part—that turned Westpac into the sustainability and profit leader it is today."[92]

Morgan made ethics and corporate responsibility integral to the bank's culture rather than top-down edicts issued by the executive suite. He appealed to employees' sense of doing the right thing, asking them to keep in sight the common good and making the bank a catalyst for multilateral collaboration. A strong emphasis on diversity helps shape the company's culture. By 2016 there were an equal number of men and women among senior executives, with leadership roles throughout the rest of the organization, 47 percent of which were filled by women.[93] Other minority groups, including working mothers, LGBT, and customers with dementia, received a high level of support. As is the case with many of the other companies in our exemplar group, frontline employees are empowered to make decisions in a distributed organizational structure. In 2018, the company was recognized as Employer of Choice for Gender Equality and was the number-one bank in the Australian Network on Disability's Inaugural Access and Inclusion Index.[94]

The results soon became evident. In 2015, Westpac was selected as socially responsible institution of the year by *Money* magazine. The award panel said, "Westpac shines as ambitious social and environmental targets are made public and senior executive bonuses are put on the line for their delivery."[95] The company's continued strong financials are a testament to the business value of its strategy aimed at prosperity and flourishing for all.

Clarke

Clarke is a public health company that provides mosquito control and aquatic habitat management to make communities around the world more livable, safe, and comfortable. They continually push to bring more environmentally responsible products and services to market that help prevent disease and create healthy waterways.

Lyell Clarke, CEO of the eponymously named company, is a self-defined environmentalist who has a long-standing commitment to taking care of the environment.[96] Since his early days he has recycled, monitored his own carbon footprint, and spent his personal time enhancing conservation practices at his family's farm.

One pivotal proof point of how his personal environmental compass has steered the company was the 2009 launch of Natular, a mosquito larvicide developed at Clarke. The product enabled Clarke to sunset an organophosphate larvicide with a public health solution that provides better control with broader habitat and environmental fit. According to the US Environmental Protection Agency, it "replaces organophosphates and other traditional, toxic pesticides and is approved for use in certified organic farming."[97] For pioneering this product Clarke received the Presidential Green Chemistry Challenge Award in 2010.

At Clarke, environmental and social performance extends far beyond a single "green" product. It has become deeply embedded in the organization's mind-set and culture. Today the company aspires to make a positive impact through "caring for the planet," "caring for people" ("doing all we can to positively impact and enrich the lives around us"), "being passionate about what we do," and "doing the right thing, even when it's hard." These goals now live in the passions and behaviors of its employees.[98]

Like many sustainability leaders, Clarke has reduced its carbon footprint, improved its fleet efficiency, and greened its facilities. At the new headquarters site more than three hundred solar panels were installed on the roof, and the entire landscape was restored to natural prairie complete with fruit trees and raised-bed gardens for employees to enjoy.[99]

Although the company is privately owned, its executives were willing to share with us that, with 175 employees and about US$100 million in sales in 2017, it has been a consistently profitable enterprise. They attribute much of Clarke's success to the use of appreciative inquiry summits, where a broad set of stakeholders are convened to uncover the unique strengths of the company's entire ecosystem, producing initiatives that have transformed the company into a more innovative and flourishing business.

Through its commitment to the appreciative inquiry process, Clarke has evolved its orientation beyond operational sustainability to creating a positive impact on the world. The Zika crisis, a mosquito-borne epidemic, led the company to realize its full potential in terms of public health. "The opportunity to serve our communities during the Zika outbreak inspired a loftier, higher vision of what our purpose is," says Julie Reiter, vice president for human resources and sustainable development. "Appreciative Inquiry has elevated our capabilities, our sense of purpose and our confidence. When the call came [for help from Florida's Miami-Dade County] there was no doubt about our abilities. We stretched the organization incredibly and saw innovation coming from every corner. . . . Everyone wanted to be involved because we were responding as an agent of public health."[100]

Greyston Bakery

Founded in 1982 by Bernie Glassman, an aeronautical engineer turned Buddhist monk, Greyston Bakery is a registered B Corporation and New York State's first benefit corporation. It provides people in Southwest Yonkers, New York, with employment, skills, and resources to lift them out of poverty. In practice this means that the company hires men and women who have little or no work experience, many of whom have histories of homelessness, incarceration, substance abuse, welfare dependence, domestic violence, or illiteracy. Greyston's Open Hiring Model "embraces an individual's potential by providing employment opportunities regardless of background or work history while offering the support necessary to thrive in the workplace and in the community."[101] This business model fuels community development and a commitment to human growth and potential. Its employees have been on a mission to pay it forward through a variety of volunteer efforts, reaching 420 "sweet service hours" in 2014.[102]

The company is a longtime supplier of brownies to Ben and Jerry's for their famous chocolate fudge brownie ice cream. In 2016 it was shipping thirty-five thousand pounds of brownies a day to this anchor customer.[103] It has a cobranded line of products with the Whole Planet Foundation that is sold exclusively at Whole Foods Market. With continued year-on-year growth and market recognition, by 2017 its 130 employees were serving more than five thousand customers.

As a social enterprise, Greyston generates a profit that goes to the Greyston Foundation, which operates a number of self-sufficiency programs in the company's market area, including affordable housing and support services for the formerly homeless; children and youth services including child care; a technology learning center; health and social services such as housing for individuals living with HIV/AIDS; and a community gardens project.

The company has been able to retire the debt incurred in building its state-of-the-art bakery. As Greyston's CFO Jennifer Solomon says, "Obviously we are here because of a mission, but that doesn't mean you have to be less focused on results—but also have results that are socially focused."[104] It is emerging as a globally recognized brand with an innovative business model and fresh value proposition.[105]

Starbucks

Starbucks has performed well for both shareholders and stakeholders. Since going public in 1992, Starbucks grew its revenues from US$74 million to US$24.7 billion through 2018. An investment of US$1,000 in Starbucks stock in 1992 was worth US$306,000 at the end of 2017, representing an astonishing annual growth rate of 26 percent over a quarter of a century.

Starbucks works closely with its suppliers to make a positive social impact everywhere it does business. It set the gold standard as one of the first ethically sourced commodity providers. By 2015, 99 percent of its supply chain met the standard. With it, Starbucks no longer viewed its suppliers in transactional terms: it saw them more relationally as critical to the health of the whole system in which it operates. Starbucks invests tens of millions of dollars annually into alternative loan programs for local farmers.[106] By 2018, the company was actively working with suppliers around the globe to combat the potentially catastrophic effects of climate change, as estimates in journals such as the *Proceedings of the National Academy of Sciences* were showing that as much as 88 percent of coffee-growing land in Latin America may be unusable by 2050.[107] Starbucks is sharing its lessons on adaptive farming with all farmers and competitors in an attempt to benefit the entire industry. Its sense of social responsibility extends also to hiring practices: for example, when, post-9/11, the company launched policies to hire veterans.

Former CEO Howard Schultz has always had a personal quest for connectedness. In 1982, he joined Starbucks as a director of retail operations and marketing. In 1983, while on a trip to Milan, Italy, he noticed that every street had an espresso bar, and these espresso bars served as a place for the community to gather and connect. From the beginning, Schultz saw an opportunity for his business to help build social cohesion by facilitating the need for conversation and connection over coffee. His original mission and vision were simple: create a "third place," a meeting spot for people to gather between work and home.[108] He believed he was selling experiences and connections, and coffee was just part of the experience. The value of his brand was in the conversations and relationships that happened over coffee between employees, customers, and their friends. He built the business on a core set of values centered around treating employees like partners and customers like friends. His sense of compassion and caring created a deep sense of self-awareness and a desire to serve others.

The Starbucks mission evolved into "to inspire and nurture the human spirit—one person, one cup and one neighborhood at a time."[109] Along with the revised vision are seven key principles or practices that focus on the world seeing Starbucks as a potential for good in society, not just as a retailer of a product. The organization believes the result of these principles will create value for shareholders. Shareholder value will not be at the expense of these principles.

"Caring is not a sign of weakness," says former Starbucks president Howard Behar, "but rather a sign of strength, and it can't be faked—within an organization, with the people we serve, or in the local or global community. Without trust and caring we'll never know what could have been possible. Without freedom from fear, we can't dream and we can't reach our potential."[110] When the goal is flourishing, caring and the well-being of others become more vital than ever to enterprise success.

The Many Paths to Flourishing

The sixteen exemplars presented here offer a range of business models, products, processes, and technologies, united by a way of seeing the world based on wholeness and connectedness. They take diverse but converging paths to quantum leadership. They highlight the many different factors that account for their success.

Natura, Tata, and Starbucks illustrate the extraordinary vision of their founders—Luiz Seabra, Jamsetji Tata, and Howard Schultz, respectively—centered on wholeness and connectedness. Nucor, Westpac, and Schuberg Philis demonstrate the power of distributed organizations, egalitarian labor practices, and caring for people and community, with Greyston Bakery's Open Hiring Model being a distinctive case, in which flat and decentralized organizational structures give employees a sense that they are trusted to carry out the company's positive-impact vision. Clarke and Eileen Fisher exemplify whole-system approaches in which all key stakeholders along the value chain are engaged in visioning, designing, and implementing the company's strategy and culture. Tesla and Tennant Company show us that a mission of social responsibility can be seamlessly integrated into smarter products that customers prefer because they simply perform better than competitors. Others have elaborate blueprints for achieving flourishing enterprise: Unilever's Sustainable Living Plan, IKEA's People and Planet Positive strategy, and the Novo Nordisk Blueprint for Change. Almost all the exemplars are high on industry-level collaboration, with Nike first among equals.

5 THE QUANTUM
LEADERSHIP MODEL

BUSINESS RESPONSIBILITY, or the lack thereof, is increasingly a tale of two cities.[1] The psychopaths portrayed in *The Wolf of Wall Street*, with their utter lack of concern for those they manipulate for personal advantage, are the denizens of one city. We are surrounded daily by tales of their exploitation and greed. Volkswagen's use of "defeat devices" to cheat on pollution emission tests and Uber's culture of discrimination and harassment under Travis Kalanick are among the more notorious examples, as is Turing Pharmaceuticals' alleged price gouging by its CEO Martin Shkreli. Less well known but equally concerning are reports about companies such as Alpha Natural Resources,[2] with its long history of environmental disasters, and WellPoint insurance (now Anthem), with its allegations of rescinding coverage to customers who had run up larger-than-average medical bills.[3]

Corporate misbehavior is hardly an American or Western phenomenon. Pharmaceutical companies—both foreign and domestic—have been accused of polluting local water supplies in India with a cocktail of up to twenty-one active pharmaceutical drugs.[4] In Bangladesh, the eight-story Rana Plaza building, which supplied garments to Benetton and Primark among other global apparel brands, killed 1,134 garment workers and injured around 2,500 in 2013. The building's owners had ignored warning signs after cracks in the building began to appear;

garment workers were ordered to return the following day, at which point the building collapsed during morning rush hour.[5] In 2008 the Chinese dairy producer Sanlu was found (along with other Chinese dairy firms) to have caused widespread harm, including some deaths, to babies after adding the toxic chemical melamine to its milk and infant formula to boost the tested protein level.[6] Unfortunately, these examples of corporate greed, and of knowingly putting people and nature in harm's way, are only the most media-exposed corporate citizens of this city.

The other city is populated by quantum leaders, whose purpose is to create shared prosperity on a healthy planet. They embody business as an agent of world benefit, pursuing full-spectrum flourishing that generates economic returns through personal well-being, community health, a fair and inclusive society, and a thriving biosphere. Neither the popular media nor business channels provide much coverage of these leaders and their positive impact. The efforts toward world betterment by the sixteen exemplar companies profiled in the previous chapter are not widely known, and, with very few exceptions, these stories do not find their way into mainstream media. This dearth of popular interest in positive business stories has led to the founding of initiatives such as AIM2Flourish,[7] which aims to bring to public attention the thousands of largely unknown examples of business as a force for good.

Lucky Iron Fish,[8] an AIM2Flourish prizewinner for its contribution to UN Sustainable Development Goal #3 (health and well-being), is an example of an extraordinarily simple yet powerful innovation that is making a huge difference in Southeast Asia among low-income populations suffering from iron deficiency. The specially formulated iron ingot, in the shape of a fish—considered to be a symbol of luck and prosperity—releases a significant portion of a person's daily iron intake requirements when boiled with a meal for as little as ten minutes.

Another AIM2Flourish prizewinner was Bureo,[9] a Chilean company that manufactures skateboards from discarded fishing nets, using designs inspired by aquatic creatures. The company collects its raw materials through its "Net Positiva" program in which it educates local fishing syndicates about the harm of discarding nets in the ocean while giving them a channel to reuse such nets in a way that benefits the environment and the Chilean shorefront community.[10]

Showcasing such positive business stories is a hugely valuable exercise in itself. When businesspeople learn about for-profit companies that have a world-changing positive impact, they become inspired to pursue greater purpose and to pay it forward by engaging other leaders and organizations.

In this chapter, our goal is to go deep into the guts of business leadership to identify and analyze the characteristics of full-spectrum flourishing. Previous chapters examine quantum leadership from the perspective of Frederick Chavalit Tsao (Chapters 2 and 3) and through case studies of businesses exhibiting quantum leadership attributes (Chapter 4). We now look more closely at the leaders and cultures of such flourishing organizations. What defines their organizational cultures? What are their daily practices? Only by answering these questions—which we aim to do through the evidence-based research—can we hope to amplify the kind of business leadership that has the potential to create flourishing for all of humanity and all life on earth.

The Consciousness Hypothesis

Why do some leaders tend toward selfishness, divisiveness, and exploitation, while others are disposed toward caring, wholeness, and compassion? Our years of combined experience led us to hypothesize that consciousness is the foundation of a leader's orientation toward meaningful social responsibility. In 2015 we set out to research and validate that intuition. Our multiyear research project was framed by the following consciousness hypothesis:

> Consciousness, the awareness by the mind of itself and the world around it, is a powerful root cause of who we are, how we behave toward others and nature, and why we act the way we do. Transforming our consciousness is the most effective tool we have for unlocking local and global change.

The hypothesis echoes the assertion of systems scientist Donella Meadows that the highest leverage point to intervene in a complex system is "the mindset or paradigm out of which the system arises."[11] Former McKinsey director Frederick Laloux, in his best-selling book *Reinventing Organizations: A Guide to Creating Organizations Inspired by the Next Stage of Human Consciousness*, observed similarly that "throughout history, the types of organizations we have invented were tied to the prevailing worldview and consciousness."[12] More recently, a team of researchers at the Center for Evolutionary Learning concluded, "The answer [to global sustainability challenges] lies in the notion of 'evolutionary leaps' in human consciousness. Such rapid, and at the same time, profound changes can yield integrative awareness, experiences, decision-making and actions in all spheres of life, including business, that are spontaneously directed toward promoting the common good."[13]

We were not the first to walk this path, but we felt the time had come to introduce it to a wider business audience. Also, what is different now is the growing awareness of new findings in science—in disciplines as diverse as quantum physics, consciousness research, evolutionary biology, epigenetics, neuroscience, economics, psychology, and organizational behavior—that are beginning to overturn conventional views about the nature of reality. These new findings are presented in the next chapter.

Transforming consciousness is not just a cognitive argument. Unlike the business case for social responsibility, which attempts to persuade managers based on rational analytic grounds, a consciousness of connectedness changes who people are at the level of their perceived reality. Currently, two very different forms of consciousness exist. Now more than ever, these two forms are at war with each other.

A CONSCIOUSNESS OF SEPARATENESS. Over the last three hundred years our fields of knowledge—in diverse disciplines across the natural and social sciences—have led us to see ourselves as separate, selfish, utility-maximizing individuals who are spiritless and existentially alone, born into a coldly mechanical universe composed of clumps of matter subject to gravitational and electromagnetic forces driving us toward meaningless extinction.

A CONSCIOUSNESS OF CONNECTEDNESS.   Fueled by a collective search for greater purpose,[14] which has always existed but is experiencing renewed urgency as we face global threats to existence, and new findings in the natural and social sciences, a new consciousness is emerging in which we see ourselves as deeply connected to one another physically, emotionally, and spiritually.[15] It is a more relational view of who we are.

. . .

The sense of being part of a whole has the potential to define our most basic impulses toward others and all life on earth. It changes how we think and act. We become more empathetic and compassionate. When we see ourselves as an integral part of the natural world rather than separate from it, we become more attuned to how our actions affect not only others but all life-forms.

The point is that our consciousness is the foundation for the stories we tell about who we are and the nature of the world we live in. These stories in turn determine the actions we take in business as in life.

The Consciousness Leap: A Visual Tour of Business Evolution

Quantum leadership is an entirely new paradigm for business. Social enterprises led by quantum leaders are not incrementally more socially responsible than other social enterprises. They are anchored in a new consciousness of connectedness that leads them to pursue well-being, prosperity, and flourishing—*because that is who they are.*

To understand the leap in consciousness from one of separateness to one of connectedness, we turn to the evolution of business along three axes: business purpose, organizing principles, and leadership mode. This multifactor evolution discussed in the following sections is presented visually in Figures 5.1–5.3 to help capture the whole-system nature of the transition to the new paradigm.

The First Transition

Since the 1960s, businesses such as Ben and Jerry's (United States), The Body Shop (United Kingdom), Danone (France), Triodos Bank

(Holland), Kyocera Corp (Japan), Natura (Brazil), and many others have been vocally embedding a social mission within their core *business purpose*—the horizontal axis of Figure 5.1—letting the world know that they were moving away from an exclusive focus on shareholder value. At the same time, CSR scholars such as Ed Freeman were formalizing alternative theories of value creation that spanned shareholders and stakeholders. In 1994, John Elkington advanced the notion of a "triple bottom line" of people, planet, and profit. Three years later, the strategist Stu Hart published "Beyond Greening," a landmark *Harvard Business Review* article that won that year's McKinsey Award. In it, he articulated the business strategies that contributed to a more sustainable world while simultaneously driving shareholder value. In 2000, Jed Emerson published his concept of "blended value" and, in 2003, Chris Laszlo proposed the "sustainable value" framework.[16]

By 2011, when Harvard Business School professor Michael Porter published his article "Shared Value," the idea was no longer new. Porter's

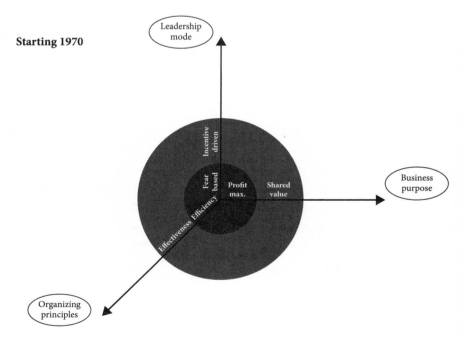

Figure 5.1. First transition from shareholder value to shared value

article simply helped cement it in the executive mind-set. Within a few years of the article's publication, global surveys of CEOs were showing that more than 80 percent believed that environmental and social sustainability was critical to competitive advantage.[17]

The second axis represents *organizing principles*. Corresponding to the first stage's shareholder value focus was a predominant style of organizing based on power and hierarchy. Efficiency was the defining concept in human resources management, with employees and external stakeholders of the firm treated instrumentally in pursuit of shareholder value. As the purpose of the firm gradually shifted to include the creation of stakeholder value, organizing principles also evolved. Effectiveness became more important than efficiency, with business performance extending to social and environmental performance and measured by new indicators such as the balanced scorecard and those of the Global Reporting Initiative (GRI). Relationships and the emotional well-being of employees and other stakeholders were becoming integral to the principle of effectiveness, although they were still seen chiefly through the lens of business performance.

The third axis represents *leadership mode*. Along with a business purpose of shareholder value and the organizing principle of efficiency was often a type of leadership in which fear was the prime driver. In a fear-based workplace, employees know that if they miss their objectives, set by their hierarchical superiors, they could lose their jobs. Senior leaders use their position to punish infractions and to control performance. In a 1995 *Harvard Business Review* article, best-selling management guru John Kotter urged leaders to create a "burning platform" in the organization, using crisis as a way to motivate people to engage change.[18] Yet in many corporate settings, fear-based leadership gradually became less popular. Although still widely used, its limits have become apparent in more complex, relationship-intensive business environments.[19]

Partially in its place grew incentive-based leadership. A popular practice in the 1990s was to issue extensive stock options as a way to reward executives of publicly traded companies for improved stock price performance. Incentive stock options (ISOs) and equity incentive plans became popular tools to motivate and retain employees. According to management consultant John Collard, the key to incentive-based management is to "set realistic goals and time frames, hold managers accountable for performance, and communicate measurement and reward methodology—then step back and let them perform."[20]

The transition from the first to the second stage of business is represented visually in Figure 5.1.

The Second Transition

The second transition in the evolution of business can be characterized as the shift from shared value to *business as a force for good*, in which creating value for societal stakeholders becomes the driving business mission. Such social purpose has a long distinguished pedigree in social entrepreneurship and in niche businesses such as Patagonia and Triodos Bank. However, new forms of mainstream businesses are appearing, such as the rapidly developing B Corps (first appearance 2007), benefit corporations (first appearance 2010), and Conscious Capitalism (part of the subtitle in Patricia Abergene's book *Megatrends 2010: The Rise of Conscious Capitalism*, and subsequently used as the title of John McKay and Raj Sisodia's 2012 book). Multinational companies Unilever and Danone's stated objective to become B Corps and IKEA's People and Planet Positive strategy are among the more visible recent examples of a mainstream business transition.

Caring and compassion now become organizing principles. The well-being of employees, suppliers, customers, and other stakeholders is seen as central to business success. Caring and compassion for oneself and others (including all life on earth) help motivate business activities. As Frederick Laloux notes, in this stage of business evolution, people are "likely to affiliate only with organizations that have a clear and noble purpose of their own. We can expect that purpose, more than profitability, growth, or market share, will be the guiding principle for organizational decision-making."[21]

Leadership mode transitions from "incentive based" to "serving others." Leaders seek fairness, equality, community, and cooperation.[22] They take multiple perspectives into account. Relationships are increasingly valued over transactional outcomes.[23] Such a leadership mode focuses on the empowerment of employees, suppliers, and customers while doing good in the communities and natural environments in which the company operates.

The transition from the second to the third stage of business is represented visually in Figure 5.2.

Is this third stage not sufficient to create the desired results for both business and society? The answer, unfortunately, is increasingly no. Evidence mounts that corporate sustainability in this stage is only slowing the rate of harm, which is very different from creating well-being, prosperity, and flourishing for all. Signal trends that we are not heading in the right direction include the year-on-year rise in atmospheric carbon emissions and the growing gap between rich and poor, vividly portrayed by a 2018 Oxfam study showing that the world's nine richest men

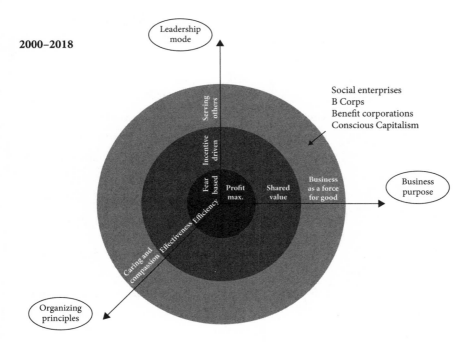

Figure 5.2. Second transition from shared value to business as a force for good

have more combined wealth than the poorest four billion people.[24] Further evidence that business is not contributing, at the aggregate level, to world betterment is summarized in Chapter 1.

The Third Transition

The third transition is characterized by the shift to full-spectrum flourishing. In the latter stage, people pursue doing good because that is who they are rather than because they are persuaded by others that it is the right thing to do or because there is a business case for it. Their mind-set and behaviors come from a place of wholeness. It is not dissimilar to the concept of *ubuntu*, a word in the Nguni Bantu language that translates roughly as "I am what I am because of what we all are." Here there is no other: the well-being of the individual becomes inseparable from the well-being of others. Humanity is no longer reduced to tribalism or nationalism or religious separatism. With regard to the natural environment, we become an intrinsic part of it rather than well-meaning stewards who are somehow separate from and above it.

The purpose of business becomes the creation of health and well-being at the level of the individual, the organization, the local community, and on upward to ever-more-complex levels until all of humanity and the biosphere are included. Here businesses are no longer content to make a positive impact as part of a separate social mission. Neither are they driven by codes of business ethics or financial analyses based on the return on investment (ROI) of doing good. Quantum leaders experience the world in a new way. Instead of seeing freedom and dignity as attributes of an individual, they hold that true freedom and dignity exist only when everyone has them.[25]

Organizing principles at this stage are based on wholeness. Feelings of empathy for others and the desire to alleviate suffering come not from a sense of separate social identities but from a place of oneness. As authors, we felt that this distinction was important, yet it remained unclear how, exactly, wholeness translated into specific social processes that shape the interactions between organizational members. We needed research to provide evidence-based answers.

Similarly, our experience suggested that leadership mode in the fourth stage went beyond notions of serving others. Anecdotal case studies suggested that self-awareness, along with the awareness of the interconnectedness of all things, was the essence of leadership in the fourth stage. Again, we needed further research to provide evidence-based answers.

The transition from the third to the fourth stage of business is visually represented in Figure 5.3.

On occasion, we are asked by skeptical business leaders and students of management whether such a model of business as an agent of world benefit is realistic and attainable. This question begged another: Is what

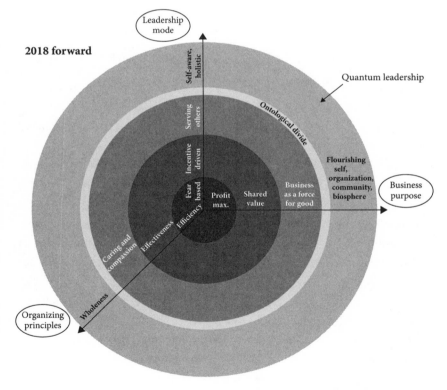

Figure 5.3. Third transition from business as a force for good to full-spectrum flourishing

we know about the past and present the only guide to human behavior? The British science-fiction writer Arthur C. Clarke formulated three laws, the third of which states, "Any sufficiently advanced technology is indistinguishable from magic."[26] The same is true in regard to the evolution of consciousness.

Our preagricultural nomadic ancestors lived in what cultural historian Morris Berman called a state of paradoxical consciousness, in which they saw themselves as embedded and inseparable from the natural world.[27] They could not have imagined either a post–Bronze Age consciousness in which the self, others, and nature developed split identities or the refined ego consciousness of the industrial era in which other people and nature are treated as inexhaustible resources on a global scale.[28] Today, we may not be able to imagine a consciousness of connectedness, but that does not mean it cannot or will not happen.

Clare Graves, Frederick Laloux, Ervin Laszlo, Peter Senge, Ken Wilber, and many others have long made the case that the next stage of human evolution will be driven by a paradigm shift in consciousness.[29] Our hypothesis was that the next stage in business evolution—to full-spectrum flourishing—will result only from such a quantum leap in collective consciousness.

Our research was aimed at exploring, testing, validating, and clarifying the consciousness hypothesis. We were interested in understanding the role of consciousness in helping business leaders cross the ontological gap from separateness and selfishness to connectedness and caring. We wanted to develop evidence-based insights into quantum leader attributes, cultures, and practices. The following sections provide a review of our research methodology and key findings.

Quantum Leadership Research

From December 2015 through June 2018, a mixed-methods study was conducted by a team of researchers in Asia, Europe, North America, and South America.[30] The mixed-methods approach had both qualitative and quantitative components.[31] The collection, analysis, and integration of qualitative data obtained from the interviews were combined with quantitative data from the survey respondents.

Qualitative Research

Forty-nine leaders of organizations were interviewed as part of this research.[32] An additional eight in-depth interviews were conducted to follow up on questions raised by the findings. Interview subjects were from a wide range of organizational sizes and industry types.[33] The primary consideration in selecting the sample was finding organizations and leaders who showed signs of embodying the fourth stage of quantum leadership. We sought out organizations with a known social-impact mission as part of their business purpose and leaders with evidence of practices of connectedness in their leadership approach. Practices of connectedness were defined early on as mindfulness or reflective in nature and later on expanded to include a much broader range of practices and routines aimed at increasing a consciousness of connectedness, such as having personal check-ins at the start of meetings, encouraging people to volunteer in the local community, and giving employees breaks outside during the work day. By this means, we excluded from the sample set those organizations operating at the first or second stage shown in Figure 5.2 and focused fully on understanding those that showed evidence of crossing the "ontological divide" from stages three to four.

The research process allowed the voices of the forty-nine interviewees to point the way forward. New questions emerged along the way that took the study in directions that could not have been determined or predicted at the start. Some of the questions pursued in the later interviews were shaped by the analysis and findings that resulted from the earlier ones.

Within the chosen sample set, the qualitative analysis used grounded theory drawn from the scholars Barney Glaser and Anselm Strauss.[34] The qualitative analysis of the interviews involved coding the findings according to theoreticians Kathy Charmaz and Johnny Saldana to explore the emerging relationships between practices of connectedness, consciousness of connectedness, leadership attributes and behaviors, and positive social impacts.[35]

All interviews were conducted using a protocol designed to explore the following four thematic categories. Open-ended questions were used at the start of each category and throughout the process to allow the interviewer to follow the pace and topics that emerged and to freely explore ideas generated during the interview.

1. **Core business purpose, organizing principles, and leadership mode.** In this category we asked interviewees about business purpose. What was the company's stated and lived purpose? How did greater purpose guide the strategy, and how was it woven into the organizational principles and culture of the company? To what extent was it shared among employees? How would the interviewee describe "the way things are done" at his or her company? Further questions explored perceptions of organizational principles and leadership style. These included themes of caring and compassion, collaborative style and relational energy, and the company's relationship to the natural environment.

2. **Practices of connectedness.** This category focused on leadership practices and routines at the individual, team, organizational, and whole-system levels. What specific practices and routines were integral to the leader's approach? A more open-ended question was followed by an inquiry into those practices that were designed specifically to increase a sense of connectedness to self, others, and the world. The questions explored the themes of compassion, empathy, and wholeness. (A prompt was used to define "wholeness" as a work identity and a personal identity that are well integrated and personal values and organizational values that are well aligned.) Another question explored whether there existed any cultural practices or traditions that helped maintain a sense of connectedness to self, others, and the world.

3. **Consciousness of connectedness.** Questions in this category explored the leaders' most fundamental mind-set about who they were and what they saw as the nature of the world around them. We began by asking what the term "consciousness" meant to the interviewee. We explored the associations, resonances, or ideas that came to mind when the interviewee reflected on the term "consciousness of connectedness." (After asking the question

in an open-ended way, the interviewer was instructed to use a prompt defining consciousness as "the story we have about who we are in the world we live in" and consciousness of connectedness as "an awareness of how one's attitudes and actions impact all life on earth and future generations.") Further questions explored the evolution or biographical journey of the interviewee as a leader in the organization. We looked for stories and anecdotes about business decisions as well as the economic results and social impacts that resulted from the leader's evolution of consciousness.

4. **Business outcomes.** This category related to the interviewee's perceptions of the organization's economic as well as social and environmental outcomes, relative to its peers. Specifically, we were interested in perceptions of the company's relative success in creating economic prosperity and positive societal impact. As the majority of our interviewees were from privately owned firms, we used perceived business outcome measures. Actual financial performance figures are not published or disclosed in a standardized way for privately held companies. Given the potential for introducing bias by lacking a secondary data source, we followed accepted protocols in the management literature related to the use of perceived business performance measures with the design of our interview questions, assessment scales, and tests for interobserver reliability.

In many but not all cases, the interviews concluded with a discussion of the interviewee's "dream vision" for business and society. What would a business-led future of prosperity and flourishing look like? What would it look and feel like to live in such a world?

Data Collection
Data collection started in December 2015 and was completed in June 2018. Interviews lasted between ninety minutes and two hours, with a few rare cases extending to four hours. They were conducted in person and in some cases via telephone or the videoconferencing service Skype.

Interview candidates were initially contacted by e-mail or telephone and were drawn from the research team's professional networks. A "snowball" approach was applied to engage additional participants.

Participants were advised of the precautions taken to protect their privacy. They were asked to sign an authorization form stating their agreement to participate in the interview. All interviews were audio-recorded. The form included consent to the audio recording. Participants were informed that they could exit the interview at any time and that they could remain anonymous if they chose this option on the authorization form.

Research was conducted in accordance with the "Belmont Report,"[36] with all plans for research submitted in advance to the Institutional Review Board of Case Western Reserve University.

Data Analysis

In keeping with the principles of grounded theory, the analysis of data began following the first interview and continued throughout the data-collection period. Axial and selective coding of the interview data was used. Axial coding involves disaggregating core themes, and selective coding regroups them in ways that are meaningful and provide fresh insight. The research team used a web-based qualitative analysis platform, Dedoose, to support the coding process.

The initial round of coding resulted in 2,695 so-called open codes. This number was progressively reduced as a result of iterative team conversations in which we analyzed ways to organize codes into meaningful categories that brought increasing clarity to the patterns of meaning that emerged across the full set of interviews.

The process led to 369 axial codes in the second round, to 225 codes in the third round, and ultimately, through selective coding, to three overriding themes.

1. **Quantum leader attributes.** Under this root code we grouped all selective codes that were descriptive of the main attributes of quantum leaders.

2. **Flourishing organizational cultures.** Here we grouped the selective codes that provided descriptions of the organizational cultures associated with quantum leadership.

3. **Practices of connectedness.** Under this code we grouped all the practices of connectedness that the interviewees identified at the individual, team, organizational, and system levels.

We were searching for insights into the nature of business leadership, organizational cultures, and practices that resulted, iteratively and in a reinforcing way, in a consciousness of connectedness. In other words, we were studying how businesses operate in the outermost ring shown in Figure 5.3.

Quantitative Research

The quantitative research involved surveying 322 respondents consisting of business owners, senior executives, and middle managers from a cross section of industries.[37] The overarching research question underlying the quantitative study was to explore how a consciousness of connectedness combined with greater purpose influences economic, social, and environmental outcomes in business. The model was developed based on the results of the earlier qualitative research described in the previous section. The goal was to further explore the relationships between a consciousness of connectedness; greater purpose; leadership behaviors and attributes; and positive economic, social, and environmental outcomes.[38]

The research also built on other quantitative studies that provided evidence of a positive relationship between sustainability leadership and financial performance. Such studies included the work of Robert Eccles, Ioannis Ioannou, and George Serafeim with their analyses showing the financial outperformance of high-sustainability firms and the research of Rajendra Sisodia, Jagdish Sheth, and David Wolfe published as *Firms of Endearment*.[39] Both studies provided compelling evidence that creating stakeholder value as part of a business strategy and culture is positively correlated to financial performance. We were interested in learning about the antecedents to such a relationship: What was it that propelled companies to pursue positive impact in the first place? Specifically, we were interested in the relationship between greater purpose and consciousness of connectedness (the independent variables) and positive economic and social and environmental outcomes (the dependent variables), mediated by the leadership variables of shared vision, compassion, and relational energy.

Survey Design and Data Collection

A survey instrument was developed and tested in a multistep process. Screening points were established to ensure that only respondents in leadership positions in their organizations completed the survey, and attention screens with minimum and maximum time thresholds were implemented to ensure engaged participation.

Four questions related to consciousness of connectedness were designed using a visual representation of oneness based on an adaptation of the oneness survey from William B. Swann and colleagues and a "connectedness to nature" survey from F. Stephan Mayer and Cynthia M. Frantz.[40] Four questions related to greater purpose were adapted from Ante Glavas and Ken Kelley.[41]

Twelve questions designed to measure leadership traits and behaviors were drawn from the "relational climate survey" developed by Richard Boyatzis, Kylie Rochford, and Scott Taylor.[42] The reference to leadership is not only to those at the hierarchical top of the organization. It is to all those who help shape the "relatively stable collective structure that represents the socio-emotional atmosphere that is created and maintained as people interact in a dyadic relationship, team, or organization."[43]

To measure the model's dependent variables, the survey asked respondents to assess the perceived performance of their organization relative to their major competitors. Three items related to economic performance, defined as the perceived evaluation of the organization's creation of economic prosperity relative to major competitors; and four items related to positive social and environmental outcomes, defined as the perceived evaluation of the organization's social and environmental outcomes relative to major competitors.

Data Analysis

The statistical analysis technique used for testing the hypotheses was structural equation modeling (SEM). Hypotheses 1 and 2 were concerned with how greater purpose and a consciousness of connectedness influenced leadership. The study confirmed a significant positive relationship existing between both greater purpose and consciousness of connectedness and each of the three leadership factors of shared vision, compassion, and relational energy. The strongest correlations were between consciousness of connectedness and compassion and between greater purpose and shared vision. The implication for business leaders is that a higher consciousness of connectedness has a measurably positive influence on the way people in their organizations relate to one another, increasing caring, compassion, and collaboration, while having a greater purpose measurably increases a sense of shared vision.

Hypotheses 3 and 4 were concerned with how greater purpose is mediated by the factors of relational climate in influencing perceived economic performance and social and environmental outcomes.

Hypotheses 5 and 6 were concerned with how consciousness of connectedness is mediated by the factors of relational climate in influencing perceived economic performance and social and environmental outcomes.

For these mediated pathways to economic performance and positive social and environmental outcomes, a mixed set of results emerged. For the path of greater purpose to economic performance, a significant indirect path was supported through shared vision and relational energy. However, a significant negative correlation emerged between compassion and economic performance (higher compassion correlating with lower perceived economic performance relative to competitors), which can be attributed to the perception that too much compassion deemphasized a culture of high performance, and vice versa.[44] For the path of greater purpose to positive social and environmental outcomes, the hypotheses of mediation were not supported.

Hypothesis 7 focused on the direct relationship between greater purpose and consciousness of connectedness to positive social and environmental outcomes. The direct relationship between greater purpose and positive social and environmental outcomes was significant and strong, while consciousness of connectedness has a positive but weak direct effect on positive social and environmental outcomes, with a much stronger relationship existing when mediated by compassion.

A synthesis and discussion of the research findings are presented in the next section.

Research Findings

Findings were organized into two groupings loosely following the differences in objectives of the quantitative and qualitative studies. The first set of findings narrates the relationships between variables: practices of connectedness, consciousness of connectedness, leadership traits and behaviors, and positive economic and social outcomes. The second grouping offers a deeper understanding of quantum leaders: who they are, their organizational cultures, and their practices. Because the findings about practices are so extensive and focus on the "how to" of quantum leadership, they are presented and discussed further in Part III.

RELATIONSHIPS.   A leader's consciousness of connectedness with other people and the natural environment is positively correlated with shared vision, compassion, and collaboration, which in turn mediate a positive relationship to economic performance as well as social and environmental outcomes. A company's mission to serve a greater purpose likewise correlates with vision, compassion, and collaboration and is also mediated to social and environmental outcomes as well as to economic performance. Taken together, these findings suggest a high level of correlation in the factors that define a quantum leader: a self-aware and holistic leadership mode, a business purpose aimed at full-spectrum flourishing, and a set of organizing principles based on wholeness. The finding of a negative correlation between compassion and economic performance opens the question of the conditions under which greater compassion does lead to better economic outcomes. Similarly, the finding that consciousness of connectedness correlates positively with shared vision, compassion, and collaboration yet weakly with positive social and environmental outcomes opens the question of how consciousness of connectedness translates into action.

ATTRIBUTES.   The coding process used in the qualitative study provided a profile of quantum leaders. In descending order of importance (as measured by code frequency), quantum leaders are (1) high on the scale of consciousness of connectedness; (2) driven by a sense of greater purpose; (3) relational, collaborative, and people-centric; (4) committed to self-cultivation; and (5) evolutionary. Each of these attributes can be expanded as follows.

High on the scale of consciousness of connectedness meant having whole-system vision, relational awareness, and attunement to a spiritual or universal energy field. Quantum leaders feel a high degree of connectedness to (in descending order of importance) community; the business they are a part of (intraorganizational); networks (interorganizational); the whole (a connection to all beings); the totality of their relationships (their relational coordination); nature; and self.

Driven by a sense of greater purpose was given meaning in terms of adherence to values and to a sense of responsibility for others. Greater purpose was aimed at (in descending order of importance) *transforming* the business, the environment, community and society, people, the world, and economic growth.

Relational, collaborative, and people-centric was given expression by (in descending order of importance) having collaborative intention; acting as a connector in the organization or community; having an experience of resonance with others; being empathetic; appreciating diversity; and habitually employing differing viewpoints in dialogue.

Committed to self-cultivation was closely associated with a deep desire to flourish. It encompassed not only the goal of personal development but also the flourishing of all people and all life on earth. The meanings given to this attribute were (in descending order of importance) a commitment to self-cultivation; flourishing in the organization; flourishing in society; and flourishing in nature.

Evolutionary meant being a learning leader who is (in descending order of importance) future driven and process oriented; sensitive to context and narrative; aware of the bigger picture; able to use constructively the feedback of others; able to turn crises and limitations into opportunities; able to continuously learn new things; and creative and adaptive.

Attributes of Flourishing Organizational Cultures

The coding process also revealed the main attributes or characteristics of the flourishing organizational cultures associated with quantum leadership. In descending order of importance (as measured by code frequency), flourishing organizational cultures are people-centric and relational; creative and innovative; designed to promote well-being inside and outside the organization; and operate from a strength-based perspective rather than a deficit-based one.

People-centric and relational cultures emphasized the interests and values of employees, clients, and other stakeholders of the organization rather than adopted the economistic paradigm in which transactions and market interests reign supreme.[45] They are defined by (in descending order of importance) collaboration and cocreation; compassion, empathy, and caring; transparency, trust, and authenticity; and communication, coordination, and team value. Additional key words in order of code frequency are "engagement," "ownership," "belonging," "sharing," and "impact" (collective and positive).

Creative and innovative cultures are distinguished by design thinking in which abductive reasoning is as important as deductive or inductive logic. They are hallmarked by an appreciation for cultural diversity and local knowledge.

Designed to promote well-being inside and outside the organization refers to cultures that enable an alignment of personal and organizational values. They allow employees to bring their whole selves to work and give priority to their work-life balance.

Operating from a strength-based perspective rather than a deficit-based one refers to cultures that embed positive psychology and positive organizational development.

These are the attributes of quantum leaders and flourishing organizational cultures that resulted from the coding process. Following are selected excerpts from the interviews, which exemplify quantum leadership attributes in the practitioners' own words.

Voices from the Interviews

Jeffrey Abramson, CEO of the Tower Companies, says, "Consciousness is a feeling of the infinite intelligence and silence, the natural experience of which is [being] more alert, mindful, clear . . . but there's a quality of consciousness beyond just alertness. . . . [It's] a term that probably is more prevalent in what is used now as a way of describing the necessity of being a global citizen to understand your own emotions, to rise above your own emotions, . . . and to allow everyone else in society to rise automatically."

According to Shannon Kaplan of In Posse, "I think it comes down to that constant awareness that everything that you do touches other people. . . . I feel like a lot of it is acknowledging that everybody influences everyone else and that together we can either choose to make that connection as meaningful and valuable as possible or we can . . . make it a horrible experience for everyone."

"It's being able to put your hand on your heart and say that I haven't exploited the environment and I haven't exploited human resources in order to get this piece of material in order to make something from it," says Deb King of Quikes.

Frank Foti, CEO of Vigor Shipyards, explains, "Connecting with people is so often done without words and [instead] done by an action, a smile, an eye contact. . . . I think of the industrial worker who is a kinesthetic learner, a visual learner, or an auditory learner. . . . They're not connecting through words . . . they're trusting [through] feelings, and I'm trusting of them. . . . That is higher-order consciousness and connection, if you ask me, right there."

"When I walk along the street, I look at each person and think, 'Behind every person there is an entire world' . . . and I feel very connected. . . . For me every person is very important; I don't know why. It is not part of any philosophical school of thought or anything like that. It's just the way it is," explains Manuel Villen of OHL.

Rod Ely of Green Mountain Coffee Roasters says, "I'm trying to live my life in harmony with the world, and . . . as I look back, I can see that was really always the case."

Roy Whitten of Whitten and Roy Partnership expresses a similar philosophy: "When I go to work . . . I'm doing it in a way that's true to who I am. I'm not pretending. I'm not bending my own ethical stance. I'm doing it in a way that I'm aware of my connection with [other] people around me and to live in a way that I'm proud of."

Says Gerwin Shuring, cofounder and head of sales at Schuberg Philis, "I think there's more to this interpersonal relationships, and professionally I really love some of the people I've worked with . . . and I think that, yeah, all these friendships in our company really help us to feel more deeply connected to each other. Also with customers—I really developed deep friendships with some of my customers [of a kind] you also don't always see. . . . The whole idea of families and how to leave the world a little better for our children is one of the reasons we do how we do things."

Catherine Chauvinc, group vice president of Aden Services, explains, "Do we go for technology only, or do we keep the human touch? There's a strong debate currently on that. I've been CEO of the company in China for five years. . . . [I believe that] we need to keep this connected human touch because this is our strength; that's the way things work; . . . it gives you agility. . . . What could change in five to seven years [will be] to go toward a social enterprise and make a bigger impact on society. . . . Most of our managers and leaders are Chinese, and I think they care about these [aspects]—the link between the environment, the company, and themselves."

"What we do to others we're doing to ourselves. I also believe that when we do business in our own community, we are more aware of that [connection]. We are more aware because there's a short distance between us as a business decision maker and the people who are affected by our decisions. Whether they are our employees or our customers or our suppliers, neighbors, or the nature environment we operate in, there's a short distance. Then it's more likely that we will make decisions for the common good," explains Judi Wicks of White Dog Café.

"I'm not a smoker, but all the breaks, I would always step out to get some fresh air. . . . I love to step outside; I think it just [is] connecting me to nature," says Srini Venkatesh, chief scientist at GOJO.

Lynnette Brown of CCP notes, "I'm not religious in that you won't see me at church every Sunday, but I'm very spiritual, and I'm very aware that there has to be something bigger than us. The spiritual thing in me is really about justice and respect and about understanding that my responsibility is to help other people."

Says Michel Fedelman of KPB, "I've always had a passion for making people feel like they're part of a community. I think that's a really important part of making a person healthy and whole. You're feeling like there are people around you who you know; you can walk outside your door and feel a part of something bigger than yourself."

What the Research Affirms

The overall findings provide compelling evidence that the transition to quantum leadership is rooted in a shift in consciousness toward connectedness and that quantum leaders embody such a consciousness of connectedness in their way of being. It is a new way of seeing, feeling, and experiencing the world. It begins with an awareness of how one's attitudes and actions affect all life on earth and future generations. A close correlation exists between such a shift in consciousness and indicators of positive social impact in business: shared values of human well-being and a long-term perspective toward the creation of economic prosperity and flourishing for all.

While a clear image of quantum leaders and flourishing organizational cultures emerged from the research, the findings nonetheless suggest that the shift in consciousness may be messy, nonlinear, and complex. In some companies there was little evidence of a consciousness of connectedness, but leaders pursued flourishing outcomes. In other cases, leaders held views that were suggestive of a consciousness of connectedness, but employees were treated poorly. Nonetheless, overall the evidence from our research points to a transformation in consciousness as the root of the emergence of a form of business in which prosperity (rather than only profit) and flourishing for all (rather than profit for the top 1 percent) are the primary outcomes.

The finding that even leading companies in our data oscillate between a consciousness of connectedness and one of separateness reflects the instability characteristic of society at this junction of history. Such instability is evidenced in the radical swings of some countries toward nationalism, racism, and protectionism; the loss of biodiversity that some observers are labeling the "sixth mass extinction";[46] and the growing incidence of terrorism spurred by various ideological causes. Will such instability remain for an extended transitory period? Will we slide backward into separateness and selfishness, lurching from one social and environmental crisis to the next? Or will business leaders make the leap to a consciousness of connectedness that allows them to play a central guiding role in humankind's next stage of evolution?

6 THE SCIENCE OF CONNECTEDNESS

IN THE SEIWA PREFECTURAL FORESTS of Japan, city residents come to walk among the towering oak trees. They are practicing *shinrin-yoku*, "forest bathing," which means taking in the sylvan air in contemplative strolls. Forest bathing became popular in Japan in the 1980s and today is a recognized preventive health-care practice. One research study measuring the physiological effects of forest bathing on 280 subjects in their early twenties concluded, "Forest environments promote lower concentrations of cortisol [a hormone associated with stress], lower pulse rate, lower blood pressure, greater parasympathetic nerve activity, and lower sympathetic nerve activity than do city environments."[1] Such immersions in nature have also been proven to bring a host of psychological benefits, as people engage in fewer negative emotions and less self-referential thinking.[2]

A group of executives set up their easels along the Lungarno. The late-evening sun illuminates the Ponte Vecchio, one of Italy's oldest bridges, a stunning example of early medieval architecture and the only bridge in Florence to have escaped destruction in World War II. Slowly, colors and forms begin to emerge on canvas. These travelers from the business world are there to explore new perspectives, hoping to find beauty in a fractured world and, obliquely, expand their leadership capabilities.[3] As MIT professor Edgar Schein observed, "Art and artists stimulate us to see more, hear more, and experience more of what is going on within us and around us."[4] Management scholars point to the importance of art for business in creating a more socially desirable future.[5] A growing body of research shows that the arts can also contribute to feelings of well-being, aid recovery to good health, and support longer lives better lived.[6]

The Helene Stureborgs kammarkör meets weekly in downtown Stockholm to practice a cappella (singing without instruments),[7] drawing on a repertoire ranging from the medieval ballad *Bältet* to Waldemar Åhlén's popular *Sommarpsalm* (Summer hymn). There is a long tradition of a cappella singing in the country; almost 5 percent of the Swedish population belongs to a choir, according to one estimate.[8] It is a practice that is proving to be good medicine.[9] Studies show that singing is associated with respiratory benefits, stress reduction and enhanced immunity, improved cognition and mitigation of the effects of Alzheimer's disease,[10] and feelings of greater social confidence.

In the Copper Canyon of northern Mexico, the reclusive Tarahumara, also known as the Rarámuri, make running part of their daily life. They often run just for fun, engaging in a social game called *rarajipari* in which runners kick a wooden ball along mountain trails in relay races that can last several days. Although poor in material terms, surviving on a staple of mostly beans and corn, the Rarámuri have unusually low rates of psychological disorders, a near absence of modern-day diseases such as cancer or type 2 diabetes, and little or no crime.[11] The benefits of not only running but all forms of exercise, such as walking, swimming, and weightlifting, are now irrefutable both for reductions in all-cause mortality rates and for improvements in feelings of well-being.[12]

In Basel's old-town quarter of St. Alban, forty-year-old Lukas engages daily in the practice of journaling. Every morning over a cup of *kaffee creme*, he writes down his thoughts and emotions as they occur to him. Like many Swiss citizens, he strives for precision and economy of thought. But also like many of his compatriots, he is overworked and stressed by his job. Journaling helps Lukas express his innermost feelings and confront his private fears and hopes. It helps him take note of his life experiences, to learn from them, and to make connections that otherwise would lie buried in his subconscious. Journaling's health benefits have been well documented and include fewer illness-related visits to the doctor, reduced burnout, and increases in positive mood, social engagement, and quality of close relationships.[13]

Practices of Connectedness and Their Benefits

Along with nature immersion, art, music, exercise, and journaling, there are countless other practices—from engaging in loving-kindness meditation (LKM) to practicing yoga and having a glass of wine with friends[14]—that offer measurable benefits in terms of individual and community well-being. We refer to these collectively as *practices of connectedness*, for reasons that we make clear in this chapter.

While each of these practices appears to operate at a different level (for example, exercise is physiological while art is a felt experience that engages sensory perception),[15] for our purposes they all have three important characteristics in common. The first is that these practices are part of a well-documented upward spiral in lifestyle that increases our positive emotions and strengthens our personal resources, which in turn can lead to increased life satisfaction and an intrinsic inclination to do good for others and the world.[16] Conversely, these practices have been shown to help avoid the downward spiral of decreased well-being and disconnection that in turn reinforce mistrustful and uncooperative behaviors.[17]

The second is that such practices expand our awareness of being one with others and the world, helping us transcend everyday preoccupations that otherwise tend to leave us feeling fearful and alone. Modern-day research into the experience of flow, defined by Mihaly Csikszentmihalyi as a state of being "in the zone" where creativity and productivity emerge effortlessly,[18] demonstrates that a realization of oneness can result from artistic and athletic endeavors.[19] These practices can elevate a person's awareness of being part of a larger whole, manifest as the sudden loss of a sense of oneself in the "flow" activity.

The third shared characteristic is that such practices engage the whole person rather than only the rational, analytic, left-brained self. Neuroscientists would say they engage the default mode network

(DMN), which plays a central role in emotional self-awareness, socially focused activity, and ethical decision making, rather than the other main cortical network, the task-positive network (TPN), which is important for problem solving, focusing attention, and controlling action.[20] While some researchers suggest that the DMN may become deactivated during sense-making practices such as focused-attention meditation, it is likely that presencing practices such as LKM increase engagement of the DMN.[21] A key finding is that the neural activity in the TPN tends to inhibit activity in the DMN, and vice versa, which may explain why highly rational, analytic, task-oriented leaders can, at times, be challenged emotionally, socially, and ethically.[22]

Practices that share these three characteristics offer an action-oriented pathway to entrepreneurial creativity and to effective collaboration in today's complex and turbulent business environments.

Inquiry into the Origins of the Benefits

Today, clinical neuroscience is able to verify that our mind-body functioning is *physically changed* by such practices.[23] Clinical studies show that they help quiet our five senses and slow the analytic cognition of the brain.[24] They activate the parasympathetic nervous system and parts of the brain associated with broader perception and greater awareness of our essential oneness with humanity and all life on earth.[25] There is persuasive evidence that the neurophysiological changes induced by practices of connectedness are associated with greater feelings of oneness with others.[26] Through functional magnetic resonance imaging (fMRI) and single-photon emission computed tomography (SPECT) imaging, meditation has been shown to reduce brain activity in the parietal lobes, which results in a blurring of the perceptual line between the meditator and the external world.[27] This explains *how* the practices lead us to experience a greater sense of connectedness with others and nature.

Until now, however, it was not clear *why* such practices induced these observed changes. Clinical studies could tell us only how neural networks are altered by practices of connectedness. For example, why does mindfulness meditation increase the cortical folds of the brain (what neuroscientists call gyrification) associated with increased cognitive functioning and emotional regulation? The current state of knowledge provides little insight.

- Why do these practices lead to psychological and neuro-physiological benefits in health and well-being?
- Why might they increase our sense of wholeness and connectedness?
- Why might they increase pro-social and pro-environmental behaviors?

Consider the research conducted in two practice areas: meditation and nature immersion. In her "broaden-and-build" studies, Barbara Fredrickson provides compelling evidence that even short periods of LKM lead to increased positive emotions, which in turn build our cognitive, psychological, social, and physical resources to better handle life's challenges.[28] The transformation in LKM practitioners was statistically significant along nine dimensions: mindfulness, pathways thinking, savoring the future, environmental mastery, self-acceptance, purpose in life, social support received, positive relations with others, and reduced illness symptoms.[29] Each of these nine dimensions is essential in building the quantum leadership capabilities defined in the previous chapter. What remains unanswered in Fredrickson's research is *why* LKM produces these highly desirable effects.

Similarly, why should nature immersion lead to improvements in mood, cognition, and health? In *The Nature Fix*, award-winning journalist Florence Williams presents evidence that even small amounts of exposure to the living world can improve our creativity, enhance our sense of well-being, and increase our sense of civic responsibility.[30] Numerous empirical studies demonstrate that a sense of connection with nature is important to our happiness and is also a predictor of pro-environmental behavior.[31] So we know of nature's restorative effects and its ability to improve emotional functioning and responsible behavior, but not what mechanism is involved. The reverse effect—the link between a disconnection from nature and stress, depression, and a lack of concern for the natural environment—has also been well documented.[32]

Best-selling author Richard Louv's *Last Child in the Woods* identified a modern-day malady he calls nature-deficit disorder. According to Louv, the health of children and the health of the earth should be considered inseparable. He notes that this is especially important at a time when children are spending increasingly less time playing in natural environments than did previous generations.[33] But why should nature immersion lead to such beneficial effects in health, well-being, and responsible behaviors?

These are the questions we tackle next in an attempt to shed light on the origins of quantum leadership. We go behind the clinical research of practices of connectedness to look at what science is now telling us about the nature of reality itself, in disciplines as diverse as quantum physics, consciousness research, evolutionary biology, epigenetics, neuroscience, economics, psychology, and organizational behavior.

Emerging Science as an Accessible Guide to Action

Our goal is to make emerging science, and its implications for business leadership, accessible to people who want to understand who we are and the nature of our world. This understanding can then serve as a foundation for a revision of their narrative of human behavior—a narrative that jumps from essentially "selfish and separate" to "connected and caring." We subsequently try to offer an informed answer—still speculative given the current state of scientific knowledge—about why the practices of connectedness work to elevate our consciousness in such a way as to transform our attitudes and actions toward others and nature.[34]

Fritjof Capra, David Bohm, Ken Wilber, Ervin Laszlo, Margaret Wheatley, and Dana Zohar are among the modern-day pioneers who have helped develop the connection between the new sciences and their implications for human behavior, specifically for leadership.[35] We are building on their work and seeking to make it more accessible to businesspeople.

The search for a comprehensive understanding of reality as a guide to action goes back much further—to at least 2,500 years ago. In the sixth century BCE, scientist-philosophers from Thales of Miletus and Anaximander (his student), Pythagoras of Samos, Empedocles of Acragas,

Parmenides of Elea, to Atreya in India, were steering clear of mythology as a means of describing the observable world, turning instead to the testable hypotheses of science.[36] According to the Chinese scholar Nan Huai-Chin, the following three founding principles of the Great Learning of Confucius,[37] which also date from the sixth century BCE, offer a link between an understanding of the world and how we should behave in it:

1. To really understand the true nature of the universe, of the human being, our existence
2. To be able to spread what you understand to all people, to all human beings
3. To be virtuous in the Chinese Middle Way, which transcends extremes and guides us on a path of moderation that seeks to harmoniously integrate all facets of human nature[38]

Quantum leadership attempts to reimagine this ancient Chinese wisdom by using new discoveries in science to reveal the true nature of the universe and of the human being and then to make this understanding accessible to as many people as possible. Doing so provides a way to engage people in practices that help them experience a heightened awareness of how their attitudes and actions affect others, leading to both greater personal well-being and the *potential increased desire to do good.*

We say "potential" because our contention is that elevated states of consciousness do not guarantee a person's inclination to do good but do make it more probable.[39] Equally, we say an "increased desire to do good" without the expectation that business leaders become paragons of virtue. Our search is for a science-based model for being and acting in the twenty-first century.

As one business leader said, "The key, in my view, is layering neuroscience on top of the meditation. . . . [It] allows people to more easily embrace the meditation exercises, greatly enhancing their effectiveness."[40] Imagine how much more powerful the case becomes for engaging in practices that elevate our consciousness when we layer a much broader view of science on top of the—still largely reductionist—neuroscience.

Toward a New Ontology

In the next section, we examine the evidence for a new ontology emerging across a broad swath of scientific disciplines. Ontology is the study of being and the nature of reality. It is the story of who we are and the world we live in. Recent findings in science are revolutionizing this narrative with evidence-based reasoning rather than ideological positioning. The emerging narrative is one of *connectedness and caring* as defining qualities of who we are and of life itself, supplanting the traditional view of *separateness and selfishness*. Humanity has the potential to move in this direction if a critical mass of people embodies the new narrative—much as the Renaissance's humanism and intellectual curiosity displaced the clerical and feudal narrative of the Middle Ages. The scientific breakthroughs we are discussing here are yet to enter the mainstream, but they have huge implications for what it means to be a leader. Just as the intellectual advances of the Renaissance permeated human consciousness at the level of whole societies and led to new ways of understanding and being, the same could happen now, manifested as a fundamental change in how we act toward others and nature.

The natural and social sciences provide critical insights into the possible causative influences that practices of connectedness exert on business leadership. Such disciplines allow us to speculate about why these practices transform who leaders are being.

A Tale of Separateness and Selfishness

Prevailing beliefs about the physical world are largely a product of the scientific advancements of the last 2,500 years, especially the last 300 since the Age of Enlightenment.[41] In this period, mainstream science gradually reinforced a materialist view in which physical reality is composed of particles and forces that account for every aspect of reality, including us and our thoughts and emotions. We learned that the particles are atoms and, in due course, that their constituent parts are protons, neutrons, and electrons, with ever-smaller units subsequently unveiled by increasingly powerful technology. The forces are gravity, the electromagnetic field, and the strong and weak nuclear forces that hold atoms together. In its most elementary form, this materialist view of science holds that the interactions of particles and forces account for every observable aspect of existence. The advent of more sophisticated notions in physics such as Einsteinian relativity and quantum mechanics did not change the widely held conception in mainstream science that mind and spirit exist only as corollaries of physical interactions in the material world. Whether intentional or not, the science of Galileo Galilei, Isaac Newton, René Descartes, Gottfried Wilhelm Leibnitz, Antoine Lavoisier, and their successors had the effect of despiriting nature.

Such a materialist conception sees the human mind and consciousness itself as the product of the brain. When such an analogy became available, the brain could then be conceived of as a 1.3-kilogram supercomputer: a form of materialistic reductionism in which all mental processes could be attributed to the synaptic firing of axons and dendrites.[42] In the twentieth century, logical positivism even came, at one point, to deny the existence of consciousness.[43]

In neo-Darwinism, the evolution of species was seen as depending on the survival of the fittest through competition and genetic inheritance. Genetic inheritance meant that organisms were completely determined by their genomes. Environmentally induced variations in genetic coding were largely rejected.

In neoclassical economics, the production and consumption of goods were determined by efficient markets. Consumers were defined by their utility preferences. Firms were considered to reach a production equilibrium when their marginal costs equaled marginal revenues. Both consumers and firms existed only to maximize outcomes such as utility and profit.[44]

In psychology and organizational behavior—relatively recent disciplines central to the scholarship and practice of leadership—the last hundred years has seen organizational life largely in terms of problems to be solved and pathologies to be cured. Businesspeople were characterized by distrust, anxiety, self-absorption, and fear. Scholars in these domains emphasized theories of problem solving (i.e., how to treat pathologies of the mind and breakdowns in organizations) as the path to achieving competitive advantage.[45] They tended to focus on the study of negative deviances—what can go wrong with people and organizations.[46] According to past president of the American Psychological Association (APA) Martin Seligman, "Scientific psychology has neglected the study of what can go right with people."[47] Organizational studies, preoccupied with managerial dysfunction (for example, the conditions that lead to declines in employee productivity), have similarly ignored the study of what can go right with organizations.

The ontological implications of the sciences of the last three hundred years can be summarized as follows:

- The known world is reducible to particles and the forces that govern their interaction.
- Objects as well as living beings have independent identities and are separate from each other.
- Physical processes are materialistic and deterministic (i.e., causally explained by known forces and their interactions).
- Humans are self-interested utility maximizers.
- The sole purpose of business is profit.
- The defining characteristics of society are competition, growth, and consumerism.
- People and organizations are problems to be fixed.
- Nature exists largely as a resource for human consumption.

The basic tenets of Western science have helped humanity accomplish extraordinary feats in industry and medicine. These accomplishments have been well documented and concern a period in which humanity has experienced significant improvements in quality of life and in well-being characterized by longer lives and greater material prosperity.[48]

But as human understanding progresses, we find ourselves at a tipping point. Einsteinian relativity did not supplant Newtonian mechanics, but it did make us realize that the latter was just one limited way of understanding the universe, at a particular (human-observable) scale. The same is true today: There are new models developing, some already widely accepted, some still on the margins, that are compelling us to consign the tenets of Western science to their historical place and to move forward to a new understanding. These are discussed in the following sections.

Quantum Physics

Quantum physics has gathered widely accepted evidence for the existence of a field of energy and information that constitutes the most fundamental fabric of reality.[49] This field conception of reality has its modern origins (1954) in the Yang-Mills theory, according to which the smallest known particles in existence should not be thought of as "little billiard balls" but rather as field "excitations" that look like particles.[50] At the finest scale of the universe, physicists find only vibrations from which matter arises. Previously, scientists assumed that it was the particles or clusters of particles that vibrated, but the contrary is turning out to be the case. There are no elemental matter particles from which the world is constituted. The physical world as we observe it is created from clusters of vibrations.[51]

In other words, while the physical world of our grandparents was made up of particles and forces, in the quantum universe, the physical world is constituted of vibrational fields. All matter is now seen as energetically excited states of a field. Fields connect phenomena.[52] They are like fishing nets so fine yet so strong that they span space unseen. Objects that move in the net cause a rippling effect instantly and nonlocally, that is, at any distance.[53] This extraordinary and bewildering view of the fundamental nature of all matter is now an accepted part of mainstream physics. It has its antecedents in David Bohm's theory of implicate order,[54] Karl Pribram's holographic model of the brain,[55] Rupert Sheldrake's theory of morphogenetic fields,[56] and Ilya Prigogine's theory of dissipative structures,[57] among others. "According to our best laws of physics," says Cambridge University's David Tong, "the fundamental building blocks of Nature are not discrete particles at all. . . . Every particle in your body—indeed, every particle in the Universe—is a tiny ripple of the underlying field, molded into a particle by the machinery of quantum mechanics."[58]

Consciousness

A resurgent interest in the science of consciousness began just a few decades ago, almost one hundred years after William James in the United States, Franz Brentano in Germany, and F. W. H. Myers in England had made it a popular intellectual endeavor.[59] A debate now rages about the very nature of consciousness, captured for popular audiences in the *New Yorker Magazine* and in business publications such as the *Economist*.[60] The physicalist camp, led by American philosopher Daniel Dennett, argues that consciousness is the product of the neuronal activity of the brain. It demystifies the notion of selfhood by explaining it in purely material (physical) terms. The opposing camp, led by Australian scientist David Chalmers, argues that consciousness is a fundamental property of all life and irreducible to physical phenomena.[61] Its adherents argue that neither the brain nor advanced artificial intelligence could ever account for the *feelings* that accompany sensory experience. Now that quantum science has moved into consciousness research,[62] the life sciences have rediscovered the nature of the human mind with surprising conclusions about the underlying unity of mind and matter, supporting Chalmers's position.

One emerging theory, still hotly debated, is that the brain is capable of processing information at the quantum level through protein structures called microtubular lattices.[63] According to this view, consciousness is not generated *by* the brain but rather exists *outside* the brain as quantum-level vibrational frequencies intrinsic to spacetime geometry. Chalmers termed this view "panpsychism" (also called neutral monism), which sees consciousness as a universal and primordial feature of the cosmos.[64] Brain scientist Ede Frecska and social psychologist Eduardo Luna suggest that there are two systems in the brain that process information.[65] There is the classical neuroaxonal network that processes sensory input from sights, sounds, smells, flavors, and textures. There is also a quantum-level network, composed of the microtubular lattices, that offers a direct-intuitive-nonlocal mode of perceiving but is mostly filtered out by the dominant perceptual-cognitive-symbolic mode.

The practices of connectedness help us achieve a more equal balance between the two ways of experiencing the world. By quieting our senses and "tuning in" to the vibrational field underlying reality as we observe it, the practices may help us experience a consciousness of connectedness that is fundamental to all life. In other words, the practices enable a direct experience of oneness and wholeness, because these are the constants of the world we live in.

Evolutionary Biology

Thanks to the work of Charles Darwin and Alfred Russel Wallace, evolution was gradually recognized as the basic dynamic of development in the living world. However, the factors responsible for evolution in the living world have been increasingly questioned by the scientific community.[66] The emerging field of evolutionary biology is showing that cooperation and mutualism—the between-species interactions beneficial to all organisms involved—lie at the heart of thriving ecosystems.[67] Nature is not always "red in tooth and claw," as sometimes portrayed in the popular imagination. It is not driven only by the survival of the fittest in a merciless form of competition.[68] Symbiosis, the physiological cooperation between organisms, is seen as one of the keys to evolution. Chilean biologist Humberto Maturano famously said, "Love is the grounding of our existence as humans, and is the basic emotioning in our systemic identity as human beings."[69] In this perspective, we experience love (connection) before we learn to fight, separate, or individualize.

Quantum Biology

Quantum biology is an emerging field that is gaining adherents in mainstream science. Early persuasive theories that attempt to explain biological phenomena in terms of quantum science concern photosynthesis, avian magnetoreception, and olfaction,[70] which are made possible by quantum tunneling, entanglement, and superposition.[71] These theories and their findings suggest that the interconnectedness and coherence observable in the quantum world may also be true at the macrolevel of living systems. A 2018 *Scientific American* article noted that "several recent studies (e.g., 2009, 2011 and 2015) have demonstrated entanglement for much larger systems. Last year, a paper reported entanglement even for 'massive' objects. Moreover, quantum superposition has been observed in systems [such as] living tissue. Clearly, the laws of QM [quantum mechanics] apply at all scales and substrates." The authors conclude that "there are no excuses left for those who want to avoid confronting the implications of QM. Lest we continue to live according to a view of reality now known to be false, we must shift the cultural dialogue towards coming to grips with what nature is repeatedly telling us about herself."[72]

Epigenetics

While the genome provides the recognized set of instructions that defines the organism, the set of instructions for activating or deactivating the action of genes is epigenetic, meaning that it is environmentally influenced during the life of the organism.[73] What you eat, where you live, who you interact with, how much you sleep and exercise—all of these factors can eventually cause chemical modifications around the genes that will turn those genes on or off over time. As Peter Medawar and Jean Medawar eloquently observed, "Genetics proposes; epigenetics disposes."[74]

Neuroscience

Neuroscience is able to show at a clinical level that humans respond better to certain stimuli than others. For example, we react better to being inspired than being dictated to because our brains are wired that way.[75] Neuroimaging techniques have also uncovered evidence of mirror neurons, a distinct class of brain neurons that fire when we observe another person's emotions as if we were experiencing those emotions ourselves.[76] For example, whether a person anticipates receiving a pin prick to the finger or observes another person receiving a pin prick, fMRI scans show that the same neurons within the anterior cingulate cortex are fired in both cases.[77] Also called empathy neurons, mirror neurons have been described as one of neuroscience's most important discoveries in the first decade of the twenty-first century.[78] Their existence points to a neurophysical basis for a person's feeling of connectedness with others. UCLA's Marco Iacoboni states that "mirror neurons embody the interdependence of ourselves and others."[79] Studies of mirror neurons suggest that "the barriers between the self and others are more nebulous than conventional paradigmatic research suggests."[80] When we feel another person's joy or suffering, we become connected in a shared reality, not just metaphorically but physically.

Economics

Replacing the *Homo economicus* model of utility-maximizing individuals and profit-maximizing firms, an emerging model of an economy in service to life aims to create prosperity and flourishing for all.[81] In an economy in service to life, "businesses and society must pivot toward a new purpose: shared well-being on a healthy planet."[82] New frameworks are being proposed, such as Kate Raworth's *Doughnut Economics*, Richard Thaler's predictably irrational *Nudging*, and Amit Goswami's beyond-materialist *Quantum Economics*.[83] In the Doughnut Model, economic activity is constrained by planetary boundaries (the outer ring of the doughnut) while being required to operate at minimum social standards (the inner ring of the doughnut). Operating within the two rings provides a safe and just space for humanity to pursue flourishing now and in the future.[84] The aim of economic activity becomes one of meeting the needs of all within the means of the planet. It conceives not of economies that need to grow whether or not they make us thrive but economies that "make us thrive, whether or not they grow."[85] The significance of Raworth's innovation in economic theory has been compared to that of Maynard Keynes's *General Theory*.[86]

Psychology and Organizational Behavior

The fields of positive psychology and positive organizational development emerged into mainstream thinking post-1998,[87] with their emphasis on the power of positive emotions in human behavior. They draw on the earlier humanistic psychology movement with its aim of unleashing human potential,[88] which itself rests on self-actualization as an intrinsic desire in each of us. The philosophical roots of positive organizational scholarship (POS) extend back to Aristotle.[89]

POS puts an increased emphasis on goodness in human nature; it sees "the desire to improve the human condition [as] universal."[90] It does not reject the study of "what is wrong," that is, negative deviances in individuals and organizations. It accepts the needs for strategies that move people and organizations from dysfunctional states to healthy states. It expands the field of study to explore what leads to positive states, positive processes, and positive relationships. It has a bias toward life-giving, generative, and ennobling human behaviors.[91]

According to this line of research, there is an innate human tendency to grow toward what is positive. Appreciative inquiry pioneer

David Cooperrider observes that "human systems are largely heliotropic in character, meaning that they exhibit an observable and largely automatic tendency to evolve in the direction of what is good. . . . Just as plants of many varieties exhibit a tendency to grow in the direction of sunlight (symbolized by the Greek god Helios), there is an analogous process going on in all human systems."[92]

In addition to emphasizing what is good, POS gives greater weight to the dynamics of whole systems and cooperative relationships. "Organizational research [is] shifting from an emphasis on competition and reductionism to partnerships, networks, high quality relationships, community, and stakeholder negotiation. This movement indicates a paradigm shift from the individual to the collective."[93]

· · ·

It is inevitable that such paradigm-changing models will meet resistance and, at the very least, incomprehension in some quarters. The physicist Niels Bohr is supposed to have said, "Those who are not shocked when they first come across quantum mechanics cannot possibly have understood it." In another variant, a classical physicist says about quantum physics, "Even if it was true, I wouldn't believe it." As we disentangle ourselves from materialistic conceptions and keep our minds open to new scientific discoveries, we can observe a tension between more traditional materialistic viewpoints and emerging models of an integral reality. Many scientists are still uncomfortable with the entanglement and nonlocality of quantum physics,[94] the mutualism and cooperativeness of evolutionary biology, and the environmentally mediated expression of phenotypes in epigenetics,[95] to say nothing of 150 years of experiments that offer evidence of extrasensory perception, such as remote viewing and precognition, for which evidence exists using the accepted methods of science.[96] We are only beginning to appreciate the implications of the idea that our consciousness can help heal our bodies or affect our well-being.[97] Statistically sound meta-analyses of such phenomena are dismissed as somehow failing to control for such things as cheating and sensory leakage, no matter how well designed and executed the experiments.[98]

The Emerging Story of Who We Are:
Connectedness and Caring

Recent developments in scientific thought have huge and immediate consequences for how we see the world around us: Instead of considering ourselves as separate and discreet from one another and from nature, the new sciences suggest that we are all part of one interconnected fabric of existence. In the language of quantum physics, we are instantly and everywhere connected to each other and the world. At the macrolevel of bionomics, epigenetics, and environmental science, living systems are dynamically connected to each other and their environment. Instead of depending on chance mutations in the genome, evolution is now seen as a finely tuned process with an extraordinarily high level of coherence between species and their environments.[99]

Yet there remains enormous resistance to translating the new sciences into everyday thinking. Says Michael Nagler, a University of California, Berkeley, professor emeritus, "I have had friends who, to my surprise, do not believe us when we speak of the unity of life, but they accept what's called in quantum physics 'non-locality,' which means exactly the same."[100] In the world of human affairs, the goal of intervention strategies for people, organizations, and systems is increasingly about the creation of positive outcomes, such as prosperity and flourishing, rather than only the elimination of dysfunctions and the reduction of negative deviances.[101]

The ontological implications of emerging science can be summarized as follows:

- The known world is composed of vibrational fields of energy and information.
- Physical reality is integral and interconnected. Objects and people are interlinked in systems.
- Physical processes are organic, are interwoven, and exhibit a high degree of coherence.
- To be human is to care for others and all life on earth.
- The purpose of business is to create well-being, prosperity, and flourishing.

- Well-being and happiness are more important than material success alone.
- People and organizations are living systems.
- Humanity is an integral part of the web of life.

The Power of the New Narrative

In the past 2,500 years, morality and ethical behaviors have been subjects for philosophical debate based on the value systems of a particular leader or culture. Thus, what was good or right conduct was essentially subjective, expounded by one religious, spiritual, or philosophical leader and then another. Even if universal notions emerged such as the Golden Rule, the ontological narrative of separateness and selfishness continued to act as a powerful behavioral pull in many parts of the world still characterized by environmentally unsustainable growth, racism, other forms of discrimination, social exclusion, and rising income inequality.

In an interconnected world, what is good for one person is also good for others and for the environment. Freedom for the individual depends on freedom for all. Life is seen as a whole that encompasses the individual and his or her environment, meaning all life on earth. Interconnectedness and coherence imply that every living being and every part of the nonliving world respond to each other not just metaphorically but in scientifically verifiable terms of an interconnected field.

According to the new narrative of connectedness and caring, doing good in the world requires more than fulfilling our individual aspirations and more than piecemeal technological solutions to societal problems. It requires a new consciousness of oneness in our relationships with others and with nature, enabled by daily practices of connectedness.

Why the Practices Connect Us and Make Us Whole

A mother says to her daughter-in-law, "My son will never change. He is who he is—it's simply his character to act like that." People are often encouraged to "be true to who they are" and to acknowledge their "true selves." Can the practices of connectedness really transform who we are being? One part of the answer lies in what the new sciences say about our evolutionary capacities as human beings. Epigenetics tells us that environmental factors alter gene expression over our lifetimes. Neuroscience points to a level of brain plasticity capable of reconfiguring our neural pathways as we get older. Cellular biology points to a regeneration of every cell in our bodies (with the exception of some in the cerebral cortex that, when they die, are not replaced) in seven- to ten-year cycles. Thus, we are not born as immutable beings with fixed identities that remain unchanged throughout our lives. Who we are depends on what we choose to do at different points in time—our choice of lifestyles, our daily practices and rituals, our experiences, and the environmental factors to which we expose ourselves.

Science offers insights into why the practices might change who we are being along our evolutionary journeys. It tells us why the practices can lead to an inner transformation of the self toward raised relational awareness. "By deeply looking into ourselves, we are reaching into the very essence of humanity and the generating depth of consciousness . . . [that] has the whole of humanity enfolded in it. Understanding the concept of enfoldment and interconnectedness is critical in evolving our consciousness."[102] While this idea is not new,[103] until recently the only way to frame it was in spiritual terms. The journey of inner transformation has always been primarily a question of faith.

Today we can turn to science, which, across a variety of disciplines, suggests that humans and all life exhibit a high degree of interconnectedness and coherence. Speculative insights from quantum science and new consciousness research are especially consequential. They suggest that, as we evolve, we interact with a universal energy and information field constituted of low-frequency long-wave vibrations. Quantum physicist David Bohm and neurosurgeon Karl Pribram were among the first scientists to propose that this interaction with the universal energy and information field holographically *creates* interconnectedness and coherence in both matter (physical systems) and mind (consciousness).[104] Over several decades and dozens of books, philosopher of science Ervin Laszlo has similarly proposed an integral map of reality, encompassing both matter and mind, in which an underlying vibrational field guides the finely tuned dynamics of complex systems—from atoms to the human body, from nature's ecologies to the biosphere, all the way up to stars and galaxies.[105] As Kathryn Pavlovich and Keiko Krahnke propose, "We live in a quantum world of coherent forces . . . [in which] boundaries between ourselves and others are blurred, and as we become more altruistic towards the other, we can reach the place of universal consciousness where we may 'live as one.'"[106]

Less Is More

The peculiar challenge for human beings is that, unlike in the case of an oak tree or pet dog, our overactive cerebral cortex may actually prevent us from accessing the quantum field, thereby denying ourselves the "in-formation" that renders us coherent and connected.[107] Citing the research of physicians Andrew Newberg and Eugene D'Aquila at the University of Pennsylvania, the Stanford University psychologist Elizabeth Mayer notes that the meditative or mystical experience of "being one with the universe" is achieved "not by . . . access to new sources of sensory information but rather by learning how to *tune down* the flow of incoming sensory information that constitutes our daily and habitual diet."[108]

This proposition has a correlate in the neuroscientific finding that when we engage the TPN in the brain, it tends to inhibit activity in the DMN. In other words, our analytic, task-oriented, problem-solving state of mind tends to suppress our emotional self-awareness, social cognition, and ethical decision-making capabilities. The existence of the quantum field adds a possible explanatory factor. By slowing the analytic cognition of the brain, the practices of connectedness allow us to be more present to the interconnecting and coherence-producing effects of the quantum field, which can guide us on our evolutionary paths in life, if we let it.

If the practices of connectedness work by tuning down our cognitive processes and tuning into the quantum field, why can we not prove that their benefits are a direct result of the interconnecting and coherence-producing effects of the quantum field? Elizabeth Mayer suggests one possible reason: the information in this realm isn't conventionally quantitative, which defies our usual notions of measurability, reliability, and predictability. Adds Princeton's Freeman Dyson, "I am suggesting that paranormal mental abilities and scientific method may be complementary. The word 'complementary' is a technical term introduced into physics by Niels Bohr. It means that two descriptions of nature may both be valid but cannot be observed simultaneously."[109]

Science now accepts indisputably the existence of quantum phenomena such as quantum entanglement, the Einstein-Podolsky-Rosen paradox,[110] and nonlocality, as demonstrated in the lab by French physicist Alain Aspect.[111] Aspect's team showed irrefutably that two paired particles such as electrons remain instantly correlated with each other even when they are separated by vast distance. This paired particles phenomena—what Einstein called spooky action at a distance—defies familiar constraints of time and space, yet it exists. Just as the interactions between the quantum world and the (macrolevel) material world remain inexplicable, interactions between the quantum field and living systems cannot be fully explained even though their effects are observable across scientific disciplines and everyday experience.

Convergence with Spiritual Traditions

Emerging science is converging on perennial insights from traditional cultures, especially those of China and India. "Inseparability, an oceanic sense, a feeling of oneness with all nature and a direct communion with others are given high value in all cultures," observes the physicist F. David Peat. "Such a sense of connection appears to lie outside the confines of space and time and resonates deeply with our experience of the world."[112]

A unifying source of "all that is" can be found in the Judeo-Christian faith traditions, from Christian gnosticism's concept of the Monad to the Kabbalah's *Ein-Sof,* just as it appears in the Chinese Tao, the Vedantic Brahma, the Buddhist Sunyata, the Zoroastrian Aša, and the inner mystical realm of Sufism. "In the beginning God created the heaven and the earth. And the earth was without form, and void; and darkness was upon the face of the deep. And the Spirit of God moved upon the face of the waters" (Genesis 1:1–2). From this spaceless and timeless void arose all the things that exist in the world. In Taoism, all things originate in the Tao and all things return to the Tao. It is both the source and destination of all things, though not directly observable or even nameable. The Tao cannot be seen by our eyes; it cannot be heard by our ears or touched by our hands. It can be thought of in terms of the veiled quantum-level vibrations that give rise to the world. Similarly in Buddhism, the manifest world of space and time as we observe it is only a surface manifestation of the deeper, beyond space and time reality of Brahman.

In one form or another, the concept of the world as in-formed vibration was recognized in the traditional cultures of China and India.[113] It was present in the Sanskrit concept of Akasha and in the Chinese concept of the Tao—the source or root of all things. Living in harmony with the Tao was seen as purifying because it refined the vibration of matter and energy.[114] Like being in tune with music, a harmonious vibration is one that leads to a flourishing life.[115] The universe is represented as an oscillation of yin and yang forces. When they are equally present, all is calm. When one is outweighed by the other, for example, as in excessive desire for wealth and power, confusion and disarray arise.

While such spiritual wisdom has been largely rejected as a basis for management scholarship or business practice, confirmational evidence from the realm of science is giving fresh relevance to these historical intuitions of oneness and what it means to be a human being.

The great Chinese philosopher and sage Lao Tzu described the Tao in the following terms:

> There was something that finished chaos,
> Born before Heaven and Earth.
> So silent and still!
> So pure and deep!
> It stands alone and immutable,
> Ever-present and inexhaustible.
> It can be called the mother of the whole world.
> I do not know its name. I call it the Way.
> For the lack of better words I call it great.
> Great means constant flow.
> Constant flow means far-reaching.
> Far-reaching means returning.

Man is ruled by Earth.
Earth is ruled by Heaven.
Heaven is ruled by the Way.
The Way is ruled by itself.[116]

Implications for Quantum Leaders

The path to quantum leadership is not only through a conceptual understanding of the new narrative of connectedness and caring. Our point is that the practices of connectedness give us an *experience* of connectedness. Layering the interconnected reality of emerging science on top of the clinical neuroscience data provides compelling evidence that practices of connectedness can boost our sense of well-being and increase our desire to make a positive impact on the world. Undertaking practices of connectedness and living life mindfully can give us a direct experience of oneness. The two together—the new narrative from emerging science and the experience of oneness from the practices—offers a critical path to quantum leadership.

A conceptual understanding of the new narrative of coherence and interconnection plus an experiential path to oneness through the practices leads to changes in who leaders are being. It is a formula for experiencing wholeness and healing and for increasing the likelihood of responsible behavior toward others and nature.

PART III   PRACTICES OF QUANTUM LEADERSHIP

PART III SETS OUT the practices of connectedness. The book transitions from the sixteen exemplars and the theoretical model supported by the science of connectedness to the daily practices that provide access for anyone intent on taking the evolutionary journey to flourishing.

Chapter 7 provides a schema for understanding the practices: a classification of types along with principal groupings and affects. Chapter 8 offers a selection of practices at the individual, organizational, and systems levels. Each of the practices selected includes guiding steps to begin incorporating it in your life.

An overall conclusion summarizes and offers a look to a future in which business plays a strengthened institutional role as agent of world benefit.

HOW THE PRACTICES ELEVATE OUR CONSCIOUSNESS

IN OUR INTERVIEW with Joseph McIntyre, president of Ag Innovations Network, a nongovernmental organization, he shared his story:

The more you practice presence, the more presence you have. So I was sitting yesterday in a barber's chair . . . in Santa Rosa, California, [which has] seen terrible, terrible fires where forty people have lost their lives and over seven thousand homes were destroyed. And our entire community was in pain, in some deep way, and trauma. And I was sitting in this barber chair because I wanted to get a haircut, and I wanted to stop thinking about things for a little bit. And I started talking with my barber, and slowly but surely, he started to tell me about how he lost everything in the fire. And how he and his wife and his children just escaped, how their possessions were destroyed—and how he had to be strong for his family because they needed him. . . . All I did was just to be present with him and just say, "I'm so sorry. That must be so hard." And while he is telling the story and cutting my hair very carefully and slowly, you could tell that this connection was being made between us. And I got up at the end of haircut, and I wanted to shake his hand because I wanted to let him know how much I cared about his story, and he pulled me into an embrace. And in that moment, [I had] this deep sense of connectedness. That's what it is. It isn't some fancy thing that only happens when you sit on the top of the mountain. It was in that moment, I could listen with my heart open, and he could feel [and be] heard and in that way begin to have these difficult experiences processed. . . . The more I practice, and the less I think about it as a practice, the more I experience it.

In our interview with Dolf van den Brink, CEO of Heineken Mexico, he explained:

I am committed to doing one week of wilderness [immersion] per year. This experience takes away the stimuli that hit us on a daily basis. The commitment is to do something off the grid, in wilderness, with no phone calls, no e-mails. . . . Meditation and sitting in a room doesn't work for me. In nature, when I slow down, I can zoom out again, rather than being absorbed in the shorter tasks that are just in front of our noses. When I spend time in nature, I show up better at work. . . . As a leader . . . you want to control things. In nature all that inflation disinflates, and you feel a deeper sense of connection to something larger than you. I am removed from my pedestal as CEO and feel that I am part of something bigger than I. In nature it doesn't feel bad to feel small. It's an experience of feeling really connected.

Stacey Tank, chief communications officer of Home Depot, explained to us her philosophy of flexibility:

I use unconventional human-centered practices: for example, how we work in time and space. [Home Depot] is a traditional business where people come to work to a building from Monday to Friday on the same schedule. And, of course, I think that sometimes it is important to be together but also that we have to have the maturity to recognize when it is important to be together and when that is not needed. I give people the flexibility and the opportunity to have to use their judgment. . . . If they want to work in Starbucks or at home, or go to a yoga class at ten a.m., that's great. We have high standards, and people know their performance goals. . . . Another nonconventional practice is that we have institutionalized the free Fridays. We kick everybody out at noon (of course with exceptions). This is a way of telling them, "I value you and trust that you will do your work in this regard," but there is another reason for doing it: no innovative thinking is going to happen when you are checking your e-mails or taking notes in a meeting. . . . Innovation won't come up in a constrained environment. The kind of experience of "it [suddenly] came to me" takes place when you are taking a shower or having a walk in nature with your dog. . . . I want our team to have protected time and space. . . . Being in silence, in solitude. . . . I do a little bit of that every day. I have some rituals since twenty years ago that work for me. Every weekday I wake up early and do something physical—some running, walking, or a yoga class—and then some meditation. During the day I drive in silence, to have a reflective space, and at night I do meditation. I try for it to be at least fifteen minutes, but I do it even if it is fifteen seconds, and I don't judge myself.

In our interview with Marta Ceroni, director of programs at the Academy for Systems Change, she revealed similar sentiments:

From these practices—not only from music, dancing, and writing but [from those that allow me to feel like] a whole person—[I keep my] vital energy going. So another practice that I love is to get my hands dirty in the garden. I have a vegetable garden, and so I just realized that if I leave out even one of these practices, I'm not complete, and my life energy suffers. And so if I'm not whole and complete and I have less vital energy, everything else suffers, you know. I am more tired, I worry more, I'm less attuned to what needs to happen. . . . There is an element of recognizing patterns. . . . Maybe in your practice you can either delve deeper into those fears or worries, or you can also trigger them a little bit in a gentle way so that you get used to becoming resilient so you can go through it. So you get accustomed to sort of go in and out. So that's the greatest skill that you can develop is that resilience.

The term "practice" implies agency—"the human ability to act upon and change the world."[1] We all have experience with practices from our childhood, whether it was learning to play a video game or sport, drive a car, or engage in an artistic endeavor such as drawing or dancing. Practices affect us, and the world around us, because they are a form of embodied knowledge that carries us out in the world. They involve know-*how* rather than know-*what* learning typical of traditional schools.[2] When we stick with a particular practice, we develop practical knowledge of how to do something, internalized in a way that often requires no conscious decision making.

In the previous chapter we define practices of connectedness as those that offer measurable benefits in terms of individual and community well-being, increasing our sense of flourishing in our own lives and the lives of those around us. The practices increase our personal effectiveness as well as that of the teams and organizations in which we work and the communities and systems of which we are a part.

What the practices all have in common is that they are part of an upward spiral in lifestyle that leads to a feeling of being more connected to self, others, and nature; they raise our awareness of being one with others and the world; and they engage the whole person in an evolutionary journey toward greater harmony and life satisfaction.

The following sections provide several critical distinctions and a classification system to help you understand how the practices work: at what level, with what skills, resulting in what effects, and using what techniques. For example, they will help you understand the difference between explicit and tacit knowledge and the role that such types of knowledge play in complex systems.

Explicit and Tacit Knowledge

A first useful distinction is that between explicit and tacit knowledge.[3] Explicit knowledge is symbolized, codified, and communicated through language. Tacit knowledge is procedural: it is put into action in a way that cannot be fully articulated in language but can be demonstrated and imitated. As Canadian journalist Malcolm Gladwell stated in *Blink: The Power of Thinking Without Thinking*, "We learn by example and by direct experience because there are real limits to the adequacy of verbal instruction."[4] Understanding these limits helps us appreciate the power of the practices to build and transmit knowledge through action. Practices internalize principles of behavior through experience and repetition, through which knowledge becomes embodied.

Causality in Complex Systems (That Would Be Us!)

The transformation in who we are, engendered by the practices of connectedness, is not the result of a linear cause and effect. Doubling the time spent in mindful meditation does not guarantee twice the benefits—we won't be twice as present, feel twice as tranquil, or be doubly as wise. The practices only prepare the ground by creating the right conditions for transformation.[5] They create a preparedness for a discontinuous shift or tipping point through the repetition of embodied actions and interactions.[6] Thus, practices of connectedness create the irreducible basis for enriching our lives and ways of being.

One of the best applications of complexity theory to leadership behavior is intentional change theory (ITC) developed by Richard Boyatzis.[7] ITC starts with the construction of a desired future vision (the ideal self), the awareness of our most genuine aspirations, longings, passions, and values, which are then compared to our strengths and weaknesses (the real self), out of which we develop a learning agenda and an action plan for practice. Boyatzis underscores the importance of practice to achieve change. By practicing, we create the conditions for change to happen. ITC is one manifestation of the process of transforming consciousness through the practices of connectedness. The vision of the ideal self will remain shallow and fail to translate into lasting behavioral change if it is not embodied and internalized by doing.

Constitutive Versus Dispersed Practices

Another useful distinction is that between constitutive and dispersed practices. Constitutive practices are those in a particular social or technical domain such as a medical practice or a business practice. Dispersed practices take place within and across domains and include such practices as questioning, appreciation, and mindfulness. While both types are needed on the evolutionary journey of quantum leaders, dispersed practices are often underemphasized in formal learning programs.

Question: How Do You Get to Carnegie Hall?
Answer: Practice, Practice, Practice

Practices usually lead to the development and acquisition of a particular skill. Practitioners become adepts, experts, or leaders in their domains. In *Outliers: The Story of Success*, Gladwell documents the extraordinary performance and success of entrepreneurs (such as Bill Gates), artists (the Beatles), and athletes (hockey star Wayne Gretzky), among others, who achieved mastery in their fields.[8] Gladwell concluded that the requirement for success in all these instances was a minimum of ten thousand hours of practice. That equates to more than four hundred continuous days (twenty-four hours a day, seven days a week).

Fortunately, to effect transformation, we are not required to find all of this extra time in addition to what we already do in life. Much of what is required can be found in the hours and days of doing what we already do: working, exercising, eating, building high-quality relationships, pursuing our passion. The key is to do those activities differently, in a more mindful and intentional way.

Mentors and Communities of Practice

People learn practices in the context of relationships and through the sharing of experience. To learn a practice often involves a close relationship with a master or mentor, an expert who initiates the discipline, requiring the development of trust so that the learner can accept being guided in a practice.[9] Thus, while initiation into a practice may happen by imitation and experimentation, it is often guided by a mentor who brings explicit knowledge until that know-how becomes embodied or, as Michael Polanyi puts it, "inarticulated."[10]

Belonging to a community of practice (CoP) is another way in which practices are learned. Educational theorist Étienne Wenger defines CoPs as groups of people who share a concern or a passion for something they do and learn how to do it better through regular interaction.[11] An oft-cited example is the informal assembly of copy-machine repair technicians at Xerox.[12] These field reps networked and shared their tips and tricks whenever they met each other; even though their efforts were not part of any formal initiative, the CoP is estimated to have saved Xerox US$100 million.

In all cases, the practices can help translate the new ontology of connectedness and caring into a way of living and leading. A renewed focus on such daily practices reflects the trend toward experiential and embodied learning aimed at changing who we are being and not just what we are doing. "Learning, therefore, is not solely a matter of what one knows, but also of whom one becomes."[13]

Types of Practices

There are many ways to classify the practices that connect us to self, others, and the world. They can be grouped according to *level* (individual, team, organizational, systems), *activity* (reflective, embodied, relational, artistic, athletic, naturecentric), *skill* (concentration power, sensory clarity, equanimity),[14] *effect* (e.g., sense making and presencing, or both), *technique* (e.g., journaling or dance), and *origin* (e.g., Theravada Buddhism), among other ways to slice and dice the terrain.

Our goal in classifying the practices is not to be exhaustive. You as a reader can add your own practice(s) to the list in the appendix. Rather, our aim is to point the way to the rich array of practices that already exists. Our categorization attempts to group them according to our interpretation of the practice literature and on our own experiences with such practices. However, we acknowledge that there are many other ways to organize and classify them, as well as many other practices that could have been included in the categories shown. The practices in the appendix can best be understood through two primary lenses or perspectives among the classifications mentioned previously. The first concerns the *level* the practice is designed for: whether individual, organizational, or system. The second is the intended *effect* of the practice, whether primarily sense making or presencing.

Lens 1: Levels of Practice

Here we classify the practices according to the primary actor affected by the outcome of the practice: the individual, a dyad, team, organization, community, or system such as supply chains or global society. Many (but not all) of the practices are designed to cultivate the self, which we call individual-level practices. As spirituality workplace scholar Judi Neal observes, "Systems transformation must begin with personal transformation."[15] Group-level practices are designed for dyads, teams, organizations, communities, or systems. Some of these group-level practices aim at self-cultivation, in that they involve two or more people, but their primary purpose is to transform the individual. Others—such as musicians playing in an orchestra—work at the collective level. So while the levels are a convenient way to approach the practices, they are not hard-and-fast categories.

Lens 2: Sense Making and Presencing

The effects of sense-making and presencing practices are not the same because they engage very different modes of being. Sense making is a process by which people construe, understand, or make sense of the world. Organizational theorist Karl Weick defined it formally as "the ongoing retrospective development of plausible images that rationalize what people are doing."[16] While sense making has been alternately described as a social activity and a language-based endeavor to create order through dialogue and narrative, the distinguishing feature for our purposes is that it engages our analytic-cognitive mode of being. "The aim [in sense making] was to focus attention on the largely cognitive activity of framing experienced situations as meaningful."[17]

Presencing practices are primarily direct-intuitive.[18] They are *embodied* in the whole person. Their effect has immediacy because these practices engage our mind and body, our heart and spirit, in a sort of instantaneous awareness.[19] Immersion in them leads to a loosening of the boundaries between the parts and the whole, the subject and the object. In presencing practices, the person is not so much in an analytic-cognitive mode but engaged in a broader perception and greater awareness of the self in relation to the whole. For instance, when listening to a poem that particularly resonates with us, something in the sound of the words, in the quality of the poem, affects us beyond its meaning. This experience of resonance can be a useful metaphor for what goes on all the time in our existence. We are affected by things and by others, by what exists with us and around us, beyond verbal meaning; we are affected by the presence of things and beings. Only on specific occasions when we are mindfully present do we develop a full awareness of what is going on, what is happening, beyond our usual meaning making. In our experiences of art and immersion in nature, to choose just two of the practices listed in the appendix, we experience something beyond our usual meaning making and sense making of those experiences.

Rather than consider sense making and presencing as separate types of practice, we need to see them dynamically, as overlapping and evolving one into the other. Just as is the case for the levels of practice, sense making and presencing are not hard-and-fast categories. Presencing can lead to sense making, and vice versa. Stanford University professor Hans Ulrich Gumbrecht, in *The Production of Presence: What Meaning Cannot Convey*, refers to the oscillation between presencing effects and meaning-making effects ("a structural form of oscillation" between the dimensions of meaning and presence in our experiences).[20] The idea is that such an oscillation or tension between presence and meaning is present in all experiences and in all cultures. There are practices such as dance, poetry, and nature immersion for which the "presence effects" are the defining dimension, just as there are cultures for which this is true. Pre-Socratic Greece and traditional Chinese, Indian, African, and Native American cultures exemplify presence-oriented cultures, while twentieth-century Western societies place a greater emphasis on meaning making.[21]

In spite of the overlapping nature of sense making and presencing, as filters or lenses for understanding the practices, they provide primary categories in the classification scheme outlined in the appendix.

Presencing

Presencing practices are especially important to quantum leaders because presencing strengthens direct-intuitive capabilities, which, as previously noted, involve holistic, immediate, and embodied perception rather than analytic-cognitive reasoning. Yet the term "presence" (or "presencing") is difficult to define simply because we are attempting to name an experience that is largely beyond language. Gumbrecht observes that we are affected by the presence of things and people, as we relate to them, beyond the meaning that can be expressed through language. Gumbrecht is not proposing a return to naïve (or direct) realism, the philosophical idea that our five senses can provide us with a direct awareness of objects as they really are. Instead, he is inviting us to explore the relationship between us and the world as one of mutual influence, beyond the meanings we construct through language and social interaction. Similarly, the early twentieth-century Cambridge University philosopher of language Ludwig Wittgenstein famously observed: "Whereof one cannot speak, thereof one must be silent."[22] What cannot be said, he claimed, lies on the other side of language, and therefore when we try to speak about it, we produce only nonsense. Our language is designed to talk about the material world as we interact with it. When we want to talk about presence, we are trying to talk about what lies *beyond* meaning and language.

None of this means that we should abandon the idea of meaning through language, only that we need to acknowledge a direct-intuitive dimension to lived experience. We know this to be true of our most creative experiences in art and in sport, in our high-quality relationships, and in our tranquil moments spent in nature.

Nobel Prize–winning economist Daniel Kahneman proposed two ways of thinking, "fast thinking" which can be related to presencing, and "slow thinking," which engages us in the analytic cognition of sense making. He calls these "System 1" and "System 2." According to Kahneman, System 1 thinking is associative, holistic, automatic, fast, and parallel and requires little cognitive capacity, and acquisition is by biology and personal experience. System 2 thinking is rules-based, analytic, logical, controlled, slow, serial, demanding of cognitive capacity, and acquisition is by culture and formal education.[23]

System 1 thinking, in Kahneman's framing, is about the recognition of patterns of relationships between things. It works well only in contexts where the practices are done repeatedly until a level of expertise is achieved and the relationships between patterns can be perceived. Kahneman goes as far as to say that "intuition is just another word for expertise."[24] For our purposes, what is important is his emphasis on the intuitive mode of System 1 thinking and the need for repetition until we master the patterns of embodied knowledge through practice.[25]

Thus, presencing practices lead to direct-intuitive experiences that engage the whole person (body, mind, spirit) in a holistic form, at once organizational, social, and biophysical. Why? Because we are better able to experience reality as it actually is: dynamically interconnected and highly coherent. By enabling us to augment our analytic cognition and privilege our direct-intuitive mode, presencing practices increase our awareness of the wholeness of life. The practices connect us to the essential oneness of reality. Doing so helps heal us and make us whole at a time when the confluence of technology, politics, economics, and environmental degradation is especially contentious, tending to fracture our individual identities and divide our communities on a global scale.

Presencing practices also make us more creative.[26] David Bohm and David Peat speak about a generative order that "is relevant to creativity in art and to . . . creative perception and understanding of nature."[27] In their view, mediocre artists content themselves with reproducing their habits of mind, while the great artist "teaches us to see the world in new ways. . . . [He or she accesses] new generative orders which ultimately lie beyond the individual work and extend to the whole of nature and experience."[28]

Albert Einstein observed, "The intellect has little to do on the road to discovery. There comes a leap in consciousness, call it intuition or what you will—the solution comes to you and you don't know how or why."[29] The American Renaissance scientist and educator George Washington Carver and the inventor Thomas Edison both credited direct-intuitive knowledge for their inspiration. "He believes that his inventions come through him from the infinite sources of the universe," said Mina Miller Edison about Thomas Edison, "and never so well as when he is relaxed."[30] For Bohm and Peat, the generative source of our intuitions arises from the implicate order, the universal energy and information field that connects all people and all things.[31]

Layers of Causality

When we engage in sense-making or presencing practices, we are connecting to something greater than ourselves. In the perspective of quantum science and consciousness research, we are synchronizing in some way with the cosmos, not only loosening our frames of mind and quieting our automatic ways of thinking but also connecting to a generative field that underlies everything and helps heal and make us whole. When we connect with this field, we have *instant* (also called "nonlocal" in quantum physics and "transpersonal" in consciousness studies) direct-intuitive experiences that help us meet the challenges we face in life.

Thus, there are multiple ways of understanding how the practices work to heighten our consciousness of connectedness, each building on the other. A psychologist and leadership expert might say that the practices help us let go of our attachments to negative emotions and gradually move toward equanimity, serenity, and wisdom; or that they help us "see what we are seeing" and become more aware of the mind-sets that shape how we think and act.

A neuroscientist might say that the practices do this by strengthening the neural networks associated with positive emotions and reducing activity in the parts of the brain that account for our sense of separateness and individuality and that they enable our brains to access quantum-level information that we process through microtubular lattices (see Chapter 6 for more discussion of quantum processing in microtubular lattices).[32]

An even deeper explanation now comes from quantum science, which suggests that the practices may be helping us connect to a universal vibrational field of energy that helps make us whole (if we just slow down a little and let it) and increases our sense of oneness with others and all life on earth. According to this view, the practices allow us to have a broader systems view because they expand our scope of seeing and being, allowing us to act from within the broader context of our lives. But they also enable us to connect with something larger than ourselves, which quantum science and consciousness research describe in terms of a universal energy and information field that underlies material reality as we observe it.

Mindfulness and Presencing

Social scientists describe these two phenomena in terms that converge on recent findings in the natural sciences about the nature of reality. They seem to come to insights similar to those of quantum scientists such as Bohm and consciousness researchers such as Hameroff, often without realizing they are doing so, much as the French playwright Molière's Monsieur Jourdain suddenly realized that he had been speaking in prose all his life without knowing it.

Mindfulness expert Jon Kabat-Zinn says,

At each level of our being there is a wholeness that is itself embedded in a larger wholeness. And that wholeness is always embodied. It cannot be separated from the body and from an exquisite and intimate belonging to the larger expression of life unfolding. . . . This web of interconnectedness extends well beyond our individual psychological self. While we are whole ourselves as individual beings, we are also part of a larger whole, interconnected through our family and our friends and acquaintances to the larger society and, ultimately, to the whole.[33]

Furthermore, he writes,

Beyond the ways in which we can perceive through our senses and through our emotions that we are connected with the world, there are also the countless ways in which our being is intimately woven into the larger patterns and cycles of nature that we only know about through science, [which] . . . affirms a view based on strong scientific evidence and reasoning that was, in essence, also held by all traditional cultures and peoples, a world in which all life, including human life, is interconnected and interdependent—and that interconnectedness and interdependence extends to the very earth itself.[34]

The process of presencing is described in Otto Scharmer's *Theory U* and in the book *Presence* by Peter Senge, Otto Scharmer, Joseph Jaworsky, and Betty Sue Flowers.[35] The process they describe is what guides us through the movement of the U: we learn to "see our seeing," in other words, to become more aware of the mind-sets that shape who we are and how we act. It requires a capacity to suspend our habitual mind frames and the courage to see freshly so that we can start seeing from the whole.[36] While the work of Senge and colleagues does not reference explicitly the new sciences, it is strongly suggestive of them, even going as far as to write about presencing in terms of becoming a force of nature and of being in dialogue with the universe.[37]

·   ·   ·

We define practices of connectedness as those in which the goal is not only to make sense of or give meaning to our lived experiences but also to also enrich the quality of our being. How? By enabling practitioners to quiet the buzz of their minds and thereby rid themselves of their automatic conditionings and then freeing them from reactive behaviors based on old patterns of thinking, focusing their attention on the present, and being responsive to life's demands and ongoing challenges in an adaptive and creative way. These practices take us off the treadmill and back onto the path to flourishing. The practices interrupt our habitual ways of thinking and help us cultivate broader perception and greater awareness of how our thinking and actions affect others and all life on earth. They deepen our capabilities to positively affect the well-being and self-realization of each person in life and at work, the thriving of the community/society at large, and the regeneration of the natural environment on which our lives depend.

8 SELECTING THE PRACTICES THAT ARE RIGHT FOR YOU

WHICH PRACTICES are right for you? Many people and organizations accidentally fall into a *practice of connectedness* either by chance (a friend urged them to try yoga) or because they learned it as a child (as in singing in a choir, hiking in nature, or volunteering in the community). Such practices can gradually take on novel significance as the years go by, when one realizes the extent to which they contribute to improved well-being and life satisfaction. In other cases, a personal or organizational crisis or a search for deeper meaning can lead a person to renew a practice or to take up a fresh one, among the countless practices that exist, many of which are described in the appendix.

Whatever the circumstances, too many people—both young and old—find themselves at a point in their lives when they feel disconnected from a sense of purpose. They feel isolated and lacking in high-quality relationships. Or as city dwellers, they suffer from an insufficient contact with the natural world, that sensation of freedom in the wind and the earth beneath their feet. And when they do feel such a disconnection, they retreat into material pursuits ("I'll buy that newest phone or latest fashion accessory") that increasingly fail to satisfy or to create meaningful value. A parallel downward spiral exists for organizations: it is in moments of isolation and disconnection from their external stakeholders that executives are most likely to make decisions and take actions to pursue short-term profit at the expense of their employees, of the communities in which they operate, and of nature.

Traditional China had seven hobbies (琴棋书画诗酒茶) illustrating the ancient origins of many of today's self-cultivation practices. These were playing the zither (a plucked stringed instrument), the game of Go, calligraphy, painting, poetry, wine, and tea.[1] They were seen as essential for pursuing a meaningful, refined life. "He who is good at playing zither would be understanding and serene, he who is good at playing *Go* would be resourceful, he who is good at reading would have good understanding of the nature of things and know courtesy, and he who is good at painting would be intelligent with an ethereal spirit."[2] Probably the most universal and contemporary of the seven hobbies is drinking tea. In China, Japan, and many other parts of the world, drinking tea is seen not only as a source of sustenance but as something to be habitually enjoyed, connecting people in a shared ritual and giving expression to a higher self while refining the senses.

In previous chapters, we make the case that a regular practice of connectedness is critical not only to a person's sense of well-being but also to the person's leadership mode. Making a daily practice an integral part of your life will, over time, shape your career choices, especially in terms of leadership for good: it will influence (but not determine) your intrinsic desire and ability to make a positive impact on your colleagues, your community, and the environment.

The selection of practices presented in this chapter includes practical steps to begin, along with the benefits associated with each case. Readers are encouraged to try different ones. Some will resonate while others may not. The sequence of practices follows the curriculum developed by the Quantum Leadership Initiative led by the AITIA Institute in Shanghai. These practices and their sequencing were designed for executive education and graduate business courses, such as the second-year MBA quantum leadership elective course taught in spring 2018 and 2019 at the Weatherhead School of Management.

Journaling

Journaling is placed first in the sequence of practices because it can help make sense of all the other practices. It is a way to record your experiences as you try different ones and note the insights that emerge from them. Over time, journaling helps you work your way through difficult challenges and see more clearly what might be possible. Why is this important for quantum leaders? Writing in the *Harvard Business Review*, McGill University professor Nancy Adler says, "A leader's unique perspective is an important source of creativity and competitive advantage. But the reality is that most of us live such fast-paced, frenzied lives that we fail to leave time to actually listen to ourselves. Gaining access to your own insight isn't difficult; you simply need to commit to reflecting on a daily basis. . . . I recommend the simple act of regularly writing in a journal."[3]

Here are five steps to begin:

1. **Find the right media.** Paper and pen, tablet, or phone. Choose what works best for you. To make a separation from work (if you use a computer) and with your online social life (much of which is on a phone), you may want to write by hand in a notebook chosen for this purpose.

2. **Start with what's going on for you right now.** Put your thoughts down about current events in your life, how your relationships are going, what you're feeling, your gratitude as well as your anxieties and highest hopes for the future. Just write down everything that comes to mind. Write without judgment, and put aside any concern about getting it exactly right.

3. **Write regularly.** Many journaling advocates recommend writing every day, at least a few sentences at a time, first thing in the morning. What is important is finding a rhythm that works for you. In the quantum leadership course, students are asked to write three pages before each class once a week. You can choose to write more or less than that. What is important is achieving consistency in how much you write and when and

not forcing the writing but letting your thoughts and feelings flow naturally.

4. **Write about how you feel.** You might want to write about what makes you happy, joyful, serene, or inspired. Or you can write about what makes you sad, angry, jealous, or despairing. Just remember that positive emotions engage a very different part of our brains and neural networks than do negative emotions, which can make it neurophysiologically confusing to try to express both during the same journaling session. That may be one reason why gratitude journals exist and why others focus exclusively on what inspires and motivates a person, their biggest dreams and accomplishments. There is growing evidence that dwelling on positive emotions tends to bring more benefits and build greater resiliency over time.[4]

5. **Do a periodic review of what you've written.** Weekly, monthly, quarterly (corporate), semester (academic)—what is important is that take stock of what you've written. Take a look at any changes that have happened in your life. What fresh insights does rereading the last entries give you? What clarity do they bring?

Should you ever feel stuck writing, you can use trigger questions or prompts such as these: How am I feeling right now? How is my work going? What projects or initiatives do I most aspire to in my life? Another novel way to approach journaling is to write about embodied learning, a moment that shifted your experience of an event or relationship. In writing about it, try to leave out thought and emotion and let all information be conveyed through the body's senses.[5]

Journaling pioneer Ira Progoff believed that what he called an "intensive journal process" could "draw each person's life toward wholeness at its own tempo. . . . It systematically evokes and strengthens the inner capacities of persons by working from a non-medical vantage point and proceeding without analytic or diagnostic categories."[6] In her research on journaling, Nancy Adler concluded that the unexpected juxtaposition between art and real-world challenges can expose concealed dynamics and surprising new insights.[7]

Mindful Meditation

Mindful meditation develops our ability to be fully present, discovering the innate perfection of this moment. Through mindfulness practice we move toward such a state by systematically developing skillful attention. Contemplative practice has existed in some form for millennia and across all the world's cultures. For various reasons, the techniques used in modern mindful meditation are most commonly derived from those developed in ancient India and China. The aim of mindful meditation is not to quiet the mind or attempt to achieve a state of eternal calm but rather to cultivate meditative awareness itself, through applied practice. The true benefit of practice can be found in such heightened awareness.

In *Time* magazine, author and journalist Dan Harris writes that the biggest obstacle to practicing meditation is finding enough minutes in the day. But, he says, "the good news is that five to 10 minutes a day is a great way to start." He continues, "The better news is that if five to 10 minutes is too much, one minute still counts."[8]

The steps to mindful meditation vary from one school of practice to another, but at their core, they center on the development of particular qualities of attention. Here's one exercise from a mindful meditation practice called unified mindfulness (UM).[9] The exercise is "See, Hear, Feel." The technique can be applied while seated or during normal activities throughout the day when in a quiet and safe place:

1. With your eyes open or closed, allow your attention to move freely.
2. At any given time, your attention may be drawn primarily to an experience you see, hear, or feel. Whether your attention is naturally drawn to a particular experience or whether you intentionally place it there, spend a few seconds paying attention to what you are detecting before allowing your attention to move freely again. As you pay attention, try to detect details about and be open to the experience you are noticing, whatever it may be.
3. To help keep your attention on track, you can say a word that identifies or labels what you're detecting. If the experience is primarily visual, say, "See"; primarily auditory, say, "Hear"; or

primarily somatic, say, "Feel." You can say the label out loud or to yourself, using a neutral tone, every few seconds. If you notice more than one of those categories at the same time, just choose one to focus on, and if an experience disappears as you focus on it, pick something new to focus on. It's also fine to focus repeatedly on the same experience.

4. Repeat this process again and again, spending a few seconds at a time noticing details about and remaining open to any experience you detect and labeling it, out loud or to yourself, whether it's "See," "Hear," or "Feel."

UM was developed by the American mindfulness teacher Shinzen Young over the past half century.[10] The system was developed by doing a fine-grained, dimensional analysis of all known contemplative approaches to determine the underlying principles of all meditative practices. It is both an approach to meditation practice and a distillation of known approaches in all the contemplative traditions.[11]

The common theme underlying any meditation technique is skill development. The emphasis is on *how* one focuses rather than on what the practitioner focuses on, such as the breath. Meditation works because it develops one's attention. Any substantive meditative practice—whether loving kindness, walking meditation, or any other practice theme—develops the attention in specific ways that are common to all. This yields positive outcomes for the practitioner, regardless of the theme chosen to explore.

In any given tradition, attention skills may be implied, or they may be made explicit through clear terms and definitions. Also, different traditions call these attention skills by different names. Shinzen Young defined them as concentration power, sensory clarity, and equanimity. Making skill development the central paradigm of the UM approach offers a unifying perspective, enabling cohesion across all meditative traditions and providing a context to clearly understand their contrasting and complementary qualities.

Any practice of connectedness we do is ultimately dependent on our capacity for skillful attention. We can look at meditation as a foundational skill for all the other practices, improving our ability to apply attention in personally meaningful ways.

Another variant of mindful meditation is mindfulness-based stress reduction (MBSR), developed by Jon-Kabat Zinn at the University of Massachusetts Medical School in 1979. It combines science, medicine, and psychology with Buddhist meditative teachings to address sources of stress in our lives. One study examined the effects of a sixteen-week MBSR program on stress levels and self-compassion of twenty-two executives of a large Indian public-sector oil company. The result concluded: "Results from the present study suggest that a 16-week MBSR intervention not only had a positive impact on various stress indicators (physical, sleep, behavioral, emotional, and personal habits) and self-compassion but also reduced systolic and diastolic blood pressure and blood cortisol levels. The findings suggest that MBSR can be a useful stress management intervention for addressing the issues of high stress for senior executives in Indian organizations."[12]

Although originally conceived of as a way to deal with what is wrong (such as physical disease, mental disorders, and stress in the workplace), MBSR has many aspects aimed at increasing flourishing and well-being in our lives. Formal practices in MBSR courses include the "body scan" technique to increase mindful awareness of our body, mindful walking, and attending to physical sensations during gentle movement of the body, as well as LKM, a practice to help cultivate compassion for oneself and others.[13]

One of our colleagues teaching at the Moroccan University business school, which is trying to model its education program on the American liberal arts system, shared this field report:

> I told my students (87 students; 3 sections) we were going to meditate together for 3 minutes at the beginning of each class for 3 weeks. At the end of 3 weeks, I would ask them to vote (by section) on whether or not they wanted to continue the meditations. I assured them that they did not have to engage, but they were required to sit quietly during the 3 minutes so that classmates who choose to do so could engage. I was hoping that at least the small section of 17 students would have 10 students enjoying the experiment enough to vote "Continue." We had our vote last week—more than 90 percent of everyone in every section voted to continue. Even the finance majors!! I'm thrilled! It seems so simple, but it also feels

like such an incredibly courageous step that these young people have taken to actually *agree* that they *want* to continue 3 minutes of guided meditation at the beginning of each class session. I can feel a palpable difference in the energy in the room, between before and after we sit together. Apparently, they can feel it too.[14]

Qigong

Qigong is a practice originating in China, where it means literally "life energy practice." It consists of slow, flowing body movement; deep rhythmic breathing; and working effortlessly to achieve a calm meditative state of mind. According to Taoist, Buddhist, and Confucian tradition, Qigong allows practitioners to access their higher states of consciousness, to awaken their "true nature," and in the process to help develop their full potential.[15]

Now increasingly popular worldwide, Qigong practices include moving and still meditation, sound meditation (such as chanting), and massage and noncontact treatment performed in a broad array of body postures. Two foundational categories are dynamic or active Qigong (*dong gong*), with slow, flowing movement, and meditative or passive Qigong (*jing gong*), with still positions and inner movement of the breath. Both are designed to open blockages in the body based on the same meridian system used in acupuncture.

Several core principles guide the practice. These include *intentional movement*, a flowing balanced style of motion; *rhythmic breathing*, which is slow, deep, and coordinated with fluid movement; *heightened awareness* in a calm and concentrated meditative state; *visualization* of the Qi (also Ch'i or energy) flow; and the use of *chanting or sound*. Additional principles are softness (as in a soft gaze); a solid stance; relaxed muscles with joints slightly bent; and balance—motion over your center of gravity.

The following steps offer a simple way to get the Ch'i flowing in your body:

1. Start by sitting forward on the edge of a chair with your feet flat on the floor in front of you.

2. With your feet firmly rooted to the ground, imagine that your body is afloat. Let your head float above your relaxed neck like a float on the surface of water.

3. To let your spine feel free, imagine a gentle sensation of someone lifting you from above, as if there were a string attached to the crown of your head.

4. Inhale, and let the energy within you allow your arms to rise to shoulder height. On the exhale, return your arms to your sides.

5. Repeat this several times, becoming increasingly aware of the energy within that propels the movement of your arms.

Another fun and often surprising Qigong exercise is one for which you can physically feel your Ch'i energy as an imaginary ball of energy (about the size of a soccer ball) that you can push against between your hands. While standing or sitting, try to feel the Ch'i between your hands as the imaginary ball rolling between them. Imagine that you are holding this energy between your palms, and begin moving it and rolling it around. If you push it left with your right hand, you will feel your left hand being pushed an equal distance by this invisible energy ball. Your hands should not try to move through the imagined ball, just as they would not go through the center of a real ball.

The goals of Qigong are to achieve equanimity (more fluidity, greater relaxation), tranquility (a feeling of peace and a heightened awareness of the self), and stillness or the shift to smaller and smaller movements on the path to complete stillness. The more advanced the practitioner, generally the less motion is used.

Denise Nagel, an American pediatrician and psychiatrist who trained at Dartmouth and Duke University Medical Schools, talks about adopting Qigong after being diagnosed with an autoimmune disease in 2005. "Let me be very clear," says Dr. Nagel. "It is not a choice between Eastern and Western medicine for me, only medicine that works. I do Qigong or Tai Chi every day [and] I think of it as medicine, too." Among the benefits she describes based on her own experience of practicing qigong are the following:

Calming the mind and calming the body allows healing. Strengthening the muscles through simple postures and movements prevents falls. Moving with flow and gentle weight bearing helps balance and can positively impact bone density. Achieving a relaxed state of the mind reduces stress.[16]

Health and well-being benefits come from supporting the body's natural tendencies to return to balance and equilibrium but also from gently building greater strength, flexibility, and balance in the muscles and joints.

Nature Immersion

The Harvard naturalist E. O. Wilson is one of many scientists to put forward the evolutionary hypothesis that nature has a restorative power.[17] He noted that we have a natural affiliation with nature that is ingrained in our biological heritage. Phrased more poetically, the pioneering environmentalist Rachel Carson wrote, "Those who contemplate the beauty of the earth find reserves of strength that will endure as long as life lasts. . . . There is something infinitely healing in the repeated refrains of nature— the assurance that dawn comes after night, and spring after winter."[18]

How much time in nature do we need to notice its positive effects? By one measure, five hours per month is sufficient to improve mood, vitality, and feelings of restoration.[19] This is the equivalent of fifteen minutes per day five days a week. The good news is that it can be in a city park just as easily as in a forest or on a grassy plain; even a park with paved paths and street noise will do.

Here are steps to begin a mindfulness approach to nature immersion:[20]

1. **Find a place in nature.** Walk until you find a good spot to stand or sit. Favorite places are a rock, log, grass, or trail.
2. **Listen.** Just listen to the natural sounds around you. As you listen, you'll begin to hear other things that at first were inaudible.
3. **Feel.** Is the wind blowing, or is it calm? Focus on the way your body feels and how it is interpreting or interacting with what's around you.

4. **Look.** Take the same approach with what you see around you. You might start with a nearby tree or a living movement that caught your eye. When looking at a tree, notice its bark. What's between the furrows? Study the leaves, their shape, texture, and how they hang.

5. **Just be.** "Nature's peace will flow into you as sunshine flows into trees. The winds will blow their own freshness into you, and the storms their energy, while cares will drop off like autumn leaves." So wrote John Muir, the early twentieth-century American naturalist.[21]

A growing body of scientific research provides evidence of the benefits of connectedness with nature.[22] Some of the benefits that have been highlighted in contemporary research on this practice include overall health improvement;[23] stress relief;[24] reduced negative emotions (for example, decreased fear and anger);[25] enhanced positive affect;[26] improvements in mood and increased subjective well-being;[27] feelings of joy and happiness;[28] a sense of reconnection with self;[29] kinship ties in teams;[30] a heightened sense of community, kinship, egalitarianism, and belongingness along with increased empathy;[31] a stronger sense of place;[32] and improved cognitive abilities, including creativity, cognitive flow, and mental performance in problem solving.[33]

In our interviews with business leaders for the quantum leadership research project, connecting with nature was a recurring theme. Here is what Hal Hamilton, the cofounder and codirector of the Sustainable Food Lab, had to say about it:

> Being in nature has been a long-term thread in my life. When I was a young adult, I had two small children and a farm to manage. It was a lot. I would work really hard, really long, and there was this place, outside this little building where I milked the cows; I would frequently walk outside and look out over the rolling hills with their farms. I would spread my arms and just breathe, feeling deeply relaxed and connected.

Such views we heard echo the memorable lines of the farmer-poet Wendell Berry in his poem "The Peace of Wild Things":

When despair for the world grows in me
and I wake in the night at the least sound
in fear of what my life and my children's lives may be,
I go and lie down where the wood drake
rests in his beauty on the water, and the great heron feeds.
I come into the peace of wild things
who do not tax their lives with forethought
of grief. I come into the presence of still water.
And I feel above me the day-blind stars
waiting with their light. For a time
I rest in the grace of the world, and am free.[34]

Yoga

Yoga is essentially a connection of the body and mind (*yoga* or "union" is from the Sanskrit verb *yuj*, meaning "to yoke"). When our physical state is imperfect, it causes a mental imbalance (*chittavritti*), which may be overcome through the practice of yoga. It has also been described as the union of the individual self with the universal self.[35] It is now so widespread in the West that often its true purpose is forgotten, with classes being attended merely as part of a physical fitness routine. Instructors sometimes offer an idealized notion of physical excellence or beauty, but such ego should have no place in yoga, which is emphatically not a competition to be the most flexible—Hatha (posture) yoga is in fact only one aspect (the physical) and includes Ananda, Anusara, Ashtanga, Bikram, Iyengar, Kripalu, Kundalini, Viniyoga, Vinyasa, and other forms.

Yoga is essentially a holistic practice, the spiritual aspects of which are often neglected. Thus, it requires you to find a teacher; understanding your reason for practicing yoga will help you find the right teacher for you. The basic tenets are described as eight "limbs": *yama* (compassion, truth, appreciation, moderation, nonmaterialism); *niyama* (purity, satisfaction, enthusiasm, study, intuition); *asana* (physical postures, purifying the body, preparing for meditation); *pranayama* (breath); *pratyahara* (withdrawing the sense inward); *dharana* (concentration of mind); *dhyana* (meditation); and *samadhi* (control of the mind, stillness, bliss). While the doorway into yoga is through the body, working with the *asanas*, it is only one method. The progress that can be accomplished in a yoga posture is tangible and measurable (unlike the stillness of the mind) and therefore easy to relate to as a beginner. "As you open your body and mind with yoga postures and breathing you become receptive to the delightful and profound experience of inner stillness."[36]

As noted, we recommend that you begin by finding a qualified instructor. However, if you wish to start on your own, here are four very basic and generalized steps to starting a yoga practice:

1. **Learn to breathe effectively.** Learn to breathe when holding the yoga poses. This includes the basic *dirga pranayama* breath to use during the postures. Breathe in and out through the nose and into the belly while practicing.

2. **Start with a brief, mindful meditation.** Sit in an easy pose or any comfortable seated position. Take a few minutes to center yourself and focus on your breath. You may also want to set an intention or goal to begin your practice with a meditative mind.

3. **Follow a beginner's sequence of postures.** Start with a basic yoga pose sequence or these simple postures: seated twist, cat, dog, down dog, child, cobra, mountain, triangle, or forward bend.

4. **End with *shavasana* (relaxation pose).** Always end your yoga practice with *shavasana*, resting on your back and consciously relaxing your body for five to ten minutes. Some practitioners recommend a short seated meditation after *shavasana* to complete your yoga practice.

Evidence-based benefits of yoga include decreased stress, less anxiety, improved quality of life, decreased levels of cortisol (associated with depression), reduced chronic pain, better sleep quality, greater flexibility and balance, and increased muscle strength.[37] The science is clear: Yoga can contribute to both your mental and physical well-being. All it requires is practice a few times per week to make a noticeable difference.

Loving-Kindness Meditation

LKM, first introduced in Chapter 6, is a meditative practice in which a person sends goodwill, kindness, and warmth toward others by silently repeating a series of mantras. In Buddhism it is used to develop the mental habit of selfless or altruistic love. A verse from the *Dhammapada*, one of the Buddhist scriptures, observes that "hatred cannot coexist with loving-kindness, and dissipates if supplanted with thoughts based on loving-kindness." LKM is thought to bring about positive change—to systematically develop the quality of loving acceptance— through a process described as a form of self-psychotherapy, a way of healing the troubled mind to free it from its pain and confusion. In the Buddhist tradition, LKM is the first of a series of meditations that produces four qualities of love: friendliness (*metta*), compassion (*karuna*), appreciative joy (*mudita*), and equanimity (*upekkha*). The quality of friendliness is expressed as warmth that reaches out and embraces others. LKM flows into compassion, which is the ground and precondition for both appreciative joy and equanimity.[38]

Today LKM has become a secular practice, not tied to any one spiritual tradition, which is widely used and studied in different cultures and traditions around the world. Several versions of LKM mantras exist. The first version focuses on loving kindness in relation to the self:

- May I be filled with loving kindness.
- May I be peaceful and at ease.
- May I be free of physical pain and suffering.
- May my heart be filled with love.

The second focuses on someone who is present in our life. This person can be someone we care about deeply, someone we don't get along with, or even someone we only briefly encountered, for example, a homeless person we passed in the street:

- May you be filled with loving kindness.
- May you be peaceful and at ease.
- May you be free of physical pain and suffering.
- May your heart be filled with love.

A third version of LKM is aimed at sending love universally to all beings:

- May all beings be filled with loving kindness.
- May all beings be peaceful and at ease.
- May all beings be free of physical pain and suffering.
- May their hearts be filled with love.

To get started with the LKM practice, the following steps may be taken:

1. Close your eyes and sit comfortably, relaxing your body with, as much as possible, your spine straight, while breathing in and out with quiet awareness.
2. Keep your eyes closed throughout the meditation, and bring your awareness inward.
3. Without straining or concentrating, just relax and gently (without forced effort) repeat any of the previous LKM mantras.

LKM has been shown to increase positive emotions (such as joy, happiness, and contentment), leading to measurable increases in personal resiliency and life satisfaction.[39] It can help strengthen or mend our relationships with others while fostering greater emotional intelligence and well-being.[40] In our experience teaching LKM to graduate students, this practice was often reported as one of the most moving and transformative experiences among the range of practices explored. Interestingly, about half the students in our sample chose to practice LKM in relation to someone they did not get along with, finding that sending such a person loving thoughts eased their anxiety about the relationship and made them feel better about themselves.

Art and Aesthetics

We have a long tradition of seeing our love for beauty as an inborn instinct—a response to the natural environment, to attractors as well as to threats, shaped by our social environment, cultural traditions, and erotic interests.[41] Beauty is related to our experience of wholeness.

Psychologist Rollo May speaks of beauty as that which gives us a sense of mystery, a sense of serenity, and at the same time a sense of exhilaration; beauty intensifies our sense of being alive.[42]

The Greek word *aisthesis* means "having to do with the senses." The senses are our doorway to the world, our way of being in the world. We use "aesthetic" in contrast to "anesthetic," that which numbs and deadens us. This sensibility is what enables us to see the world beyond scientific terms or as a collection of resources for our consumer appetites. Swiss scientist and artist Paolo Knill refers to our capacity to respond to what is beautiful as our aesthetic responsibility, an ethical call to care for the beauty of life and a fundamental aspect of what it means to be a human being.[43] The Navajo word *hozho* is translated into English as "beauty," and it features prominently in Navajo chants, which invoke a blessing to walk in beauty, to walk with beauty before, behind, above, and within oneself. *Hozho* also implies harmony, goodness, and wholeness. For the Navajo, beauty is more than a quality of an object or a person. Beauty is expressed as being in relationship with other humans and with all of life, enabled by this primary aesthetic response of taking in, breathing in, and taking to heart.[44]

A repeated theme of this book is the potential for creativity in each one of us. Artist and art therapist Stephen Levine describes this potential for creativity as the very ground of our being.[45] Because human experience has a sensory basis, we are called to create, shape, and give form to our sensory response to the world. This giving form to experience is an act of care for the life we are given. Art making is seen as a primary mode of inquiry combining creative imagination with embodied experience. The arts, when approached as an expressive act, offer a pathway that can open us to a fuller experience of being and becoming in the world.

Expressive art is a powerful path for personal development and positive change. Expression through the arts is an effective means of addressing issues of human suffering, building community, and facilitating change.[46] Since the beginning of history, human beings have sung, danced, created images, built artifacts, and engaged in arts-infused ritual and ceremony.

The following is an exercise that you can do alone or use in a group dynamic or in a retreat with facilitators. The aim of this practice is to explore how art shapes your perceptions and influences your ways of being.

1. Select a piece of art.
2. Contemplate it slowly.
3. Be aware of its effects on you physically, mentally, emotionally, and spiritually.
4. Respond without words, using only movement such as dancing or drawing.
5. Only then write down your experience and share it with another person.
6. Ask what it might say to you if the artwork had a voice. You can even give it a name or title. Literally, how does it speak to you?

Some of the healing effects of practicing art in its various forms, and highlighted by expert art therapists, include embracing surprise, appreciating differences, and developing trust. Human beings experience feelings of awe at the richness and beauty of the world. Exploring the world through the arts and the creative aesthetic process can enhance our curiosity and increase mental flexibility and open-mindedness. Through exploring different artistic languages of expression, one is able to feel really at home with many different persons and with many different ways of being in the world, with a new appreciation for its beauty and diversity. Trusting the artistic process teaches us to trust ourselves. This personal security enhances our trust in others.

Personal expression through art and aesthetics is a way of navigating through crises and finding new meanings or possibilities. Re-creating our identities and ways of being in the world (for example, Frida Kahlo, who recounts in her autobiography that, after having an accident that kept her bedridden for years, she was kept alive by her art and the process she developed through her painting, the expression and transformation of her anguish, suffering, fears, and desires). When we fall apart, experience crisis, distress, or despair, art is a resource that gives shape to our emotions and thoughts. It offers us a way out, through catharsis and the re-creation of our selves. "If we can let go of our previous identities and move into the experience of the void, then the possibility arises for new forms of existence to emerge."[47]

Appreciative Inquiry

Appreciative inquiry (AI) is a radically different systems-level approach to change. It is based on a new way of looking at the world, one that builds on strengths and generative relationships within a whole rather than reductionist problem solving using forms of root-cause analysis. AI is particularly well suited to complex business challenges with a diversity of strategic stakeholders. It has been used by organizations as varied as the US Navy, the United Nations, Walmart, Hewlett Packard, McKinsey, and the US dairy industry.[48]

Here we offer a practice-oriented introduction to AI for business students and executives. The theoretical assumptions and applied research into AI's effectiveness for flourishing enterprise have been presented elsewhere.[49] What is important to know is that AI focuses on the power of strengths rather than on shortcomings. It uses an inquiry process that builds cooperative capacity in whole systems, allowing the voices of all key stakeholders to be heard. The AI summit methodology is designed for self-managed groups scalable up to one thousand people (in some cases even more) convened over three or more days.

The following questions form the basis of an introductory AI exercise. They are asked sequentially (person A asks all three questions to person B; then B asks the same questions to A) in dyads as part of a larger organizational transformation process:[50]

1. What was a high-point moment for you in leading positive change or collaborative innovation? Share the story: What were the most memorable parts of the initiative, including challenges, innovations, and insights? Reflect on root causes of success. What are your three best qualities or special strengths?
2. When do people in your organization feel most engaged and passionate? Share your observations of moments when people feel

most passionate and connected in your organization. Can you share an example of a hot team, a great innovation, high engagement, or extraordinary performance? What are your organization's signature strengths? Assuming your organization will change in the future, what are those best qualities or signature strengths that you would want to keep or build on, even as it moves into an emerging future? Please offer a few examples of those strengths in action.

3. Reflecting on what your organization could become in the next ten years, what are some powerful images of an extraordinarily desirable future that come to mind? We wake up in the year 2030: What do you see that is new, different, changed, better?

These questions are best asked in a spirit of discovery. Their purpose is to explore and amplify strengths, aspirations, opportunities, and desired results.

AI is not only a summit methodology; it is a fresh way of seeing the world, one that can infuse all our relationships and communications. AI can provide fresh insights into complex multistakeholder dynamics, build strong relationships, and stimulate extraordinary levels of creativity by harnessing the collective intelligence of the whole system. Importantly, it enables aligned action even among constituencies who have a history of confrontation and counterproductive relations.[51]

Group and Systems-Level Practices

Rituals at the community level and practices that attempt to shape society as a whole range from the World Café and AI summits to CoPs aimed at creative and regenerative societal projects.

To consider one example of group-level practices, we return to the world of art and aesthetics. Creating art in a group setting offers participants the opportunity of sharing something of themselves with others. The presentation of their artwork invites the possibility that both the artist and the group become authentically present to each other. Building community is an important capacity of the arts.[52] Cocreative processes, where the whole group creates collectively, give participants many opportunities to explore leading and following, giving and taking, creating and letting go.

The following steps are a simple way to begin a group art practice:

1. In a group setting, draw a line from one side to the other on a piece of cardboard. This is the line of your life.
2. Above and below the baseline are your peaks and nadirs at different stages of your life. Intuitively draw the ups and downs from birth to the present, and then imagine what it might look like ten years into the future.
3. Now draw symbols on each stage that represent meaningful events, persons, places, and objects.
4. On the same or another surface, draw the line of your life in an artistic way, using any and all materials you wish to use.
5. Share first in dyads and then with the group as a whole.

The experience of having one's art witnessed and honored by others can be life changing, offering insight and clarity that are transformative.[53] The artwork contains a mystery that keeps it from being an object of knowledge; it will always be more than what we can say about it in our verbal interpretations.

Hal Hamilton, one of the executives we interviewed, spoke about group-level engagements that combine different practices to transform leaders into agents of world benefit:

> The most consistently effective experience that we create in [our organization] is that we take people in small groups; we make sure each group is very diverse, with corporate, NGOs, government, and farmers and many others. We take them on for at least a couple of days on different visits on a field trip; we have people do a lot of journaling, silence, and reflecting on particular questions. And then after each visit we have people sharing one at a time their answers to some simple questions about what they noticed, what surprised them, what inspired them, what worried them. And what happens there is that they notice how different the lenses are through which they see and through which they hear. . . . There is a way in which when people can share respectfully the different ways

their vision works, the different data that they take in and interpret; they also notice over time the common humanity with which they're experiencing these different visits and observations and conversations. I thought for a long time about just what a lesson it is in mental models to have people experience how they see the same thing differently. It's really interesting the kind of bonds that develop between people who see things extremely differently, but by sharing that experience and going around over and over again, and then of course sharing the experience of traveling together, uncomfortably and tired in a van, bouncing over roads through the countryside, there is something else that happens too. People get a little shaken up physically. So they are a little more available in a certain way, in a human way. But these relationships that have been formed on these simple little two- to four-day trips have led to projects where organizations like Oxfam and big corporations are doing things together to try to improve the lives of small farmers in different places; and this wouldn't have ever happened without the personal relationships that they've developed between people who see the world very differently but who understand that there is something that underlies these differences, which is some kind of common caring.

The value of group-level practices that bond teams and connect organizations internally and externally was a recurring theme in our interviews of quantum leaders.

.   .   .

Consciousness is the mother of all capital, and mindfulness practices are the gateway to our deep investigation of humanity and to developing the relational skills to finding purpose. The AITIA Quantum Leadership Center and Octave help provide a holistic system of learning for mindfulness practices, to quiet ourselves and shift consciousness. The practices are designed to align internal and external consciousness and allow its expression in the form of creativity. It is a lifelong learning journey that integrates self-cultivation, family learning, community building, and universal harmony, which is awakening humanity to love and the evolving self. Such learning programs are a process to rewire, reframe, reskill, and renew ourselves across all the systems of the self (mind-body-spirit), family, organization, and humanity.

Conclusion

Most of us are hit daily with a barrage of stories about the worsening circumstances and growing malaise of a majority of the world's population. From food insecurity and public health crises to growing income inequality, social divisiveness, and ecological destruction, the 24/7 news feed reveals that all is not well. There is a much deeper story—about who we are and the nature of the world—that is showing signs of no longer serving us. We urgently need a new narrative to replace the current plotlines of profit maximization, endless growth, material consumption, and lack of caring for each other and future generations.

Throughout this book we point to consciousness as the most powerful lever for changing who we are and how we behave toward others and nature. We show how transforming consciousness can be the most effective tool we have for unlocking local and global change.

A spectrum of consciousness exists, at one end characterized by separateness and selfishness and at the other, by connectedness and caring. Now more than ever, these polar opposites are at war with each other, mirroring a budding scientific revolution that suggests the coming of a fundamentally new understanding of what it means to be human and the nature of reality. The following two paragraphs sum up these warring narratives.

A consciousness of separateness and selfishness. In the last three hundred years the natural and social sciences led us to see ourselves as separate, selfish, utility-maximizing individuals who are spiritless and existentially alone, born into a cold mechanical universe composed of clumps of matter subject to gravitational and electromagnetic forces driving us toward meaningless extinction. Such a narrative has a long and distinguished pedigree in Newtonian physics, Cartesian dualism, the biological evolution of Darwinism, the utility theory of John Stuart Mill, and the mathematical laws of economic behavior expounded by William Stanley Jevons.

A consciousness of connectedness and caring. New findings in the natural and social sciences suggest that we are deeply connected to one another, not only metaphorically but also through energy and information fields. Quantum physics reveals properties of entanglement and nonlocality at the finest scale of reality; quantum biology and epigenetics show that this interconnectedness extends to the scale of life; and a growing body of research suggests that consciousness may be a field property of the universe rather than a localized result of brain activity. In the social sciences, the rapid rise of positive psychology and new economic theory embedded in society and the natural environment reinforce a more relational view of life.

These very different narratives are not only about competing science. They shape our thoughts and, ultimately, our ways of *being* and *acting*. Leaders who embrace mindfulness and direct-intuitive practices in their daily lives can, over time, elevate their consciousness of connectedness. They are able to move toward flourishing because that is who they *are* rather than only because doing so has financial benefits. The practices that elevate our consciousness enable us to tap into a universal source of energy from which enormous creativity and relational intelligence drive evolution toward flourishing. This outcome is a must for business at a time when civilization is undergoing enormous upheaval with hyperfast changes.

Business is at its most relevant when it is able to generate wealth, broadly defined to include not only economic but also physical, relational, emotional, and spiritual wealth, *and* serve humankind. The fullest expression of a leader-as-integrator is as an enlightened entrepreneur who spurs creativity and collaboration as a way to serve the well-being of the whole. Quantum leaders take the "Middle Way," avoiding blame and judgment of others, letting go of the past, showing empathy and compassion, while being open to the emerging future. Quantum leaders grow when they help others grow along their own leadership journeys.

The focus has morphed from the strong-armed bosses of early entrepreneurial capitalism to bureaucrats in siloed operations, to managers who use a combination of fear- and incentive-based systems to motivate others, to those who take the giant step to pursue prosperity and flourishing from a place of wholeness and relational intelligence. Today's challenges are greater than ever because the sociopolitical and economic fabric of society no longer has the cohesiveness needed to absorb the disruptions we experience. There is a need to elevate the consciousness of connectedness in business leaders and to strengthen their sense of greater purpose to give them the adaptive and direct-intuitive skills needed to succeed in perpetually turbulent times. Only then will they be able to align their people with a business purpose in service of flourishing.

A key task of quantum leaders is thus to inspire others to deal effectively with rapid and discontinuous change. They must cultivate the ability to recognize change and to adapt to it in ways that create positive economic, social, and environmental value. At its most fundamental level, this requires a heightened consciousness of connectedness to see the world from an expansive, relational, and loving perspective.

Quantum leaders are regularly challenged by systemic drag: the weight of existing organizational structures and processes that unintentionally act to preserve the status quo and function as barriers to evolution. When change is the only constant, learning is the ultimate tool. The trick is to go beyond analytic-cognitive approaches that emphasize only conceptual understanding. Managing change from the perspective of the whole requires embodied learning through direct-intuitive experience that builds relational and spiritual intelligence in additional to technical skills.

Quantum leaders must be creative and strategic, possess curiosity and open-mindedness, and lead and manage change proactively, staying ahead of the market and the competition. They must carry out insightful analyses to anticipate change, be able to develop innovative strategies and business models, and be capable of strategic integration to execute those strategies. They must be proactive and capable of driving strategic thinking while remaining prudent. They also need to have a hands-on frontline presence. To do all this, they must build an organizational culture in which practices of connectedness are part of the company's "way of doing things."

Whether through Fred's personal life story and the evolutionary journey of his organization; the sixteen exemplar companies presented as mini–case studies; the field research supporting the quantum leadership model; or the science of connectedness, you have now seen evidence of everyday practices that can help leaders and organizations shift their consciousness from one of separateness and selfishness to one of connectedness and caring. From meditation to walking in nature, from music to exercise and prayer, such practices help quiet our five senses and slow the analytic cognition of the brain. They help cultivate broader perception and greater awareness of how our actions affect others and future generations.

Having a consciousness of connectedness changes how we think and act. We become more empathetic and compassionate. When we see ourselves as an integral part of the natural world rather than separate from it, we become more attuned to how our actions affect not only people but all life on earth.

The path to quantum leadership is above all an experiential one. It is not achieved through conceptual learning alone. Mindfulness, which engages the heart-body-spirit and not only the mind, is the gateway to awakening an experience of wholeness. Leaders who successfully pursue it find greater purpose and meaning through the pursuit of positive social impact.

The point is that our consciousness, influenced by both science and our values and beliefs, and shaped by our daily practices, is the foundation for the stories we tell about who we are and the nature of the world in which we live. These stories in turn determine the actions we take in business as in life.

APPENDIX CLASSIFICATION SCHEME FOR UNDERSTANDING THE PRACTICES OF CONNECTEDNESS

I. Presencing Practices

   A. Meditative and contemplative practices: We include here many of the meditative and contemplative practices that come from the world's main spiritual traditions, along with a broad range of secular practices. All of the practices emphasize to one degree or another the importance of silence, embodied awareness, nonattachment, compassion for others, and attunement to nature.

      1. Secular practices

         a. Contemplative time (taking time to "just be")

         b. Gestalt sensory awareness

         c. Workplace mindfulness practices

            i. Use of meditation rooms

            ii. Moments of silence before meetings

            iii. Retreats or time off for reflection

         d. Mindfulness-based stress reduction (MBSR)

            i. Body scan

            ii. Loving-kindness meditation (LKM)

            iii. Self-compassion and compassion for others

            iv. Mindfulness for creativity development

            v. Mindful eating

            vi. Mindful working

            vii. Mindful relating to others

2. Practices from the world's great religious and spiritual traditions
   a. Practices in the Christian spiritual tradition, such as contemplative silence, prayer, and Quaker meetings
   b. Practices in the Judaic tradition, such as Hasidic practices and the Kabbalah
   c. Practices in the Islamic spiritual tradition, including Sufi practices
   d. Practices developed in the Hindu spiritual tradition from yoga (e.g., Hatha, Iyengar, Vinyasa, and Tantra) to transcendental meditation
   e. Practices developed in the Buddhist spiritual tradition
      i. Practices developed in the Theravada tradition: Shamata, Anapanasati, and Vipassana
      ii. Practices developed in the Mahayana tradition: Zen practices such as Zazen and Koans
      iii. Practices developed in the Vajrayana tradition: Dzogchen (Ati Yoga)
   f. Taoist meditation, including disciplines such as Qigong and Tai-Chi
   g. Shamanism
B. Embodied/somatic practices: Practices that involve the body as actor consist of different types of "body work" that, through the interiorization of a corporeal discipline, promote a holistic change in the body-mind-spirit. They most often involve a sequence of forms and postures that are repeated and perfected over time.
   1. Somatic awareness practices
      a. Hakomi psychotherapy
      b. Shiatsu massage
      c. Craniosacral therapy
      d. Healthy posture and movement
         i. Rolfing
         ii. SomatoEmotional release
         iii. Gokhale method
         iv. Zero balancing

2. Active embodiment
    a. Eastern active embodiment practices (also overlapping with meditative and contemplative practices)
        i. Yoga
        ii. Qigong (China)
        iii. Jorei (Japan)
        iv. Dzogchen (Nyingma, Tibetan)
        v. Martial arts (various)
    b. Western active embodiment practices (athletic in nature)
        i. Team sports, such as soccer, football, basketball, and cricket
        ii. Recreational sports for individuals, such as distance running (e.g., roads and trails), cycling, swimming, and weightlifting
        iii. Competition sports for individuals, such as track running (in a stadium), jumping, throwing (e.g., javelin and discus)
        iv. Outdoor community activities, such as aquatics, running games (e.g., *rarahipari* [Tarahumara Indian]); hunting and fishing
        v. Indoor community recreation, such as eSports (e.g., League of Legends [LoL] and Dota)
C. Nature practices
    1. Immersion in nature
        a. Sitting or being outdoors (individual, interpersonal, group, and family levels)
        b. Forest bathing (individual, interpersonal, family, team, and organizational levels)
        c. Hiking/walking (individual, interpersonal, family, team, and organizational levels)
        d. Nature adventures for team building (team level)
    2. Gardening (individual, interpersonal, group, and family levels), including wilderness retreats
    3. Observing and caring for nonhuman life forms (flora and fauna)

D. Aesthetics and artistic practices
   1. Processing or receiving an artistic or aesthetic experience
   a. Listening to music
   b. Seeing exhibits/theater/movies
   c. Sensing journeys
   2. Creating or expressing an artistic or aesthetic experience
      a. Playing music
         i. Playing an instrument (individual and group levels)
         ii. Jazz band (group level)
         iii. Choir (group level)
         iv. Drum circles (group level)
      b. Dancing
         i. Free dancing
         ii. Open floor and soul motion
         iii. Contemplative dance
         iv. Authentic movement
         v. Expressive movement
         vi. World dances such as tango or flamenco
         vii. Christian, Sufi, and other religious dances
      c. Narrative practices
         i. Storytelling (dyad and group levels)
         ii. Creative writing
      d. Theater practices
         i. Classical theater
         ii. Improvisation theater/spontaneity theater
         iii. Social presencing theater
         iv. Noh and Kabuki theater
         v. Theatre of the Oppressed (TO)
      e. Visual arts
         i. Drawing and doodling
         ii. Painting with oils or watercolors
         iii. Sculpting in clay, wood, and ceramics
         iv. Photography
         v. Floral arts (e.g., Ikebana)

E. Relational practices
   1. Relational practices inside the organization
      a. Water-cooler conversations (informal socializing)
      b. Family presence (e.g., bring your child to work)
      c. Caring practices (various)
   2. Relational practices outside the organization
      a. Socializing (spending time together outside the organization)
      b. Sharing interests/learning something new together
      c. Communities of practice (CoPs)
F. Space/place practices
   1. Space-based rituals, such as feng shui
   2. Place-based rituals (finding your place of peacefulness)
II. Sense-Making Practices
   A. Reflective practices: Emphasis is on the introspective processes that give meaning and that help make sense of our experiences and intuitions. As human beings, we have an existential need to put our experiences into words as a way to give meaning and to make sense of them.
      1. Introspection, where the reflective practice involves concentration or focus on an image, object, or topic
      2. RAIN (Recognition, Acceptance, Investigation, and Nonattachment), a practice designed to work through feelings of overwhelm
      3. Journaling, such as the intensive diary method of Ira Progoff and stream-of-consciousness writing practiced daily when we wake up
      4. Automatic writing practice in groups or workshops to explore what emerges in individual narratives and then sharing those narratives in the group, followed by reflective dialogues about the topics that emerge as important for the group
      5. Interviewing and storytelling as the basis of action research projects, where qualitative analysis is done on the collected stories to find patterns of meaning making in common as

well as building on shared strengths, concerns, longings, and needs (team and organizational levels)

B. Relational/communication oriented practices: The focus is on the relationships and the communication processes.

   1. Generative dialogues (team level)
   2. Dialogical practices (team level)
   3. Collaborative practices (team level)
   4. Open room (after organizational meetings a time is given for people to develop open conversations) (organizational level)
   5. World Café (organizational level)

C. Future vision–building practices: These include interpersonal-level coaching using participatory organizational development methodologies.

   1. Coaching for building a shared vision (team and organizational levels)
   2. AI processes and summits (team, organizational, and system levels)

D. Innovation/creativity development

   1. Creative writing (individual and group levels)
   2. Design thinking and human-centric design methodologies for innovation (team level)
   3. Lateral and parallel thinking (Edward de Bono's Six Thinking Hats) (team level)
   4. Role-playing and creativity development (team level)

E. Health/well-being/happiness/personal development–oriented practices

   1. Life coaching and lifestyle design (individual level)
   2. Personal development programs (interpersonal and team levels)
   3. Wellness and health programs (biopsychosocial and holistic models of health) (group and organizational levels)

F. Values-oriented practices: values, ethics, and greater purpose

   1. Internal
      a. Horizontal practices: being in service to others, exercising compassion toward others, and contributing to create

a good relational atmosphere (interpersonal, team, and organizational levels)

b. Vertical practices: mentoring (interpersonal level)

2. External

a. Community/society volunteering

b. Environmental stewardship

c. Multiactor networks for shared greater purposes

NOTES

Preface

1. See EMRG, "Einstein Enigmatic Quote," *Icarus Falling* (blog), June 24, 2009, http://icarus-falling.blogspot.com/2009/06/einstein-enigma.html.

2. Michael Bendenwald, "Sustainability Fatigue, Disruptive Innovation and the Flourishing Enterprise," *GreenBiz*, June 20, 2013, https://www.greenbiz.com/blog/2013/06/20/sustainability-fatigue-disruptive-innovation-and-flourishing-enterprise.

3. Chris Laszlo and Nadya Zhexembayeva, *Embedded Sustainability: The Next Big Competitive Advantage* (Stanford, CA: Stanford University Press, 2011).

Chapter 1. A New Consciousness in Business

1. Milton Friedman, "The Social Responsibility of Business Is to Increase Its Profits," *New York Times Magazine*, September 13, 1970, http://umich.edu/~thecore/doc/Friedman.pdf.

2. In the United States, the Environmental Protection Agency was founded in 1970, the same year that the Clean Air Act was passed. The Clean Water Act was passed in 1971.

3. Thomas Donaldson and James P. Walsh, "Toward a Theory of Business," *Research in Organizational Behavior* 35 (2015): 183, http://www.jamespwalsh.com/Resources/Donaldson%20and%20Walsh%20-%202015%20-%20Toward%20a%20Theory%20of%20Business-1.pdf.

4. For a more complete list, see the UN Global Goals for Sustainable Development, at http://www.globalgoals.org. In late 2016, Pope Francis met with select global Fortune 500 CEOs to address the need for a global economic system that both encourages growth and spreads its benefits more broadly. A *Business Wire* headline announced, "Prominent Business and Thought Leaders Present Solutions to the Pope on How the Private Sector Can Be a Driving Force in Ending Poverty and Creating a More Sustainable World." This event was one of a growing number of similar efforts in recent years to promote business for good. See "His Holiness Pope Francis Addresses Time Inc.'s 2016 Fortune/Time Global Forum at the Vatican," *Business Wire*, December 3, 2016, http://www.businesswire.com/news/home/20161203005054/en/Holiness-Pope-Francis-Addresses-Time-Inc.%E2%80%99s-2016.

5. Marc J. Epstein, Adriana Rejc Buhovac, and Kristi Yuthas, "Managing Social, Environmental and Financial Performance Simultaneously," *Journal of Long Range Planning* 48 (2015): 35–45. This empirical study finds that managers "always think about the business case first. But at the same time, when the details of any specific decisions are discussed,

the importance of social and environmental goals comes through" (40). These decisions tend to be related to boundary conditions such as bribery or a supplier's use of child labor, where it might be more expensive to comply than to pay a fine but where the implied unethical behaviors are considered unacceptable to management. The study also shows empirically that innovation is how middle- and upper-level managers break through the apparent trade-offs between financial performance and social and environmental outcomes.

6. Surveys include those by the Sloan Management Review with the Boston Consulting Group, Accenture, Deloitte, and McKinsey.

7. The 2016 UN Global Compact/Accenture CEO study says that "80 percent of CEOs say that demonstrating a purpose-driven commitment to sustainability is already a differentiator in their industry." UN Global Compact and Accenture Strategy, "Agenda 2030: A Window of Opportunity," 2016, https://www.accenture.com/t20161216T041642Z __w__/us-en/_acnmedia/Accenture/next-gen-2/insight-ungc-ceo-study-page/ Accenture-UN-Global-Compact-Accenture-Strategy-CEO-Study-2016.pdf.

8. Accenture and UN Global Compact, "The UN Global Compact–Accenture CEO Study on Sustainability, 2013: Architects of a Better World," September 2013, http://www .unglobalcompact.org/docs/news_events/8.1/UNGC_Accenture_CEO_Study_2013.pdf.

9. WeSpire, "The State of Employee Engagement Report, 2018," 2018, http://www .wespire.com/resource/the-state-of-employee-engagement_qs_whitepaperqs_resource _name2018report-2.

10. Johan Rockström, W. Steffen, Kevin J. Noone, Åsa Persson, F. Stuart Chapin III, E. F. Lambin, T. M. Lenton, et al., "A Safe Operating Space for Humanity," *Nature* 461, no. 1 (2009): 472–475.

11. Simon L. Albrecht, "Work Engagement and the Positive Power of Meaningful Work," in *Advances in Positive Organizational Psychology*, ed. Arnold B. Bakker (Bingley, UK: Emerald Group, 2013), 237–260.

12. John R. Ehrenfeld and Andrew J. Hoffman, *Flourishing: A Frank Conversation About Sustainability* (Stanford, CA: Stanford University Press, 2013).

13. See Michael Pirson, *Humanistic Management: Protecting Dignity and Promoting Well-Being* (Cambridge: Cambridge University Press, 2017).

14. See, for example, the Barrett shared vision and values approach. Barrett Values Centre, "Culture and Vision/Mission," https://www.valuescentre.com/mapping-values/ culture/culture-vision (accessed November 16, 2018).

15. Stuart Hameroff and Roger Penrose, "Consciousness in the Universe: A Review of the Orch OR Theory," *Physics of Life Reviews* 11, no. 1 (2014): 39–78.

16. Dirk K. F. Meijer and Hans J. H. Geesink, "Consciousness in the Universe Is Scale Invariant and Implies an Event Horizon of the Human Brain," *NeuroQuantology* 15, no. 3 (2017): 41–79.

17. A useful practical definition of transformation that points to an expansion in consciousness is given in Judi Neal, "An Overview of the Field of Transformation," in *The Handbook of Personal and Organizational Transformation*, ed. Judi Neal (New York: SpringerNature, 2018), 3–46. Neal cites a contributing author's definition: "Transformation is the evolution or revolution of an operating paradigm to one that is more encompassing of realities not allowed, considered, accounted for, or contained in the previous frame of ref-

erence. It generally occurs when we bump up against the limitations of our current frame of reference. Things are happening that we can't explain, or we see that we are consistently re-creating events and situations that we don't like because of the decisions we make" (14).

18. Donella H. Meadows, "Places to Intervene in a System," *Whole Earth*, Winter 1997, http://www.wholeearth.com/issue/2091/article/27/places.to.intervene.in.a.system. A second version of the article appears as Donella Meadows, "Leverage Points: Places to Intervene in a System," Donella Meadows Project, http://donellameadows.org/archives/leverage-points-places-to-intervene-in-a-system (accessed November 16, 2018).

19. Ray Anderson, personal communication, 2006.

20. Meadows, "Leverage Points." Meadows also argues that there is one leverage point that is even higher than changing a paradigm. This is "the power to transcend paradigms." For her, this means letting go into not knowing, into what the Buddhists call enlightenment and Chinese traditional wisdom has long espoused as the path to right living. "It is in this space of mastery over paradigms," she writes, "that people throw off addictions, live in constant joy, bring down empires, get locked up or burned at the stake or crucified or shot, and have impacts that last for millennia." In Part II we discuss this power to transcend paradigms and its implication for business leadership.

21. Thomas S. Kuhn, *The Structure of Scientific Revolutions*, 3rd ed. (Chicago: University of Chicago Press, 1996).

22. Meadows, "Leverage Points."

23. Peter Senge, Hal Hamilton, and John Kania, "The Dawn of System Leadership," *Stanford Social Innovation Review*, Winter 2015, https://ssir.org/articles/entry/the_dawn_of_system_leadership.

24. Chris Laszlo and Nadya Zhexembayeva, *Embedded Sustainability: The Next Big Competitive Advantage* (Stanford, CA: Stanford University Press, 2011), 42–54.

25. Richard E. Boyatzis, Kylie Rochford, and Scott N. Taylor, "The Role of the Positive Emotional Attractor in Vision and Shared Vision: Toward Effective Leadership, Relationships, and Engagement," *Frontiers in Psychology*, May 21, 2016, http://journal.frontiersin.org/article/10.3389/fpsyg.2015.00670/abstract.

26. Management thought leader and author Dana Zohar observes that such creative thinking "originates crucially in the spiritual level of the self [and] issues from a brain dynamic that functions very much like the processes and systems described by quantum physics and complexity science." Dana Zohar, *The Quantum Leader: A Revolution in Business Thinking and Practice* (New York: Prometheus Books, 2016), 47.

27. Jeremy Hunter and Michael Chaskalson, "Making the Mindful Leader: Cultivating Skills for Facing Adaptive Challenges," in *The Wiley-Blackwell Handbook of the Psychology of Leadership, Change, and Organizational Development*, ed. H. Skipton Leonard, Rachel Lewis, Arthur M. Freeman, and Jonathan Passmore (Chichester, UK: Wiley-Blackwell, 2013), 195–220.

28. See Chapters 6 and 7 for the social and natural science defining the practices.

29. Jonathan Porritt, "Jonathan Porritt Reviews *Designing Regenerative Cultures*," *Age of Awareness*, June 24, 2017, https://medium.com/@designforsustainability/jonathon-porritt-reviews-designing-regenerative-cultures-6baa2177340c.

30. See the evidence presented in Chapter 6.

31. For example, a study by N. A. Farb and colleagues shows that after eight weeks of mindfulness training, subjects had higher levels of insula activation, which is central to our sense of human connectedness, by helping mediate empathy in a more visceral way. See Norman A. S. Farb, Zindel V. Segal, Helen Mayberg, Jim Bean, Deborah McKeon, Zainab Fatima, and Adam K. Anderson, "Attending to the Present: Mindfulness Meditation Reveals Distinct Neural Modes of Self-Reference," *Social Cognitive and Affective Neuroscience* 2 (2007): 313–322. Additional clinical neuroscientific studies covering a variety of practices are presented in Chapter 6.

32. See also Sandra Waddock, "Integrity and Mindfulness: Foundations of Corporate Citizenship," *Journal of Corporate Citizenship* 1 (Spring 2001): 25–37.

33. See Peter Guy Northouse, *Leadership: Theory and Practice* (London: Sage, 2009). James MacGregor Burns founded the field of leadership studies with the publication of his book *Leadership* in 1978. Two of his major contributions were (1) a shift away from studying the traits and actions of great leaders toward the study of the interaction between leaders and their constituencies and (2) delineating two forms of leadership: transactional leadership and transformational leadership. Cited in Neal, "Overview of the Field of Transformation," 17.

34. Todd Spangler, "Top 20 Most Pirated Movies of 2014 Led by 'Wolf of Wall Street,' 'Frozen,' 'Gravity,'" *Variety*, December 28, 2014, http://variety.com/2014/digital/news/top -20-most-pirated-movies-of-2014-led-by-wolf-of-wall-street-frozen-gravity-1201388403.

35. United Nations, "We Can End Poverty, 2015," September 2010, http://www.un .org/en/mdg/summit2010/pdf/MDG_FS_1_EN.pdf. Counted as living in "extreme poverty" were originally those living on less than US$1.00 a day, adjusted by the World Bank to US$1.25 in 2008. "Extreme poverty" was originally defined by the United Nations in 1995 as "a condition characterized by severe deprivation of basic human needs, including food, safe drinking water, sanitation facilities, health, shelter, education and information." United Nations, "Report of the World Summit for Social Development," April 19, 1995, http://www.un.org/documents/ga/conf166/aconf166-9.htm.

36. See the works of Richard Boyatzis, Martin Seligman, Barbara Frederickson, and Shinzen Young.

37. Michael Puett and Christine Gross-Loh, *The Path: What Chinese Philosophers Can Teach Us About the Good Life* (New York: Simon and Schuster, 2016). This book is based on a course taught at Harvard University. It has become the third most popular undergraduate course with more than seven hundred students registered at any given time. The popularity of the course and of the book reflects a renewed interest in reimagining ancient Chinese wisdom based on the writings of Lao Tzu, Confucius, Mencius, Zhungzi, Xunzi, Mozi, and others who offer fresh insights into the secrets of living a prosperous and flourishing life.

38. Jay H. Bragdon, *Companies That Mimic Nature: Leaders of the Corporate Renaissance* (Sheffield, UK: Greenleaf, 2016), 12–13.

Chapter 2. A Personal Experience

1. The treaties were with the British and French, respectively, as outcomes of the deplorable Opium Wars, and hugely favorable in both cases to the Europeans. The Treaty

of Nanking granted Hong Kong to the British (relinquished only in 1997), and Shanghai, a "treaty port," grew into a major commercial center.

2. Michael Zakkour, "The China Miracle Isn't Over—It Has Entered Its Second Phase," *Forbes*, March 30, 2017, https://www.forbes.com/sites/michaelzakkour/2017/03/30/the-china-miracle-isnt-over-it-has-entered-its-second-phase/#659be3b76635.

3. Adam Smith, "Conclusion to the Mercantile System," in *The Wealth of Nations*, by Adam Smith (New York: Random House, 1994), 715.

4. For a complete list of the goals, see http://www.undp.org/content/undp/en/home/sustainable-development-goals.html.

5. *Daodejing* is also transliterated as the *Tao Te Ching*. A good English-language edition is Philip J. Ivanhoe, *The Daodejing of Laozi* (Indianapolis, IN: Hackett, 2001).

6. It is in no way patronizing to direct the curious to a quick overview titled "A Children's Picture-Book Introduction to Quantum Field Theory," by Brian Skinner, a physicist and a postdoctoral researcher at MIT. See Brian Skinner, "A Children's Picture-Book Introduction to Quantum Field Theory," *Ribbon Farm*, August 20, 2015, https://www.ribbonfarm.com/2015/08/20/qft.

7. Johnjoe McFadden and Jim Al-Khalili, *Life on the Edge: The Coming of Age of Quantum Biology* (London: Bantam Press, 2014).

8. Much new research, as discussed in Chapter 6, suggests that consciousness itself is not generated by the brain but exists outside the brain as quantum-level vibrational frequencies intrinsic to spacetime geometry.

9. See Chapter 6 for discussions of the emerging theories of and evidence for universal quantum energy fields.

Chapter 3. An Organization's Journey

1. See Business and Sustainable Development Commission, "Better Business, Better World," January 2017, http://report.businesscommission.org/uploads/BetterBiz-BetterWorld.pdf.

2. See Peter Drucker, *The Landmarks of Tomorrow* (Portsmouth, NH: Heinemann, 1959).

3. For more on the roles of culture and sustainability in family businesses, see Joseph P. H. Fan and Chavalit F. Tsao, "Culture and Sustainability: An Analysis of the Chinese Culture and Families," Family Business Academy Research Paper No. 2016-01, October 12, 2016.

4. Russell Brandom, "A Real Hyperloop Is Almost Here—and It's Not What Elon Musk Envisioned," *The Verge*, August 2, 2017, https://www.theverge.com/2017/8/2/16084154/hyperloop-one-test-size-speed-loop-elon-musk.

5. Rebecca Harrington, "By 2050, the Oceans Could Have More Plastic than Fish," *Business Insider*, January 26, 2017, http://www.businessinsider.com/plastic-in-ocean-outweighs-fish-evidence-report-2017-1.

6. Josh Allan Dykstra, "Why Millennials Don't Want to Buy Stuff," *Fast Company*, July 13, 2012, https://www.fastcompany.com/1842581/why-millennials-dont-want-buy-stuff.

7. Marcel Proust, *In Search of Lost Time*, vol. 5, *The Captive*, trans. C. K. Scott Moncrieff and Terence Kilmartin (New York: Modern Library, 1993), 343. The exact wording

is "The only true voyage . . . would be not to visit strange lands but to possess other eyes, to see the universe through the eyes of another."

8. Jody Fry and Eleftheria Egel offer a model of spiritual leadership that inherently embeds sustainability into the triple bottom line. They define spirituality as "concerned with qualities of the human spirit and that intangible reality at the core of personality, the animating life principle or life-breath that . . . alerts us to look for the deepest dimension of human experience. It is at the heart of the quest for self-transcendence and the attendant feeling of interconnectedness with all things in the universe." Louis W. (Jody) Fry and Eleftheria Egel, "Spiritual Leadership: Embedding Sustainability in the Triple Bottom Line," *Graziadio Business Review* 20, no. 3 (2017), https://gbr.pepperdine .edu/2017/12/spiritual-leadership.

9. Dustin DiPerna and H. B. Augustine, eds., *The Coming Waves: Evolution, Transformation, and Action in an Integral Age* (San Francisco: Integral, 2014).

10. Stephen R. Covey, *The Seven Habits of Highly Effective People* (New York: Simon and Schuster, 1989), 70.

11. Willis Harman, *Global Mind Change: The Promise of the 21st Century* (Oakland, CA: Berrett-Koehler, 1998).

Chapter 4. Sixteen Exemplar Companies

1. Jonathan Storper, "What's the Difference Between a B Corp and a Benefit Corporation?," *Conscious Company Media*, April 4, 2015, https://consciouscompanymedia .com/sustainable-business/whats-the-difference-between-a-b-corp-and-a-benefit -corporation.

2. Certified B Corporation, "About B Corps," https://www.bcorporation.net/what -are-b-corps (accessed November 19, 2018).

3. B Corps' legal structure expands corporate accountability to include making decisions that are good for society, not just their shareholders. To become a certified B Corp, a company has to take and pass the benchmark B Impact Ratings System; adopt the B Corporation Legal Framework; and sign a Term Sheet that makes the certification official.

4. Benefit corporations are required to produce an annual public "benefit report" that assesses their overall social and environmental performance against a third-party standard.

5. John Mackey, cited in Francesca Fenzi, "4 Ways to Become a (More) Conscious Capitalist," *Inc.*, April 8, 2013, https://www.inc.com/francesca-fenzi/4-ways-to-become -a-more-conscious-capitalist.html. See also John Mackey and Rajendra Sisodia, *Conscious Capitalism: Liberating the Heroic Spirit of Business* (Boston: Harvard Business Review Press, 2013).

6. Otto Scharmer, "Transforming Capitalism: 7 Acupuncture Points," *Huffington Post*, April 1, 2017, http://www.huffingtonpost.com/entry/transforming-capitalism-seven -acupuncture-points_us_58e006cce4b03c2b30f6a6fa (emphasis in original).

7. Ibid.

8. Nedbank, "Sustainability Approach," https://www.nedbank.co.za/content/nedbank/desktop/gt/en/aboutus/green-and-caring/sustainability/sustainability-approach.html (accessed November 19, 2018).

9. Dana Zohar, *Quantum Leaders* (Amherst, NY: Prometheus Books, 2016). See also Peter Fisk, "Haier's 'Rendanheyi' Business Model," *Gamechangers*, November 6, 2015, http://www.thegeniusworks.com/2015/11/haier-thinking.

10. See the initiative's website, at https://aim2flourish.com.

11. See Business and Sustainable Development Commission, "Better Business, Better World," January 2017, http://report.businesscommission.org/uploads/BetterBiz-BetterWorld.pdf.

12. In 2017 Unilever was ranked among *Fast Company*'s "Most Innovative Companies" for "prioritizing sustainability throughout its portfolio of brands." That year it was also ranked the number-one company in the world in the GlobeScan SustainAbility Survey for the sixth year in a row. Unilever, "Awards and Recognition," 2018, https://www.unilever.com/sustainable-living/our-strategy/awards-and-recognition.

13. Unilever, "The Unilever Sustainable Living Plan," https://www.unilever.co.uk/sustainable-living/the-unilever-sustainable-living-plan (accessed November 19, 2018).

14. Dove, "Why the Campaign for Real Beauty?," https://web.archive.org/web/20070816112659/http://www.campaignforrealbeauty.ca/supports.asp?url=supports.asp&section=campaign&id=1560 (accessed November 19, 2018).

15. See Axe, "Is It OK for Guys . . . ," http://www.axe.com/us/en/is-it-ok-for-guys.html (accessed November 19, 2018).

16. Tim Nudd, "Axe Tackles 'Toxic Masculinity' by Revealing How Deeply Young Men Struggle with It," *AdWeek*, May 17, 2017, http://www.adweek.com/brand-marketing/axe-tackles-toxic-masculinity-by-revealing-how-deeply-young-men-struggle-with-it.

17. See Vaseline, "The Vaseline Healing Project," http://healingproject.vaseline.us (accessed November 19, 2018).

18. Lillian Cunningham, "The Tao of Paul Polman," *Washington Post*, May 21, 2015, https://www.washingtonpost.com/news/on-leadership/wp/2015/05/21/the-tao-of-paul-polman.

19. Joe Confino, "Unilever's Paul Polman: Challenging the Corporate Status Quo," *The Guardian*, April 24, 2012, https://www.theguardian.com/sustainable-business/paul-polman-unilever-sustainable-living-plan.

20. Cunningham, "The Tao of Paul Polman."

21. Ibid.

22. "Company Profile for Unilever," *The Guardian*, October 11, 2010, https://www.theguardian.com/sustainable-business/profile-unilever; "Profile: Unilever PLC (ULVR.L)," *Reuters*, https://www.reuters.com/finance/stocks/companyProfile/ULVR.L (accessed November 19, 2018); Trefis Team, "Unilever's Acquisition Spree in 2015 and 2016 Could Help Boost Its Revenues and Profits," *Nasdaq*, December 30, 2016, http://www.nasdaq.com/article/unilevers-acquisition-spree-in-2015-and-2016-could-help-boost-its-revenues-and-profits-cm728080.

23. Jay H. Bragdon, *Companies That Mimic Nature: Leaders of the Corporate Renaissance* (Sheffield, UK: Greenleaf, 2016), 23.

24. James Murray, "How Unilever Integrates the SDGs into Corporate Strategy," *GreenBiz*, October 15, 2018, https://www.greenbiz.com/article/how-unilever-integrates-sdgs-corporate-strategy.

25. Marcus Fairs, "IKEA Aims to Take 200,000 People out of Poverty in Massive Social Sustainability Drive," *De Zeen*, April 18, 2017, https://www.dezeen.com/2017/04/18/ikea-massive-social-sustainability-drive-production-centres-refugee-camps-jordan.

26. Michael Holder, "IKEA Argues for Businesses to Go All-In on Sustainability," *GreenBiz*, July 7, 2016, https://www.greenbiz.com/article/ikea-argues-businesses-go-all-sustainability.

27. "#180: IKEA," *Forbes*, September 5, 2018, https://www.forbes.com/companies/ikea.

28. Statista, "IKEA's Revenue Worldwide from 2001 to 2018 (in billion euros)," 2019, https://www.statista.com/statistics/264433/annual-sales-of-ikea-worldwide.

29. Woolworths Holdings Limited, "2017 Annual Financial Statements," December 2017, https://www.woolworthsholdings.co.za/wp-content/uploads/2017/12/WHL_Annual_Financial_Statements_2017.pdf.

30. National Biodiversity and Business Network, "NBBN Partner Profile: Woolworths Holdings Limited," December 2016, https://ewt.org.za/BUSINESS DEVELOPMENT/news/Dec%202016/National%20Biodiversity%20and%20Business %20Network%20(NBBN)%20-%20December%20Newsletter.htm.

31. Woolworths Holdings Limited, "2016 Integrated Report," August 2016, p. 36, https://www.woolworthsholdings.co.za/wp-content/uploads/2017/12/WHL-Integrated-Report-2016.pdf.

32. In 2017, WSA topped the South African Customer Satisfaction Index (SAcsi) among all supermarkets. It had the highest loyalty score (77.3 versus 74.2 for the sector average), the highest perceived value (81 versus 77), and the highest likelihood of consumers recommending it to friends and family. Woolworths scored 50 percent versus the average of 32 percent.

33. Ashlee Vance, "Elon Musk, the 21st Century Industrialist," *Bloomberg*, September 14, 2014, https://www.bloomberg.com/news/articles/2012-09-13/elon-musk-the-21st-century-industrialist.

34. Christine Rowland, "Tesla, Inc's Mission Statement and Vision Statement (an Analysis)," Panmore Institute, August 29, 2018, http://panmore.com/tesla-motors-inc-vision-statement-mission-statement-analysis. See also Tesla, "About Tesla," https://www.tesla.com/about (accessed February 1, 2019).

35. Justin Bariso, "This Email From Elon Musk to Tesla Employees Is a Master Class in Emotional Intelligence," *Inc.*, https://www.inc.com/justin-bariso/elon-musk-sent-an-extraordinary-email-to-employees-and-taught-a-major-lesson-in.html (accessed December 11, 2018).

36. Certified B Corporation, "B Impact Report: Eileen Fisher," https://www.bcorporation.net/community/eileen-fisher-inc (accessed November 19, 2018).

37. Eileen Fisher, "What We Do," http://www.eileenfisher.com/social-consciousness/what-we-do (accessed November 19, 2018).

38. Eileen Fisher, "Annual Benefit Corporation Report, Fiscal Year 2017," 2018, https://www.eileenfisher.com/ns/images/company/18s_nys_benefit_hv_R11.pdf.

39. "Eileen Fisher," *Wikipedia*, October 6, 2018, https://en.wikipedia.org/wiki/Eileen_Fisher; Marc Bain, "For Eileen Fisher, a Leader in Sustainable Fashion, Perfection Isn't the Point," *Quartz*, April 22, 2016, https://qz.com/661315/for-eileen-fisher-a-leader-in-sustainable-fashion-perfection-isnt-the-point. For estimated 2018 sales, see Barry Samaha, "How Eileen Fisher's DesignWork Initiative Is Effectively Strengthening Sustainability in Fashion," *Forbes*, August 28, 2018, https://www.forbes.com/sites/barrysamaha/2018/08/28/best-sustainable-fashion-companies-eileen-fisher-designwork/#4c41637d4b67.

40. Robert Safian, "'Business as a Movement': Eileen Fisher," *Fast Company*, October 14, 2014, https://www.fastcompany.com/3036582/business-as-a-movement-eileen-fisher.

41. Laynie Rose, "Eileen Fisher Is Growing Her Business by Reducing Its Environmental Impact," *Fast Company*, November 3, 2016, https://www.fastcompany.com/3065315/eileen-fisher-is-growing-her-business-by-reducing-its-e.

42. Claire Whitcomb, "The Bumpy Path to the High Road," Eileen Fisher, http://www.eileenfisher.com/human-rights/the-bumpy-path-to-the-high-road (accessed December 11, 2018).

43. The company's commitment to social justice was never worn on its sleeve. It quietly integrated sustainability performance throughout the product life cycle, from ensuring organic and "green" sourcing of materials to its marketing and selling campaign aimed at making women feel good about themselves. An integrated part of the company's process auditing was its monitoring and engaged prevention of human trafficking and slavery in the apparel industry. The company also created opportunities for women in emerging countries to partner in harvesting and production as a part of the company's national and global commitment to helping women and girls attain business and leadership opportunities.

44. By 2016, 92 percent of Eileen Fisher's cotton was organic, as was 83 percent of its linen. The goal was to use 100 percent organic fibers for each by 2020. Hall says the company will hit those marks well ahead of schedule.

45. Certified B Corporation, "B Impact Report" (emphasis added).

46. Lauren Effron, "How Fashion Icon Eileen Fisher Brought Mindfulness into Business with Huge Success," *ABC News*, October 5, 2016, http://abcnews.go.com/Health/fashion-icon-eileen-fisher-brought-mindfulness-business-huge/story?id=42484462.

47. Allison Engel and Margaret Engel, "Eileen Fisher Wants Those Clothes Back When You're Done," *Washington Post*, August 31, 2018, https://www.washingtonpost.com/business/economy/eileen-fisher-wants-those-clothes-back-when-youre-done/2018/08/31/cd873aea-ac58-11e8-b1da-ff7faa680710_story.html.

48. Tata, "Tata Group Business Profile," https://www.tata.com/business/overview (accessed February 1, 2019); Tata, "About Us: Values and Purpose," http://www.tata.com/aboutus/articlesinside/Values-and-purpose (accessed February 1, 2019).

49. Cited in Mackey and Sisodia, *Conscious Capitalism*, 137.

50. Jamshedpur, "Out of India," *The Economist*, March 3, 2011, http://www
.economist.com/node/18285497.

51. Tata, "Tata Group Financials," http://www.tata.com/htm/Group_Investor
_GroupFinancials.htm (accessed November 19, 2018); Tata, "Welcome to the Investors'
Page," March 31, 2018, https://www.tata.com/investors.

52. "Tata Group Looks at $350 Billion Market Cap by 2025," *The Hindu*, December
6, 2015, http://www.thehindu.com/business/Industry/tata-group-eyes-usd-350-billion
-market-cap-by-2025/article7954691.ece.

53. "Tata Group Records $103 Billion Revenue in FY16: Cyrus Mistry," *NDTV Profit*,
July 30, 2016, http://profit.ndtv.com/news/corporates/article-tata-group-records-103
-billion-revenue-in-fy16-cyrus-mistry-1437925.

54. Kala Vijayraghavan and Satish John, "Use Tata Group's Leverage as Force Multi-
plier: Chandrasekaran," *Economic Times*, July 31, 2017, http://economictimes.indiatimes
.com/news/company/corporate-trends/use-tatas-group-leverage-as-force-multiplier
-chandrasekaran/articleshow/59836776.cms.

55. Sujata Agrawal, "Reaching Out to Rural India," Tata, July 2006, http://www.tata
.com/article/inside/m73PWlDIJmU%3D/TLYVr3YPkMU%3D.

56. David Wolman, "Want to Help Developing Countries? Sell Them Good Stuff—
Cheap," *Wired*, September 27, 2010, http://www.wired.com/magazine/2010/09/st_essay
_pennies.

57. Tennant, "About Tennant Company," https://www.tennantco.com/en_us/about
-us.html (accessed February 1, 2019). Research on Tennant Company in this section
draws on Chris Laszlo, Eric Aheam, Indrajeet Ghatge, and Garima Sharma, "Tennant
Company: Can 'Chemical-Free' Be a Pathway to Competitive Advantage?," *Ivey*, March
19, 2012, https://www.iveycases.com/ProductView.aspx?id=53837.

58. The ec-H2O technology platform was introduced at an industry trade show
in the fall of 2007. The technology was incorporated in a new line of floor scrubbers.
Operators had only to put water in their tank and go. The ionic activity of the con-
verted water then helped lift and break up dirt, effectively cleaning the floor's surface.
At the end of the process, the user had to dispose of what was essentially only dirty
tap water.

59. Karsten Strauss, "The World's Most Sustainable Companies, 2018," *Forbes*, January 23, 2018, https://www.forbes.com/sites/karstenstrauss/2018/01/23/the-worlds-most
-sustainable-companies-2018/#3f615f7332b0.

60. Cited in Luciana Hashiba, "Innovation in Well-Being: The Creation of Sustainable Value at Natura," *Management Innovation Exchange*, May 18, 2012, http://www
.managementexchange.com/story/innovation-in-well-being.

61. Ibid.

62. Ibid.

63. "The World's Most Innovative Companies."

64. "Equities: Natura Cosmeticos SA," *Financial Times*, https://markets.ft.com/data/
equities/tearsheet/financials?s=NATU3:SAO&mhq5j=e2 (accessed December 11, 2018).

65. Schuberg Philis, "Schuberg Philis First IT Company to Win European Anti-stress Award," https://www.schubergphilis.com/2015/04/27/schuberg-philis-first-it-company-to-win-european-anti-stress-award (accessed November 19, 2018).

66. Schuberg Philis, "Our DNA," https://schubergphilis.com/our-dna (accessed December 11, 2018).

67. Schuberg Philis, "2017 Annual Report," 2018, https://annualreport2017.schubergphilis.com/article/financial-statements.

68. "United States Steel Production [1969–2017]," *Trading Economics*, https://tradingeconomics.com/united-states/steel-production (accessed December 11, 2018).

69. Ken Iverson, *Plain Talk: Lessons from a Business Maverick* (New York: John Wiley, 1997), 5, cited in Bragdon, *Companies That Mimic Nature*, 51.

70. Ken Iverson with Tom Varian, *Plain Talk: Lessons from a Business Maverick* (New York: Wiley, 1998), 98.

71. Ross Kohan, "Nucor CEO Says Trust Is Key to Being a Great Leader," *Fortune*, October 11, 2016, http://fortune.com/video/2016/10/11/nucor-ceo-on-leadership.

72. "Spotlight: How Will One of the World's Leading Companies Work with the SDGs?," *Global Opportunity Network*, http://www.globalopportunitynetwork.org/spotlight-how-will-one-of-the-worlds-leading-companies-work-with-the-sdgs (accessed December 11, 2018).

73. Vicky Valet, "The World's Most Reputable Companies for Corporate Responsibility, 2018," *Forbes*, October 11, 2018, https://www.forbes.com/sites/vickyvalet/2018/10/11/the-worlds-most-reputable-companies-for-corporate-responsibility-2018/#435ff35d3371.

74. Lars Sorensen, president and CEO of Novo Nordisk, emphasized this goal of universal access to basic health care in a UNGC report published in 2013. Novo Nordisk, "United Nations Global Compact Communication on Progress, 2013," 2013, p. 2, https://www.unglobalcompact.org/system/attachments/62791/original/Novo-Nordisk-UNGC-2013.pdf?1391584998.

75. Aon Hewitt, *2015 Trends in Global Employee Engagement*, 2015, http://www.aon.com/attachments/human-capital-consulting/2015-Trends-in-Global-Employee-Engagement-Report.pdf.

76. Ed Silverman, "Novo Nordisk Becomes Second Major Drug Maker to Limit Price Hikes," *STAT*, December 5, 2016, https://www.statnews.com/pharmalot/2016/12/05/novo-nordisk-drug-prices.

77. A global footwear, apparel, and sports equipment company headquartered in Oregon, Nike recently refocused sales and marketing on its own brand and brand variants such as Nike+, Nike Golf, and Nike Pro. It has two key subsidiaries, Converse Inc. and Hurley International, and operates retail stores under the Niketown name. The company sponsors high-profile athletes and sports teams around the world with the trademark "Just Do It" and the Swoosh logo.

78. Kate Abnett, "Just Fix It: How Nike Learned to Embrace Sustainability," *Business of Fashion*, November 1, 2016, https://www.businessoffashion.com/articles/people/just-fix-it-hannah-jones-nike.

79. Ibid.

80. Barbara Farfan, "Nike's Mission Statement," *Balance Small Business*, October 9, 2018, https://www.thebalancesmb.com/nike-mission-statement-and-maxims-4138115.

81. For example, in 2018 the company launched a hijab for female Muslim athletes, becoming the first major sports apparel maker to offer a traditional Islamic headscarf designed specifically for competition.

82. Nike, "Nike, Inc. FY10/11 Sustainable Business Performance Summary," 2012, p. 4, https://sbi-stg-s3-media-bucket.s3.amazonaws.com/wp-content/uploads/2018/05/14214952/Nike_FY10-11_CR_report.pdf.

83. "Nike's LAUNCH Project Expands Search for Sustainable Materials Innovations," *The Guardian*, March 14, 2014, https://www.theguardian.com/sustainable-business/nike-launch-search-sustainable-materials-innovation.

84. Bart King, "Nike, Gap, Target Among Founders of Sustainable Apparel Coalition," *Sustainable Brands*, March 2, 2011, http://www.sustainablebrands.com/news_and_views/articles/nike-gap-target-among-founders-sustainable-apparel-coalition.

85. Other open-source collaboration initiatives in which Nike is a lead player include Business for Innovative Climate and Energy Policy, a revolving fund called Gamechangers aimed at building sustainable and safe places for children to play in underserved communities, the GreenXchange, and the Plant (PET) Technology Working Group.

86. Nike, "Nike, Inc. FY12–13 Sustainable Business Performance Summary," 2014, p. 4, https://sbi-stg-s3-media-bucket.s3.amazonaws.com/wp-content/uploads/2018/05/14214951/FY12-13_NIKE_Inc_CR_Report.pdf.

87. Millward Brown, "BrandZ Top 100 Most Valuable US Brands, 2019," Ranking the Brands, https://www.rankingthebrands.com/The-Brand-Rankings.aspx?rankingID=423&year=1245 (accessed February 1, 2019).

88. Corporate Knights, "Global 100 Most Sustainable Corporations 2014," *Syncforce Ranking the Brands*, 2014, https://www.rankingthebrands.com/The-Brand-Rankings.aspx?rankingID=107&year=748.

89. Westpac, "Sustainability," https://www.westpac.com.au/about-westpac/sustainability (accessed November 19, 2018).

90. David Morgan, "Speech to the Committee for Economic Development of Australia, August 21, 2000," cited in Bragdon, *Companies That Mimic Nature*, 159.

91. Ibid.

92. Ibid., 160.

93. "Deloitte Top 200: Diversity Leadership—Westpac," *NZ Herald*, November 27, 2015, http://www.nzherald.co.nz/business/news/article.cfm?c_id=3&objectid=11551715.

94. Westpac, "Ratings and Recognition," https://www.westpac.com.au/about-westpac/sustainability/news-resources-and-ratings/ratings-and-recognition (accessed February 1, 2019).

95. Money Team, "Bank of the Year 2015," *Money*, June 15, 2015, http://moneymag.com.au/bank-of-the-year-2015.

96. See Clarke, "Every Action, Every Person, Every Voice: The Clark 2009–2010 Sustainability Report," 2010, p. 2, https://www.clarke.com/filebin/PDF_Docs/Sustainability _Reports/The_Clarke_2009-2010_Sustainability_Report.pdf.

97. US EPA, "Presidential Green Chemistry Challenge: 2010 Designing Greener Chemicals Award," 2010, https://www.epa.gov/greenchemistry/presidential-green -chemistry-challenge-2010-designing-greener-chemicals-award.

98. Internal company documents provided to the authors in 2018.

99. Jennifer Keirn, "From Pesticides to Public Health," *Beyond*, June 28, 2017, https://beyond.case.edu/articles/7OgGcm5M/pesticides-to-public-health.

100. Ibid.

101. Yale Office of Career Strategy, "Greyston Bakery," https://ocs.yale.edu/career -resource/greyston-bakery (accessed February 1, 2019).

102. Ben and Jerry's, "Sweet Success: How Greyston Bakery's Good Deeds Go Beyond Baking Brownies," December 17, 2014, http://www.benjerry.com/whats-new/2014/ greyston-bakery-service.

103. Internal company documents provided to the authors.

104. REDF Workshop, "Greyston Bakery," https://redfworkshop.org/case-studies/ greyston-bakery (accessed December 11, 2018).

105. Mike Brady and Jonathan J. Halperin, "Greyston Social Enterprise: Using Inclusion to Generate Profits and Social Justice," *B the Change*, April 25, 2017, https:// bthechange.com/greyston-social-enterprise-using-inclusion-to-generate-profits-and -social-justice-6847e7ae0832.

106. Starbucks, "What Is the Role and Responsibility of a For-Profit Public Company?," https://www.starbucks.com/responsibility/global-report (accessed December 11, 2018).

107. Cited in Yale Environment 360, "Latin America Could Lose up to 90 Percent of Its Coffee-Growing Land by 2050," *E360 Digest*, September 12, 2017, https://e360.yale .edu/digest/latin-america-could-lose-up-to-90-percent-of-its-coffee-growing-land-by -2050.

108. Howard Schultz with Joanne Gordon, *Onward: How Starbucks Fought for Its Life Without Losing Its Soul* (Emmaus, PA: Rodale Books), 13.

109. Starbucks, "Our Mission," https://www.starbucks.com/about-us/company -information/mission-statement (accessed February 1, 2019).

110. Howard Behar, with Janet Goldstein, *It's Not About the Coffee: Leadership Principles from a Life at Starbucks* (New York: Portfolio, 2013), cited in Mackey and Sisodia, *Conscious Capitalism*, 227.

Chapter 5. The Quantum Leadership Model

1. As in the opening lines of Charles Dickens's widely read book by this name, "It was the best of times, it was the worst of times, it was the age of wisdom, it was the age of foolishness, it was the epoch of belief, it was the epoch of incredulity, it was the season of Light, it was the season of Darkness, it was the spring of hope, it was the winter of despair, we had everything before us, we had nothing before us, we were all going direct

to Heaven, we were all going direct the other way—in short, the period was so far like the present period, that some of its noisiest authorities insisted on its being received, for good or for evil, in the superlative degree of comparison only." Charles Dickens, *A Tale of Two Cities* (London: J. M. Dent, 1914), 5.

2. Philip Mattera, "Alpha Natural Resources: Corporate Rap Sheet," Corporate Research Project, May 28, 2017, http://www.corp-research.org/alpha-natural-resources.

3. Philip Mattera, "Anthem: Corporate Rap Sheet," Corporate Research Project, September 14, 2016, http://www.corp-research.org/anthem.

4. CHS-Sachetan, "India: Environmental Damage Caused by Western Pharmaceutical Companies," GlobalResearch, June 21, 2015, https://www.globalresearch.ca/india-environmental-damage-caused-by-western-pharmaceutical-companies/5457296.

5. Reuters in Dhaka, "Rana Plaza Collapse: 38 Charged with Murder over Garment Factory Disaster," *The Guardian*, July 18, 2016, https://www.theguardian.com/world/2016/jul/18/rana-plaza-collapse-murder-charges-garment-factory.

6. Paul Mooney, "The Story Behind China's Tainted Milk Scandal," *U.S. News*, October 9, 2008, https://www.usnews.com/news/world/articles/2008/10/09/the-story-behind-chinas-tainted-milk-scandal.

7. See the initiative's website, at http://aim2flourish.com.

8. See the company's website, at https://luckyironfish.com.

9. See the company's website, at https://bureo.co.

10. Weatherhead School of Management, "Announcing the 2017 Flourish Prizes," May 17, 2017, https://weatherhead.case.edu/news/2017/05/17/announcing-the-2017-flourish-prizes.

11. Donella H. Meadows, "Places to Intervene in a System," *Whole Earth*, Winter 1997, http://www.wholeearth.com/issue/2091/article/27/places.to.intervene.in.a.system.

12. Frederick Laloux, *Reinventing Organizations: A Guide to Creating Organizations Inspired by the Next Stage of Human Consciousness* (Brussels: Nelson Parker, 2014), 50.

13. Center for Evolutionary Learning, *The Evolutionary Leap to Flourishing Individuals and Organizations* (Abingdon, UK: Routledge, 2017).

14. See, for example, Andrew J. Hoffman, *Finding Purpose: Environmental Stewardship as a Personal Calling* (Sheffield, UK: Greenleaf, 2016).

15. See Louis W. (Jody) Fry and Eleftheria Egel, "Spiritual Leadership: Embedding Sustainability in the Triple Bottom Line," *Graziadio Business Review* 20, no. 3 (2017), https://gbr.pepperdine.edu/2017/12/spiritual-leadership.

16. Chris Laszlo, *The Sustainable Company* (Washington, DC: Island Press, 2003).

17. "The UN Global Compact–Accenture CEO Study on Sustainability, 2013: Architects of a Better World," September 2013, http://www.unglobalcompact.org/docs/news_events/8.1/UNGC_Accenture_CEO_Study_2013.pdf.

18. John P. Kotter, "Leading Change: Why Transformation Efforts Fail," *Harvard Business Review*, May–June 1995, https://hbr.org/1995/05/leading-change-why-transformation-efforts-fail-2.

19. Pacific Institute, "Fear-Based Leadership Is a Thing of the Past," April 16, 2017, http://thepacificinstitute.com/blog/2017/04/16/fear-based-leadership-is-a-thing-of-the-past.

20. John M. Collard, "Show Them the Money: A Case for Incentive-Based Management," *Smart CEO*, 2016, http://www.strategicmgtpartners.com/sceoincentives.pdf.

21. Laloux, *Reinventing Organizations*, 50.

22. Ibid. These leadership characteristics correspond to the green pluralistic meme.

23. Chris Laszlo and Nadya Zhexembayeva, *Embedded Sustainability: The Next Big Competitive Advantage* (Stanford, CA: Stanford University Press, 2011), chap. 5.

24. Sarah Jacobs, "Just Nine of the World's Richest Men Have More Combined Wealth Than the Poorest 4 Billion People," *The Independent*, January 17, 2018, https://www.independent.co.uk/news/world/richestbillionairescombinedwealthjeffbezos billgateswarrenbuffettmarkzuckerbergcarlosslimwealth-a8163621.html.

25. See also the Leading for Wellbeing website, at http://leading4wellbeing.org.

26. Gerald Jonas, "Arthur C. Clarke, Author Who Saw Science Fiction Become Real, Dies at 90," *New York Times*, March 19, 2018, https://www.nytimes.com/2008/03/19/books/19clarke.html.

27. Morris Berman, *Wandering God* (Albany, NY: SUNY, 2000), 9.

28. Barbara Dowds, "The Evolution of Human Consciousness and Spirituality," *Inside Out: Irish Association for Humanistic and Integrative Psychotherapy* 61 (2010), http://iahip.org/inside-out/issue-61-summer-2010/the-evolution-of-human-consciousness-and-spirituality.

29. Clare W. Graves, "Levels of Existence: An Open System Theory of Values," *Journal of Humanistic Psychology* 10, no. 2 (1970): 131–155; Laloux, *Reinventing Organizations*; Ervin Laszlo, *The Self-Actualizing Cosmos: The Akasha Revolution in Science* (Rochester, VT: Inner Traditions–Bear, 2014); Peter Senge, Hal Hamilton, and John Kania, "The Dawn of System Leadership," *Stanford Social Innovation Review*, Winter 2015, https://ssir.org/articles/entry/the_dawn_of_system_leadership; Ken Wilber, *The Spectrum of Consciousness* (Wheaton, IL: Quest Books, 2003).

30. The research presented in this chapter draws on the doctoral work of Joseph Leah and Maria Munoz-Grandes. With guidance from the authors, they codirected the overall research for this book. They were further assisted by Sook Yee Tai, Linkang Gong, and Gareth Craze. The researchers worked as part of the Quantum Leadership Project (QLP) and are indebted to the generous sponsorship of the Weatherhead School of Management at Case Western Reserve University (USA) and the AITIA Institute of the IMC Pan Asia Alliance (Singapore).

31. For more information on the mixed-methods approach to social science research, see Charles Teddlie and Abbas Tashakkori, *Foundations of Mixed Methods Research: Integrating Quantitative and Qualitative Approaches in the Social and Behavioral Sciences* (Thousand Oaks, CA: Sage, 2009); and John W. Creswell and Vicki L. Plano Clark, *Designing and Conducting Mixed Methods Research* (Thousand Oaks, CA: Sage, 2011).

32. The qualitative study described in this section was designed with the assistance of Joe Leah while he was a PhD student working under the supervision of Chris Laszlo. The data collection and analysis were directed by Maria Munoz-Grandes. This study is part of her doctoral thesis under the supervision of Chris Laszlo. Her research served

the QLP, for which she served as a co–research director with Joseph Leah. This type of research is designed to construct new theory from "past and present involvements and interactions with people, perspectives, and research practices." Kathy Charmaz, *Constructing Grounded Theory: A Practical Guide Through Qualitative Analysis* (Thousand Oaks, CA: Sage, 2006), 10. It is intended to help the researchers uncover and understand the meaning of lived experiences by applying a coding process to recorded interviews. The goal is to develop a theoretical understanding and to uncover new patterns aimed at adding to the existing body of knowledge on a given topic.

33. Leaders were characterized in terms of the following descriptors: (1) gender: twenty-three females, twenty-six males; (2) age range: three under thirty-five; twenty-nine between thirty-five and fifty-five; seventeen over fifty-five; (3) level of "consciousness of connectedness": thirty-six high, ten average, three low; (4) number engaged in specific "practices of connectedness": forty-two. Organizations were characterized in terms of the following descriptors: (1) annual revenue of the organization: twenty-seven under US$100 million; thirteen from US$100 million to US$1 billion; nine more than US$1 billion; (2) number of employees: thirty-one under one hundred; nine between one hundred and one thousand; nine more than one thousand; (3) industry types represented: thirty-two service, fourteen manufacturing, one retail, two other; (4) region: twenty-eight from North America, seven from Europe, four from China, three from Latin America, seven (total) from New Zealand, Australia, and Asia Pacific; (5) family businesses: seven; (6) companies with an acknowledged sense of "greater purpose": forty-two.

34. Barney Glaser and Anselm L. Strauss, *The Discovery of Grounded Theory: Strategies for Qualitative Research* (Berlin: Aldine de Gruyter, 1967). "Grounded Theory is an inductive methodology. It is a general method. It is the systematic generation of theory from systematic research. It is a set of rigorous research procedures leading to the emergence of conceptual categories." Grounded Theory Institute, "What Is Grounded Theory?" http://www.groundedtheory.com/what-is-gt.aspx (accessed November 20, 2018).

35. Charmaz, *Constructing Grounded Theory*; Johnny Saldana, *The Coding Manual for Qualitative Researchers* (Thousand Oaks, CA: Sage, 2012).

36. United States National Commission for the Protection of Human Subjects of Biomedical and Behavioral Research, "The Belmont Report," April 18, 1979, https://www.hhs.gov/ohrp/regulations-and-policy/belmont-report/index.html.

37. The quantitative study described in this section was conducted by Joseph Leah as part of his doctoral thesis, which he successfully defended in May 2017 at Case Western Reserve University's Weatherhead School of Management. The underlying research served the QLP, for which he served as a co–research director. The respondent mix included a gender breakdown of 171 males and 151 females; an organizational-level breakdown of 91 owners/C-level executives, 110 directors/division-level managers, and 121 middle managers; and an age-range breakdown of 46 Baby Boomers (over fifty-five), 141 Generation X members (thirty-six to fifty-five), and 135 Millennials (under thirty-five).

38. Joseph S. Leah, "Positive Impact: Factors Driving Business Leaders Toward Shared Prosperity, Greater Purpose and Human Wellbeing," PhD diss., Case Western Reserve University, 2017, p. 35.

39. Robert G. Eccles, Ioannis Ioannou, and George Serafeim, "The Impact of Corporate Sustainability on Organizational Processes and Performance," *Management Science* 60, no. 11: 2835–2857; Rajendra Sisodia, Jagdish Sheth, and David Wolfe, *Firms of Endearment: How World-Class Companies Profit from Passion and Purpose*, 2nd ed. (Upper Saddle River, NJ: Pearson Education, 2014).

40. William B. Swann, Jolanda Jetten, Angel Gómez, Harvey Whitehouse, and Brock Bastian, "When Group Membership Gets Personal: A Theory of Identity Fusion," *Psychological Review* 119, no. 3 (2012): 441–456; F. Stephan Mayer and Cynthia M. Frantz, "The Connectedness to Nature Scale: A Measure of Individuals' Feeling in Community with Nature," *Journal of Environmental Psychology* 24, no. 4 (2004): 503–515.

41. Ante Glavas and Ken Kelley, "The Effects of Perceived Corporate Social Responsibility on Employee Attitudes," *Business Ethics Quarterly* 24 (2014): 165–202.

42. Richard E. Boyatzis, Kylie Rochford, and Scott N. Taylor, "The Role of the Positive Emotional Attractor in Vision and Shared Vision: Toward Effective Leadership, Relationships, and Engagement," *Frontiers in Psychology*, May 21, 2015, http://journal.frontiersin.org/article/10.3389/fpsyg.2015.00670/abstract.

43. Ibid.

44. We can speculate about possible explanations for this. It may be that people in high-compassion organizations care more about people than profit, and, conversely, those reporting lower compassion were from companies where compassion is deemphasized and the emphasis is on economic performance. Indeed, this could be a reflection of an "Amazon" type of high-performance corporate culture, as reported in the *New York Times*, with little time for the niceties of human relationships in the workplace. Leah, "Positive Impact." See also Jodi Kantor and David Streitfeld, "Inside Amazon: Wrestling Big Ideas in a Bruising Workplace," *New York Times*, August 15, 2015, https://www.nytimes.com/2015/08/16/technology/inside-amazon-wrestling-big-ideas-in-a-bruising-workplace.html.

45. See, for example, Michael Pirson, *Humanistic Management: Protecting Dignity and Promoting Well-Being* (Cambridge: Cambridge University Press, 2017).

46. Damian Carrington, "Earth's Sixth Mass Extinction Event Under Way, Scientists Warn," *The Guardian*, July 10, 2017, https://www.theguardian.com/environment/2017/jul/10/earths-sixth-mass-extinction-event-already-underway-scientists-warn.

Chapter 6. The Science of Connectedness

1. Bum-Jin Park, Yuko Tsunetsugu, Tamami Kasetani, Takahide Kagawa, and Yoshifumi Miyazaki, "The Physiological Effects of Shinrin-yoku (Taking in the Forest Atmosphere or Forest Bathing): Evidence from Field Experiments in 24 Forests Across Japan," *Environmental Health and Preventive Medicine* 15, no. 1 (2010): 18–26. Evidence also exists to support the finding that there is ionic exchange between the body and the ground (literally, grounding) if the forest bathing is done barefoot on the earth (grass or dirt). This technique is known as "earthing" and is a specific form of forest bathing. See Earthing, "What Is Earthing?," https://www.earthing.com/what-is-earthing (accessed November 20, 2018).

2. Gregory N. Bratman, J. Paul Hamilton, Kevin S. Hahn, Gretchen C. Daily, and James J. Gross, "Nature Experience Reduces Rumination and Subgenual Prefrontal Cortex Activation," *Proceedings of the National Academy of Sciences of the United States of America* 112, no. 8 (2017): 8567–8572.

3. Nancy J. Adler, "Finding Beauty in a Fractured World: Art Inspires Leaders—Leaders Change the World," *Academy of Management Review* 40, no. 3 (2015): 480–494.

4. Edgar Schein, "The Role of Art and the Artist," *Organizational Aesthetics* 2 (2013): 1.

5. Adler, "Finding Beauty," 482.

6. All-Party Parliamentary Group on Arts, Health and Wellbeing, "Creative Health: The Arts for Health and Wellbeing," 2nd ed., July 2017, http://www.artshealth andwellbeing.org.uk/appg-inquiry/Publications/Creative_Health_Inquiry_Report_ 2017_-_Second_Edition.pdf.

7. ChoirPlace, "Helene Stureborgs kammarkör," August 5, 2107, https://www .choirplace.com/choirs/1631/helene-stureborgs-kammark-r.

8. John David White, *New Music of the Nordic Countries* (Hillsdale, NY: Pendragon Press, 2002), 560.

9. Berkeley Wellness, "Singing Is Good Medicine," December 18, 2015, http://www .berkeleywellness.com/healthy-mind/stress/article/singing-good-medicine.

10. Mary L. Gick and Jennifer J. Nicol, "Singing for Respiratory Health: Theory, Evidence and Challenges," *Health Promotion International* 31, no. 3 (2016), https://www .ncbi.nlm.nih.gov/pubmed/25784304; Katsuhisa Sakano, Koufuchi Ryo, Yoh Tamaki, Ryoko Nakayama, Ayaka Hasaka, Ayako Takahashi, Shukuko Ebihara, Keisuke Tozuka, and Ichiro Saito, "Possible Benefits of Singing to the Mental and Physical Condition of the Elderly," *Biopsychosocial Medicine* 8 (2014): 11; Sara E. Osman, Victoria Tischler, and Justine Schneider, "'Singing for the Brain': A Qualitative Study Exploring the Health and Well-Being Benefits of Singing for People with Dementia and Their Carers," *Dementia* (London) 15, no. 6 (2016): 1326–1339.

11. See Anthony Kales, Chester M. Pierce, and Milton Greenblatt, eds., *The Mosaic of Contemporary Psychiatry in Perspective* (New York: Springer-Verlag, 1992), 10. According to this source, there are no police and no jails among the Rarámuri communities. See also Christopher McDougall, *Born to Run: A Hidden Tribe, Superathletes, and the Greatest Race the World Has Never Seen* (New York: Knopf, 2009).

12. Rod S. Taylor, Allan Brown, Shah Ebrahim, Judith Jolliffe, Hussein Noorani, Karen Rees, Becky Skidmore, James A. Stone, David R. Thompson, and Neil Oldridge, "Exercise-Based Rehabilitation for Patients with Coronary Heart Disease: Systematic Review and Meta-analysis of Randomized Controlled Trials," *American Journal of Medicine* 116 (2004): 682–692. This widely cited meta-analysis involving almost nine thousand patients found that cardiac rehabilitation exercise was positively correlated with reduced all-cause mortality and improvements in health-related quality of life.

13. James W. Pennebaker and Martha E. Francis, "Cognitive, Emotional, and Language Processes in Disclosure," *Cognition and Emotion* 10 (1996): 601–626; Lynda J. Dimitroff, Linda Sliwoski, Sue O'Brien, and Lynn W. Nichols, "Change Your Life

Through Journaling: The Benefits of Journaling for Registered Nurses," *Journal of Nursing Education and Practice* 7, no. 2 (2017): 90–98; Michael Grothaus, "Why Journaling Is Good for Your Health (and 8 Tips to Get Better)," *Fast Company*, January 29, 2015, https://www.fastcompany.com/3041487/8-tips-to-more-effective-journaling-for-health.

14. Emma Seppälä, "A Gift of Loving Kindness Meditation," May 28, 2014, https://emmaseppala.com/gift-loving-kindness-meditation. A study by James A. Raub concludes, "Over the last 10 years, a growing number of research studies have shown that the practice of Hatha Yoga can improve strength and flexibility, and may help control such physiological variables as blood pressure, respiration and heart rate, and metabolic rate to improve overall exercise capacity." See James A. Raub, "Psychophysiologic Effects of Hatha Yoga on Musculoskeletal and Cardiopulmonary Function: A Literature Review," *Journal of Alternative and Complementary Medicine* 8, no. 6 (2002): 797–812. See also UHN Staff, "The Health Benefits of Red Wine: Scientific Evidence Is Compelling," *UHN Daily*, June 6, 2017, https://universityhealthnews.com/daily/nutrition/the-health-benefits-of-red-wine-scientific-evidence-is-compelling.

15. Hans Hansen and Erika Sauer, "Aesthetic Leadership," *Leadership Quarterly* 18 (2007): 544–560.

16. See Barbara L. Fredrickson, "Positive Emotions Trigger Upward Spirals Toward Emotional Wellbeing," *Psychological Science* 13, no. 2 (2002): 172–175; see also Barbara L. Fredrickson and Thomas Joiner, "Reflections on Positive Emotions and Upward Spirals," *Perspectives on Psychological Science* 13, no. 2 (2018): 194–199.

17. Cendri A. Hutcherson, Emma M. Seppälä, and James J. Gross, "Loving-Kindness Meditation Increases Social Connectedness," *Emotion* 8, no. 5 (2008): 720.

18. Mihaly Csikszentmihalyi, *Flow: The Psychology of Optimal Experience* (New York: Harper and Row, 1990).

19. Scott Barry Kaufman, "The Creative 'Flow': How to Enter That Mysterious State of Oneness," *Huffington Post*, November 26, 2012. https://www.huffingtonpost.com/scott-barry-kaufman/consciousness-and-flow_b_1108113.html.

20. Richard E. Boyatzis, Kylie Rochford, and Anthony I. Jack, "Antagonistic Neural Networks Underlying Differentiated Leadership Roles," *Frontiers in Human Neuroscience* 8, no. 114 (2014): 1–15.

21. Anthony Jack (associate professor and principal investigator, Brain, Mind and Consciousness Laboratory, Case Western Reserve University), personal communication, June 5, 2018.

22. Richard E. Boyatzis, Kylie Rochford, and Scott N. Taylor, "The Role of the Positive Emotional Attractor in Vision and Shared Vision: Toward Effective Leadership, Relationships, and Engagement," *Frontiers in Human Neuroscience* 6, no. 670 (2015): 1–13.

23. Matthieu Ricard, Antoine Lutz, and Richard J. Davidson, "The Mind of the Meditator," *Scientific American*, November 2014, pp. 39–45. Three forms of meditation (focused attention, open monitoring, and loving kindness) are shown to rewire brain circuits. Mindfulness-type practices physically change the brain (a consequence of neuroplasticity) with activation/deactivation of brain areas associated with reduced anxiety and stress. The authors conclude, "These studies are now starting to demonstrate that

contemplative practices may have a substantive impact on biological processes critical for physical health" (45).

24. Center for Evolutionary Learning, *The Evolutionary Leap to Flourishing Individuals and Organizations* (Abingdon, UK: Routledge, 2017).

25. Richard E. Boyatzis, Melvin L. Smith, and Nancy Blaize, "Developing Sustainable Leaders Through Coaching and Compassion," *Academy of Management Learning and Education* 5, no. 1 (2006): 8–24.

26. Fred Travis, Joe Tecce, Alarik Arenander, and R. Keith Wallace, "Patterns of EEG Coherence, Power, and Contingent Negative Variation Characterize the Integration of Transcendental and Waking States," *Biological Psychology* 61 (2002): 293–319.

27. Studies conducted by radiologist Andrew Newberg and physician Eugene D'Aquila found that these bundles of neurons in the posterior superior parietal lobe went dark during deep meditative or prayer states. Cited in Elizabeth Lloyd Mayer, *Extraordinary Knowing: Science, Skepticism, and the Inexplicable Powers of the Human Mind* (New York: Bantam Dell, 2007), 64–65.

28. Barbara Fredrickson, Michael A. Cohn, Kimberly A. Coffey, Jolynn Pek, and Sandra M. Finkel, "Open Hearts Build Lives: Positive Emotions, Induced Through Loving-Kindness Meditation, Build Consequential Personal Resources," *Journal of Personality and Social Psychology* 95 (2008): 1045–1062. The path from positive emotions to life satisfaction has been well documented. Compared to negative "fight-or-flight" emotions that narrow our attention for survival purpose, positive emotions broaden people's attention, enabling them to make higher-level connections between different ideas—a key to creativity—and to hold a greater diversity of perspectives at any given moment. In turn, this broadened outlook helps people build what Fredrickson calls consequential personal resources, such as the ability to give and receive emotional support and to maintain a sense of mastery over life's challenges. "Put simply," says Frederickson, "the broaden and build theory states that positive emotions widen people's outlooks in ways that, little by little, reshape who they are" (1045).

29. Ibid., 1054.

30. Florence Williams, *The Nature Fix: Why Nature Makes Us Happier, Healthier, and More Creative* (New York: W. W. Norton, 2017).

31. Paul Sparks, Joe Hinds, Susan Curnock, and Louisa Pavey, "Connectedness and Its Consequences: A Study of Relationships with the Natural Environment," *Journal of Applied Social Psychology* 44 (2014): 166–174. One meta-analysis of twenty-one studies with thirty nonoverlapping samples on this topic found that people who were more connected to nature experienced more positive affect, vitality, and life satisfaction than those less connected to nature. See Colin A. Capaldi, Raelyne L. Dopko, and John M. Zelenski, "The Relationship Between Nature Connectedness and Happiness: A Meta-analysis," *Frontiers in Psychology* 5, no. 976 (2014): 9.

32. See, for example, Bill McKibben, *The End of Nature* (London: Bloomsbury, 2003).

33. Richard Louv, *Last Child in the Woods: Saving Our Children from Nature-Deficit Disorder* (New York: Algonquin Books, 2008).

34. Leadership education in MBA and executive training programs has tended to focus on cognitive, technical, and emotional skills. While also valuing such skills, quantum leadership emphasizes the journey of self-cultivation through practices that elevate our consciousness. The practices change who leaders are *being* through affective experience rather than only through the task-oriented logic traditionally expected of business leaders. Cultivating the self helps these leaders go beyond the analytic reasoning for clean energy and zero waste, for example, or the cognitive arguments for treating employees ethically. The result is that quantum leaders are more likely to do the right thing because *that is who they are*, not only because they have been persuaded by data-driven analysis and moral instruction.

35. Fritjof Capra, *The Web of Life: A New Synthesis of Mind and Matter* (New York: Anchor Books, 1976); David Bohm, *Wholeness and the Implicate Order* (Boston: Routledge and Kegan Paul, 1980); Ken Wilber, *Quantum Questions: Mystical Writings of the World's Greatest Physicists* (Boston: Shambhala, 1984); Ervin Laszlo, *Evolution: The Grand Synthesis* (Boston: Shambhala, 1987); Margaret Wheatley, *Leadership and the New Science: Discovering Order in a Chaotic World* (San Francisco: Berrett-Koehler, 1992); Dana Zohar, *The Quantum Self: Human Nature and Consciousness Defined by the New Physics* (New York: Morrow, 1990).

36. Geoffrey Stephen Kirk, John Earle Raven, and Malcolm Schofield, *The Presocratic Philosophers: A Critical History with a Selection of Texts* (Cambridge: Cambridge University Press, 1983).

37. Presencing Institute, "Entering the Seven Meditative Spaces of Leadership: Interview with Nan Huai-Chin," October 25, 1999, https://www.presencing.org/#/aboutus/theory-u/leadership-interview/nan-huai-chin.

38. Ming-Jer Chen, "Transcending Paradox: The Chinese 'Middle Way' Perspective," *Asia Pacific Journal of Management* 19, no. 2–3 (2002): 179–199. One of the Four Books of Confucianism is the *Zhongyong*, meaning "the Middle Way," written by Zisi Tsu during the life of Confucius's grandson. Many elements of the Middle Way philosophy were originally taken from Buddhism.

39. See the research presented in Chapter 5.

40. Brett Topche (managing director, MentorTech Ventures), quoted in Calm Clarity, "Calm Clarity November Workshop at Villanova University," 2018, https://calmclarity.ticketleap.com/nov2018retreatatnova/details.

41. Ervin Laszlo, *The Self-Actualizing Cosmos: The Akasha Revolution in Science and Human Consciousness* (Rochester, VT: Inner Traditions, 2014). Much of the material on the new sciences is from the work of this author and is found in a dozen different books on the topic published over three decades.

42. See Robert Epstein, "The Empty Brain," *Aeon*, May 18, 2016, https://aeon.co/essays/your-brain-does-not-process-information-and-it-is-not-a-computer.

43. Allan Combs, *Consciousness Explained Better: Towards an Integral Understanding of the Multifaceted Nature of Consciousness* (St. Paul, MN: Paragon House, 2009).

44. William Stanley Jevons, a nineteenth-century pioneer of neoclassical economics, used mathematics previously reserved for the hard sciences to articulate concepts

such as marginalism and utility theory. He wrote, "My theory of Economics . . . consists in applying differential calculus to the familiar notions of wealth, utility, value, demand, supply, capital, interest, labour, and all the other quantitative notions belonging to the daily operations of industry." See William S. Jevons, *The Theory of Political Economy*, 3rd ed. (London: Macmillan, 1888), https://oll.libertyfund.org/titles/jevons-the-theory -of-political-economy/simple.

45. Kim S. Cameron, Jane E. Dutton, and Robert E. Quinn, eds., *Positive Organizational Scholarship: Foundations of a New Discipline* (San Francisco: Berrett-Koehler, 2003), 3, 14–27.

46. Since at least the publication of *Principles of Psychology* by William James in 1890, the emphasis has largely been on the analysis of disease, disorder, and distress rather than on human goodness and excellence.

47. Christopher M. Peterson and Martin E. Seligman, "Positive Organizational Studies: Lessons from Positive Psychology," in Cameron, Dutton, and Quinn, *Positive Organizational Scholarship*, 15.

48. Richard J. Estes and Joseph Sirgy, *The Pursuit of Human Well-Being: The Untold Global History* (New York: Springer, 2017).

49. Physicists have variously referred to this energy and information field that underlies reality as we know it as the quantum vacuum, the zero-point field, grand-unified field, cosmic plenum, string-net liquid, or "nuether."

50. Yang-Mills fields, also called gauge fields, are used in modern physics to describe physical fields that play the role of carriers of an interaction, such as the electromagnetic field in electrodynamics, the field of vector bosons (carriers of the weak interaction in the Weinberg-Salam theory of electrically weak interactions), the gluon field (the carrier of the strong interaction), and the gravitational field. See "Yang-Mills Field," *Encyclopedia of Mathematics*, March 24, 2012, https://www.encyclopediaofmath .org/index.php/Yang-Mills_field.

51. The Nobel Prize–winning physicist Max Planck was an early pioneer of this view. In one of his last lectures in Florence, he noted, "As a man who has devoted his whole life to the most clear-headed science, to the study of matter, I can tell you as a result of my research about atoms this much: There is no matter as such. All matter originates and exists only by virtue of a force which brings the particles of an atom to vibration and holds this most minute solar system of the atom together." Planck was not alone in stating the concept of the universe as forces and vibrations. Two years prior to Planck's pronouncement, Nikola Tesla is thought to have said that if you want to know the secrets of the universe, you should think in terms of energy, frequency, and vibration. Max Planck, "Das Wesen der Materie" [The nature of matter], speech given in Florence, Italy, 1944, Abt. Va, Rep. 11 Planck, Nr. 1797, Archiv der Max-Planck-Gesellschaft, Berlin.

52. As discussed later in the chapter, physicists now speculate that the quantum field interacts with the material and mental world as we know it. It shapes and guides the evolution of mind and matter by giving them properties of wholeness and coherence. The universal field does not have what are called vectorial forms of energy, mean-

ing that there is no measurable energy amplitude; instead, it is composed of scalar waves that have effects that do not diminish with distance and time, accounting for nonlocal interactions. We explore the nature of the interaction and its effect on human beings later in this chapter.

53. The nonlocal effect occurs when a pair of particles are connected in such a way that a measurement of one particle appears to affect the state of another particle, no matter how distant. Hundreds of experiments have confirmed that this is a very real characteristic of our universe. See Dan Falk, "New Support for Alternative Quantum View," *Quanta Magazine*, May 16, 2016, https://www.quantamagazine.org/pilot-wave -theory-gains-experimental-support-20160516.

54. Bohm, *Wholeness and the Implicate Order*.

55. Karl Pribram, *Languages of the Brain* (North Hollywood, CA: Brandon House, 1971); Karl Pribram, *Brain and Perception: Holonomy and Structure in Figural Processing* (Mahwah, NJ: Lawrence Erlbaum, 1991).

56. "Through morphic resonance, the patterns of activity in self-organizing sys-tems are influenced by similar patterns in the past, giving each species and each kind of self-organizing system a collective memory." Rupert Sheldrake, "Morphic Resonance and Morphic Fields: An Introduction," https://www.sheldrake.org/research/morphic -resonance/introduction (accessed November 20, 2018).

57. Ilya Prigogine, "Time, Structure and Fluctuations," Nobel Lecture, December 8, 1977, https://www.nobelprize.org/uploads/2018/06/prigogine-lecture.pdf.

58. David Tong, "What Is Quantum Field Theory?," http://www.damtp.cam.ac.uk/ user/tong/whatisqft.html (accessed November 20, 2018).

59. Combs, *Consciousness Explained Better*.

60. Gary Marcus, "The Riddle of Consciousness," *New Yorker*, May 28, 2013, https:// www.newyorker.com/tech/annals-of-technology/the-riddle-of-consciousness; Joshua Rothman, "Daniel Dennett's Science of the Soul," *New Yorker*, March 27, 2017, https:// www.newyorker.com/magazine/2017/03/27/daniel-dennetts-science-of-the-soul; "What Is Consciousness?," *The Economist*, March 2, 2017, http://www.economist.com/news/ international/21717973-what-consciousness.

61. See David J. Chalmers, "Consciousness and Its Place in Nature," http://consc .net/papers/nature.pdf (accessed December 14, 2018).

62. See Stuart Hameroff and Roger Penrose, "Consciousness in the Universe: A Re-view of the Orch OR Theory," *Physics of Life Reviews* 11, no. 1 (2014): 39–78.

63. See, for example, Hameroff and Penrose, "Consciousness in the Universe."

64. The universe is not coextensive with the cosmos. In Bohmian terms, the former is the explicate order while the latter is both the implicate and the explicate order. All that can be deduced (through scientific method) but neither measured nor observed directly pertains to those dimensions beyond the physical universe. The universe is the manifest component of the cosmos, and consciousness is the "in-forming" component. The latter is most closely expressed in science as the zero-point energy field, the quantum vacuum, the field of quantum potential, or the plenum. Since it is not amenable to the five senses or any of the technologies by which they are extended, it lies outside the domain of tradi-

tional science. But new paradigm science extends this domain to include the perceptual field and ways of knowing (that can be replicated, independently verified, and are open to being disproved). Consciousness cannot be seen, touched, isolated or contained, yet it is generally recognized as a legitimate phenomenon amenable to scientific study (especially in the now popular, though still largely reductionistic, area of neurobehavioral science).

65. Ede Frecska and Luis Eduardo Luna, "Neuro-ontological Interpretation of Spiritual Experiences," *Official Journal of the Hungarian Association of Psychopharmacology* 8, no. 3 (2006): 143–153.

66. For example, Henri Bergson postulated an élan vital that could explain the countertrend to the degradation of energy in physical systems, and biologist Hans Driesch called for a counterentropic drive in nature he termed "entelechy." Teilhard de Chardin spoke about syntony as a uniting force behind the evolution of complex organisms, a construct that the systems scientist Alexander Laszlo developed as a praxis in evolutionary learning communities where people "engage in lifelong learning and human development in partnership with Earth." See Alexander Laszlo, "Evolutionary Systems Design: A Praxis for Sustainable Development," *Organisational Transformation and Social Change* 1, no. 1 (2004): 29.

67. Douglas H. Boucher, *The Biology of Mutualism: Ecology and Evolution* (New York: Oxford University Press, 1988).

68. See Richard Dawkins, *The Selfish Gene* (Oxford: Oxford University Press, 1989).

69. Humberto Maturano Romesin and Gerda Verden-Zoller, "Biology of Love," http://members.ozemail.com.au/~jcull/articles/bol.htm (accessed December 14, 2018).

70. See Philip Ball, "Physics of Life: The Dawn of Quantum Biology," *Nature* 474 (2011): 272–274.

71. Johnjoe McFadden and Jim Al-Khalili, *Life on the Edge: The Coming of Age of Quantum Biology* (London: Bantam Press, 2014).

72. Bernardo Kastrup, Henry P. Stapp, and Menas C. Kafatos, "Coming to Grips with the Implications of Quantum Mechanics," *Scientific American*, May 29, 2018, https://blogs.scientificamerican.com/observations/coming-to-grips-with-the-implications-of-quantum-mechanics.

73. E. Laszlo, *The Self-Actualizing Cosmos*.

74. Quoted in Hernán A. Burbano, "Epigenetics and Genetic Determinism," *História Ciências Saúde-Manguinhos* (Rio de Janeiro) 13, no. 4 (2006): 851–863.

75. David L. Cooperrider and Ronald E. Fry, "Mirror Flourishing and the Positive Psychology of Sustainability," *Journal of Corporate Citizenship* 46 (Summer 2012): 3–12.

76. "First Direct Recording Made of Mirror Neurons in Human Brain," *Science Daily*, April 13, 2010, https://www.sciencedaily.com/releases/2010/04/100412162112.htm.

77. William Duncan Hutchinson, Karen D. Davis, Andres M. Lozano, Ron R. Tasker, and Jonathan O. Dostrovsky, "Pain-Related Neurons in the Human Cingulated Cortex," *Nature Neuroscience* 2, no. 5 (1999): 403–405.

78. Sourya Acharya and Samarth Shukla, "Mirror Neurons: Enigma of the Metaphysical Modular Brain," *Journal of Natural Science, Biology and Medicine* 3, no. 2 (2012): 118–124.

79. Cited in Kathryn Pavlovich and Keiko Krahnke, "Empathy, Connectedness, and Organization," *Journal of Business Ethics* 105 (2012): 133.

80. Ibid.

81. Chris Laszlo, Robert Sroufe, and Sandra Waddock, "Torn Between Two Paradigms: A Struggle for the Soul of Business Schools," *AI Practitioner* 19, no. 2 (2017): 108–119.

82. This comes from an early draft of a white paper by the group Leading for Wellbeing, cited in ibid., 110.

83. Richard Thaler and Cass Sunstein, *Nudge: Improving Decisions About Health, Wealth, and Happiness* (London: Penguin Books, 2009); Amit Goswami, *Quantum Economics: Unleashing the Power of an Economics of Consciousness* (Faber, VA: Rainbow Ridge, 2015).

84. Kate Raworth, "What on Earth Is the Doughnut? . . . ," https://www.kateraworth.com/doughnut (accessed December 14, 2018).

85. George Monbiot, "Finally, a Breakthrough Alternative to Growth Economics—the Doughnut," *The Guardian*, April 12, 2017, https://www.theguardian.com/commentisfree/2017/apr/12/doughnut-growth-economics-book-economic-model.

86. Ibid.

87. See Kim S. Cameron, Jane E. Dutton, and R. E. Quinn, "An Introduction to Positive Organizational Scholarship," in Cameron, Dutton, and Quinn, *Positive Organizational Scholarship*, 3–13.

88. Carl Rogers (client centered), Abraham Maslow (self-actualization), and Kurt Lewin (sensitivity training) were all pioneers in applied research and practices aimed at unleashing the human potential.

89. See book 2 of Aristotle's *Nicomachean Ethics*. Aristotle's notion of "potency" (becoming) was presented as the counterpoint of "act" (being). Reality was composed of a potential that influenced the change and dynamism of being. Human beings were seen as occupying a natural place in a cosmos that was alive with the potential for the full development of being.

90. Cameron, Dutton, and Quinn, *Positive Organizational Scholarship*, 5, 10.

91. David L. Cooperrider and Suresh Srivastva, "Appreciative Inquiry in Organizational Life," in *Research in Organizational Change and Development*, ed. William A. Pasmore and Richard W. Woodman (Greenwich, CT: JAI Press, 1987), 129–169.

92. David Cooperrider, "Positive Image, Positive Action: The Affirmative Basis of Organizing," in *Appreciative Inquiry: An Emerging Direction for Organization Development*, ed. David Cooperrider, Peter F. Sorensen Jr., Therese F. Yaeger, and Diana Whitney (Champaign, IL: Stipes, 2001), 31–76.

93. Pavlovich and Krahnke, "Empathy, Connectedness, and Organization," 131.

94. "Entanglement occurs when two particles are so deeply linked that they share the same existence. . . . Entangled particles can become widely separated in space. But even so, the mathematics implies that a measurement on one immediately influences the other, regardless of the distance between them. . . . CERN physicist John Bell resolved [the paradox] by thinking of entanglement as an entirely new kind of phenomenon,

which he termed 'nonlocal.'" "Einstein's 'Spooky Action at a Distance' Paradox Older Than Thought," *MIT Technology Review*, March 8, 2012, https://www.technologyreview .com/s/427174/einsteins-spooky-action-at-a-distance-paradox-older-than-thought.

95. For a good overview of the field of epigenetics, see Carrie Deans and Keith A. Maggert, "What Do You Mean, 'Epigenetic'?," *Genetics* 199, no. 4 (2015): 887–896.

96. Dean Radin, *Supernormal: Science, Yoga, and the Evidence for Extraordinary Psychic Abilities* (New York: Deepak Chopra Books, 2013); Elizabeth L. Mayer, *Extraordinary Knowing: Science, Skepticism, and the Inexplicable Powers of the Human Mind* (New York: Bantam Dell, 2007).

97. Bruce Lipton, *The Biology of Belief: Unleashing the Power of Consciousness, Matter, and Miracles*, rev. ed. (Carlsbad, CA: Hay House, 2007). Bruce Lipton is an American developmental biologist whose ideas are still on the margins of mainstream science. His research presaged the field of epigenetics and aims to show that all the cells of your body are affected by your thoughts, merging leading-edge science with mind-body medicine and spiritual principles. Lipton's work has been attacked as insufficiently evidence based. However, many other scientists have reached similar conclusions, including Dr. Candace Pert, who wrote "Molecules of Emotion: The Science Behind Mind-Body Medicine" (1999); Dr. Gerald Epstein, who researches how the mind can heal the body through the use of what he called imaginal medicine; Dr. Daniel J. Siegel, who wrote "The Power of Emotion" and a book on the science and practice of presence (2018); Dr. Norman Doidge, who approaches biology of belief from a neuroplasticity perspective; and Dr. Andrew Newberg, who studies the relationship between spiritual experiences and human health and psychological well-being.

98. Radin, *Supernormal*.

99. The argument here is that the evolution of species cannot be explained by Darwin's theory, in which chance mutations lead to the kind of finely balanced complexity we observe today. According to mathematical physicist Fred Hoyle, the probability of a viable species emerging from random mutations in the genome is about the same as that of a tornado blowing through a scrapyard and assembling a working airplane. See the discussion of Hoyle's claim in Lawrence Auster, "The 'Tornado in a Junk Yard' Analogy Is Correct After All," *View from the Right*, January 31, 2009, http://www.amnation.com/ vfr/archives/012411.html. This view becomes even more compelling in light of Harvard biologist Stephen Jay Gould's work on "punctuated equilibrium," which shows that new species evolve much faster than previously thought. See Stephen Jay Gould, *Punctuated Equilibrium* (Cambridge, MA: Harvard University Press, 2007).

100. "Roadmap: A Movement of Movements by Michael Nagler," *New Story Hub*, December 4, 2014, http://newstoryhub.com/2014/12/roadmap-a-movement-of -movements-by-michael-nagler.

101. To experience the possibility of increased coherence and connectedness, we must accept the possibility of their opposite—in other words, fragmentation and destruction. Both possibilities are part of the same reality—not distinct events but two faces of the same coin. Consider our sensations of love and hate. When we experience a feeling of pure unconditional love, we are taking our feelings to one extreme, which

implies the potential existence of its opposite (hate). For any field of energy to be constructive—that is, moving toward wholeness and life—the possibility of fragmentation and death must also exist. Both are part of the same field or system of reality.

102. Pavlovich and Krahnke, "Empathy, Connectedness, and Organization," 135.

103. See, for example, Ian I. Mitroff and Elizabeth A. Denton, "A Study of Spirituality in the Workplace," *Sloan Management Review*, Summer 1999, https://sloanreview.mit .edu/article/a-study-of-spirituality-in-the-workplace; Louis W. Fry, "Toward a Theory of Spiritual Leadership," *Leadership Quarterly* 14, no. 6 (2003): 693–727; and Louis Fry and Eleftheria Egel, "Spiritual Leadership: Embedding Sustainability in the Triple Bottom Line," *Graziadio Business Report* 20, no. 3 (2017), https://www.researchgate.net/publication/322150882_Spiritual_Leadership_Embedding_sustainability_in_the_triple _bottom_line.

104. Bohm, *Wholeness and the Implicate Order*; Pribram, *Languages of the Brain*; Pribram, *Brain and Perception*.

105. Ervin Laszlo, *What Is Reality? The New Map of Cosmos, Consciousness, and Existence* (New York: SelectBooks, 2016).

106. Pavlovich and Krahnke, "Empathy, Connectedness, and Organization," 135–136.

107. In-formation—also called "active information"—was first advanced by quantum physicist David Bohm to account for the formative effect of the "implicate order" on the observable "explicate order," Bohm's ontological concepts that help us comprehend quantum reality: the implicate order is a deeper and more fundamental order of reality; the explicate order includes the abstractions that humans normally perceive, such as time and space. See Bohm, *Wholeness and the Implicate Order*.

108. Mayer, *Extraordinary Knowing*, 66.

109. Freeman Dyson, *The Scientist as Rebel* (New York: New York Review of Books, 2006).

110. This is a thought experiment intended to demonstrate that the wave function does not provide a complete description of physical reality.

111. See, for example, Chad Orzel, "Three Experiments That Show Quantum Physics Is Real," *Forbes*, July 20, 2015, https://www.forbes.com/sites/chadorzel/2015/07/20/three -experiments-that-show-quantum-physics-is-real/#3663469a1ae5.

112. Cited in Mayer, *Extraordinary Knowing*, 256.

113. In the Vedas its function was identified with *shabda*, the first vibration, the first ripple that constitutes the universe, and also with *spanda*, the "vibration/movement of consciousness." The Indian scholar I. K. Taimni wrote, "There is . . . a mysterious integrated state of vibration from which all possible kinds of vibrations can be derived by a process of differentiation. That is called *Nāda* in Sanskrit. It is a vibration in a medium . . . which may be translated as 'space' in English. But . . . it is not mere empty space but space which, though apparently empty, contains within itself an infinite amount of potential energy." I. K. Taimni, *Man, God and the Universe* (Madras: Theosophical Society, 1969), 203.

114. Khoo Boo Eng, *A Simple Approach to Taoism: Festivals, Worship and Rituals* (Singapore: Trafford, 2012), 49–50.

115. Scott Ramsey, "Taoism, a/k/a Daoism," *Awareness of Nothing*, October 23, 2016, http://www.awarenessofnothing.com/taoism-aka-daoism.html.

116. Lao Tzu, *Tao Te Ching*, chap. 25, stanzas 1, 2, and 4, http://www.taoistic.com/taoteching-laotzu/taoteching-25.htm.

Chapter 7. How the Practices Elevate Our Consciousness

1. John Postill, "Introduction: Theorising Media and Practice," in *Theorising Media and Practice*, ed. Birgit Bräuchler and John Postill (Oxford: Berghahn, 2010), 7.

2. Alice Lam explains that the concept of know-how is attributed to Gilbert Ryle, who makes the distinction between "know-that" knowledge, or knowledge of propositions, and "know-how" knowledge. He offers an appreciation of know-how knowledge in the context of an intellectualist tendency in traditional education to require only explicit knowledge (know-that knowledge). Alice Lam, "Tacit Knowledge, Organizational Learning and Societal Institutions: An Integrated Framework," *Organization Studies* 21, no. 3 (2000): 487–513.

3. The authors are indebted to Maria Muñoz-Grandes for much of the research into practices presented in this chapter.

4. Malcolm Gladwell, *Blink: The Power of Thinking Without Thinking* (Boston: Little, Brown, 2005), 70.

5. Richard E. Boyatzis, "An Overview of Intentional Change from a Complexity Perspective," *Journal of Management Development* 25, no. 7 (2006): 607–623.

6. Richard E. Boyatzis, "Leadership Development from a Complexity Perspective," *Consulting Psychology Journal: Practice and Research* 60, no. 4 (2008): 298–313.

7. Richard E. Boyatzis and Annie McKee, *Resonant Leadership: Renewing Yourself and Connecting with Others Through Mindfulness, Hope, and Compassion* (Boston: Harvard Business School Press, 2005); see also Annie McKee, Richard E. Boyatzis, and Frances Johnston, *Becoming a Resonant Leader: Develop Your Emotional Intelligence, Renew Your Relationships, Sustain Your Effectiveness* (Boston: Harvard Business School Press, 2008).

8. Malcolm Gladwell, *Outliers: The Story of Success* (Columbus, GA: Back Bay Books, 2011).

9. Richard E. Boyatzis, Melvin L. Smith, and Ellen B. Van Oosten, "Coaching for Change," *People Matters* 1, no. 5 (2010): 68–71.

10. Michael Polanyi, *Personal Knowledge: Towards a Post-critical Philosophy* (Chicago: University of Chicago Press, 2015), xix.

11. Étienne Wenger, "Communities of Practice: A Brief Introduction," http://neillthew.typepad.com/files/communities-of-practice.pdf (accessed December 14, 2018).

12. John S. Brown and Paul Duguid, "Balancing Act: How to Capture Knowledge Without Killing It," *Harvard Business Review*, May–June 2000, https://hbr.org/2000/05/balancing-act-how-to-capture-knowledge-without-killing-it.

13. Kathryn Pavlovich and Keiko Krahnke, "Empathy, Connectedness, and Organization," *Journal of Business Ethics* 105 (2012): 134.

14. Shinzen Young, *The Science of Enlightenment: How Meditation Works* (Louisville, CO: Sounds True, 2016).

15. Judi Neal, "Overview of the Field of Transformation," in *The Handbook of Personal and Organizational Transformation*, ed. Judi Neal (New York: SpringerNature, 2018), 10.

16. Karl E. Weick, Kathleen M. Sutcliffe, and David Obstfeld, "Organizing and the Process of Sensemaking," *Organization Science* 16, no. 4 (2005): 409.

17. Ibid.

18. The term "direct-intuitive" refers to the immediacy and noncognitive aspects of perception. It can be assimilated with instinctual perception. Some intuitive forms of perception are slow and/or empirically based: they emerge from a process of intuiting a truth about something. Direct-intuitive experience is immediate in the quantum physics sense of nonlocal. It is instantaneous and does not require empirical evidence for cognitive confirmation.

19. Dana Zohar describes "quantum cognition" as whole-brain thinking, thinking that synthesizes and synchronizes the mental activity from all over the brain, including its bodily cues. Although she uses the language of thinking rather than of practice, her framing "integrate[s] and analyzes[s] all the data of experience simultaneously . . . and unifies all the millions of sensory data and information impinging upon the brain at any moment, as well as integrates it into a unified field of experience." In this way, Zohar's quantum cognition embraces both the explicit knowledge of language-based learning and the tacit knowledge of practice. See Dana Zohar, *Quantum Leaders* (Amherst, NY: Prometheus Books, 2016), 65, 66.

20. Hans Ulrich Gumbrecht, *Production of Presence: What Meaning Cannot Convey*, Kindle ed. (Stanford, CA: Stanford University Press, 2004), Kindle loc. 261–262.

21. Ibid., Kindle loc. 269–271.

22. This expression has also been translated as "About what one cannot speak, one must remain silent" (*Wovon man nicht sprechen kann, darüber muss man schweigen*). Ludwig Wittgenstein, *Tractatus Logico-Philosophicus*, Proposition 7 (New York: Cosimo Classics, 2007).

23. Daniel Kahneman, *Thinking, Fast and Slow* (New York: Farrar, Straus and Giroux, 2011), 13.

24. Ibid., 419.

25. Zohar, *Quantum Leaders*. In chapter 3, Zohar proposes quantum thinking as a kind of unification of Kahneman's System 1 and System 2 thinking.

26. Studies of mindfulness in the business context have shown that it is associated with increased creativity and productivity as well as decreased burnout. See Ellen J. Langer, "The Construct of Mindfulness," *Journal of Social Issues* 56, no. 1 (2000): 1–9.

27. David Bohm and David Peat, *Science, Order and Creativity* (New York: Bantam Books, 1987), 190.

28. Ibid., 171.

29. Quoted in "Physics: Discovery and Intuition," *Connections Through Time*, April–June 2003, http://www.p-i-a.com/Magazine/Issue19/Physics_19.htm.

30. Quoted in Joseph Jaworski, *Source: The Inner Path of Knowledge Creation* (Oakland, CA: Berrett-Koehler, 2012), 149.

31. Bohm and Peat, *Science, Order and Creativity*, 181.

32. Stuart Hameroff and Roger Penrose, "Consciousness in the Universe: A Review of the Orch OR Theory," *Physics of Life Reviews* 11, no. 1 (2014): 39–78.

33. Jon Kabat-Zinn, *Full Catastrophe Living: Using the Wisdom of Your Body and Mind to Face Stress, Pain, and Illness*, rev. ed. (New York: Random House, 2013), 180.

34. Ibid.

35. C. Otto Scharmer, *Theory U: Leading from the Future as It Emerges*, 2nd ed. (Oakland, CA: Berrett-Koehler, 2016); Peter M. Senge, C. Otto Scharmer, Joseph Jaworsky, and Betty Sue Flowers, *Presence: Human Purpose and the Field of the Future* (New York: Crown, 2008).

36. Senge et al., *Presence*, 71–91.

37. Ibid., 145–163.

Chapter 8. Selecting the Practices That Are Right for You

1. Huidi Ma and Er Liu, *Traditional Chinese Leisure Culture and Economic Development: A Conflict of Forces* (London: Palgrave Macmillan, 2017).

2. Ibid., 45.

3. Nancy J. Adler, "Want to Be an Outstanding Leader? Keep a Journal," *Harvard Business Review*, January 13, 2016, https://hbr.org/2016/01/want-to-be-an-outstanding -leader-keep-a-journal.

4. David Cooperrider, "Positive Image, Positive Action: The Affirmative Basis of Organizing," in *Appreciative Inquiry: An Emerging Direction for Organization Development*, ed. David Cooperrider, Peter F. Sorensen Jr., Therese F. Yaeger, and Diana Whitney (Champaign, IL: Stipes, 2001), 31–76.

5. Barbara Abercrombie, *Kicking In the Wall: A Year of Writing Exercises, Prompts and Quotes to Help You Break Through Your Blocks and Reach Your Writing Goals* (Novato, CA: New World Library, 2013).

6. Ira Progoff, *At a Journal Workshop: Writing to Access the Power of the Unconscious and Evoke Creative Ability* (New York: TarcherPerigee, 1992).

7. Adler, "Want to Be an Outstanding Leader?"

8. Dan Harris, "Meditation Can Help in an Era of Angry Politics," *Time*, January 15, 2018, p. 15.

9. Julianna Raye, personal communication, January 11, 2018. See also Jerry Slutsky, Brian Chin, Julianna Raye, and J. David Creswell, "Mindfulness Training Improves Employee Well-Being: A Randomized Controlled Trial," *Journal of Occupational Health Psychology*, October 2018, http://psycnet.apa.org/doiLanding?doi=10.1037%2Focp0000132.

10. Shinzen Young, *The Science of Enlightenment: How Meditation Works* (Louisville, CO: Sounds True, 2016).

11. Shinzen Young, "What Is Mindfulness? A Contemplative Perspective," in *Handbook of Mindfulness in Education: Integrating Theory and Research into Practice*, ed. Kimberly A. Schonert-Reichl and Robert W. Roeser (New York: Springer, 2016), 29–45.

12. Zubin R. Mulla, Kalaiselvan Govindaraj, Srinivasa Rao Polisetti, Elis George, and Nagraj Rao S., "Mindfulness-Based Stress Reduction for Executives: Results from a Field Experiment," *Business Perspectives and Research* 5, no. 2 (2017): 113–123.

13. See "Mindfulness Based Stress Reduction (MBSR)," MedStar Georgetown University Hospital, https://www.medstargeorgetown.org/our-services/psychiatry/treatments/mindfulness-based-stress-reduction-mbsr/#q={} (accessed November 20, 2018).

14. Mary Grace Neville (professor of organizational development, Moroccan University), personal communication, 2016.

15. Shou-Yu Liang, Wen-Ching Wu, and Denise Breiter-Wu, *Qigong Empowerment: A Guide to Medical, Taoist, Buddhist, and Wushu Energy Cultivation* (East Providence, RI: Way of the Dragon, 1997).

16. Denise Nagel, "Health Benefits of Tai Chi and Qigong," *Huffington Post*, June 23, 2015, https://www.huffpost.com/entry/health-benefits-of-tai-ch_b_7641712.

17. E. O. Wilson, *Biophilia*, reprint ed. (Cambridge, MA: Harvard University Press, 2009), 1–2.

18. Rachel Carson, *Silent Spring* (Boston: Houghton Mifflin, 1962), cited in David Suzuki, *The Sacred Balance: Rediscovering Our Place in Nature* (Vancouver, BC: Greystone Books, 1999), 221.

19. Florence Williams, *The Nature Fix: Why Nature Makes Us Happier, Healthier, and More Creative* (New York: W. W. Norton, 2017), 140.

20. These are drawn in part from Madison Woods, "What Is Nature Immersion? It's *Not* Being Immersed in Natural Disasters," *Wild Ozark*, August 27, 2017, https://www.wildozark.com/nature-immersion.

21. John Muir, *Our National Parks* (Boston: Houghton, Mifflin, 1901), 56.

22. For an introductory overview, see Julie Beck, "Nature Therapy Is a Privilege," *The Atlantic*, June 23, 2017, https://www.theatlantic.com/health/archive/2017/06/how-to-harness-natures-healing-power/531438.

23. Wilbert Gesler, "Therapeutic Landscapes: Medical Issues in Light of the New Cultural Geography," *Social Science Medicine* 34, no. 7 (1992): 735–746.

24. Nancy M. Wells and Gary W. Evans, "Nearby Nature: A Buffer of Life Stress Among Rural Children," *Environment and Behavior* 35, no. 3 (2003): 311–330, cited in Craig Chalquist, "A Look at the Ecotherapy Research Evidence," *Ecopsychology* 1, no. 2 (2009): 64–74.

25. See the Zuckerman Inventory of Personal Reactions (ZIPERS), cited in Howard Frumkin, *Environmental Health: From Global to Local*, 2nd ed. (San Francisco: Jossey-Bass, 2010).

26. Ibid.

27. F. Stephan Mayer and Cynthia McPherson Frantz, "The Connectedness to Nature Scale: A Measure of Individuals' Feeling in Community with Nature," *Journal of Environmental Psychology* 24, no. 4 (2004): 503–515.

28. Finbarr Brereton, J. Peter Clinch, and Susana Ferreira, "Happiness Geography and the Environment," *Ecological Economics* 65, no. 2 (2008): 386–396.

29. Koleva Mikael Korpela, "Place-Identity as a Product of Environmental Self-Regulation," *Journal of Environmental Psychology* 9, no. 3 (1989): 241–256, cited in Chalquist, "A Look at the Ecotherapy Research Evidence," 70.

30. Elizabeth A. Beverly and Robert D. Whittemore, "Mandinka Children and the Geography of Well-Being," *Ethos* 21, no. 3 (1993): 235–272, cited in Chalquist, "A Look at the Ecotherapy Research Evidence," 70.

31. Williams, *The Nature Fix.*

32. Edward S. Casey, *The Fate of Place: A Philosophical History* (Berkeley: University of California Press, 1998), cited in Chalquist, "A Look at the Ecotherapy Research Evidence."

33. Chalquist, "A Look at the Ecotherapy Research Evidence."

34. Wendell Berry, "The Peace of Wild Things," in *The Selected Poems of Wendell Berry* (Berkeley, CA: Counterpoint, 1998), 30. Copyright © 1998 by Wendell Berry. Reprinted by permission of Counterpoint Press.

35. B. K. S. Iyengar, *Yoga: The Path to Holistic Health* (London: Dorling-Kindersley, 2001).

36. Christina Brown, *The Yoga Bible: The Definitive Guide to Yoga Postures* (Alresford, UK: Godsfield, 2003).

37. Rachael Link, "13 Benefits of Yoga That Are Supported by Science," *Healthline Newsletter*, August 30, 2017, https://www.healthline.com/nutrition/13-benefits-of-yoga #section13.

38. See "An Overview of Loving-Kindness Meditation," http://www.buddhanet.net/ metta_in.htm (accessed November 20, 2018).

39. Barbara Fredrickson, Michael A. Cohn, Kimberly A. Coffey, Jolynn Pek, and Sandra M. Finkel, "Open Hearts Build Lives: Positive Emotions, Induced Through Loving-Kindness Meditation, Build Consequential Personal Resources," *Journal of Personality and Social Psychology* 95 (2008): 1045–1062.

40. Emma Seppälä, "A Gift of Loving Kindness Meditation," May 28, 2014, https:// emmaseppala.com/gift-loving-kindness-meditation.

41. Cited in Sally Atkins, *Presence and Process in Expressive Arts Work: At the Edge of Wonder*, Kindle ed. (London: Jessica Kingsley, 2014), Kindle loc. 39–40.

42. Rollo May, *My Quest for Beauty* (New York: W. W. Norton, 1985).

43. Atkins, *Presence and Process*, Kindle loc. 40.

44. Ibid., 42–43.

45. Stephen K. Levine, *Poiesis: The Language of Psychology and the Speech of the Soul*, 2nd ed. (London: Jessica Kingsley, 1997).

46. Atkins, *Presence and Process*, Kindle loc. 27.

47. Levine, *Poieisis*, Kindle loc. 63–65.

48. Chris Laszlo and Judy Sorum Brown, *Flourishing Enterprise: The New Spirit of Business* (Stanford, CA: Stanford University Press, 2014), 130–135.

49. Ibid., 127–150.

50. These questions were personally communicated by David Cooperrider and Ronald Fry to the authors in workshops jointly conducted with corporate clients. Our esteemed thanks go to both of them.

51. Laszlo and Brown, *Flourishing Enterprise*, 128.

52. Atkins, *Presence and Process*, Kindle loc. 52.

53. Ibid., Kindle loc. 51.

INDEX

Italic page numbers indicate material in figures.

Abramson, Jeffrey, 133
a cappella singing, 138
acceptance, 45
accordion structure of leadership, 56–58
active information, 156, 158, 233–234n64,
   237n107
Aden Services, 134
Adidas, 103–104
Adler, Nancy, 179, 180
aesthetics and art, 137–138, 191–194, 195–196,
   206
agency, 165
AIM2Flourish, 87, 112–113
AITIA Institute, 69–70, 71, 178
AITIA Quantum Leadership Initiative, xi,
   178
Anderson, Ray, 8
appreciative inquiry (AI), 194–195
appreciative joy (*mudita*), 190
Aristotle, 69, 151, 235n89
art and aesthetics, 137–138, 191–194, 195–196,
   206
asanas (yoga postures), 188–189
Aspect, Alain, 157
Axe campaign, 88

Bangladesh garment workers, 111–112
bankers, shadow side of, 27–28
B Corps, 84, 118, 216n3
beauty (*hozho*), 192
Behar, Howard, 109
Bell, John, 235–236n94
bem estar bem ("Well Being and Being
   Well"), 97–98
benefit corporations, 84, 216n4

Bergson, Henri, 234n66
Berry, Wendell, 187–188
"Beyond Greening" (Hart), 116
biology, 149, 153, 234n66, 236n99
Blink (Gladwell), 166
Blueprint for Change, 101–102, 110
Bohm, David, 155, 173, 237n107
Bohr, Niels, 152, 157
Book of Changes (*I Ching*), 40
Boyatzis, Richard, 167
Bragdon, Joseph H., 22, 89, 104
breathing, 189
Brink, Dolf van den, 164
Brown, Lynette, 135
Buddhism, 37, 41, 42, 61, 158, 190, 231n38
Bureo, 112–113
Burns, James MacGregor, 214n33
business: as force for good, 84–85, 118–120,
   119; purpose in, 9, *10*, 32–33, 115–117, *118*,
   120, 124; role and responsibilities of, 3–4
business evolution: first transition, 115–118,
   116; second transition, 118–120, *119*; third
   transition, 120–122, *121*
business outcomes in quantum leadership
   research, 125
Business Sustainability Mandate (IMC),
   60, 61

caring, as organizing principle, 118. *See also*
   consciousness of connectedness and
   caring
Carson, Rachel, 186
causality, 166–167, 173–174
Center for Evolutionary Learning, 114
CEO guidelines, 52